PRINCIPLES AND PRACTICES OF TQM

Also available from Quality Press

TQM: A Step-by-Step Guide to Implementation
Charles N. Weaver, PhD

A TQM Approach to Achieving Manufacturing Excellence
A. Richard Shores

An Approach to Quality Improvement That Works, Second Edition
A. Donald Stratton

Management Excellence Through Quality
Thomas J. Barry

Total Quality Management: Performance and Cost Measures
Dorsey J. Talley

Baldrige Award Winning Quality
Mark Graham Brown

Leadership, Perspective, and Restructuring for Total Quality
Richard J. Pierce, editor

The Quality Master Plan
J. P. Russell

A Leader's Journey to Quality
Dana Cound

To request a complimentary catalog of publications, call 800-248-1946.

PRINCIPLES AND PRACTICES OF TQM

T. J. Cartin

ASQC Quality Press
Milwaukee, Wisconsin

Principles and Practices of TQM
T. J. Cartin

Library of Congress Cataloging-in-Publication Data

Cartin, T. J. (Thomas J.)
Principles and practices of TQM/T. J. Cartin.
p. cm.
Includes index.
ISBN 0-87389-153-8
1. Total quality management. I. Title.
HD62.15.C364 1993
658.5'62 — dc20 92-25369
CIP

Table appearing on page 224 reprinted from *Introduction to Quality Engineering* by Dr. Genichi Taguchi with permission of the publisher Asian Productivity Organization. Distributed in the U.S., Canada, and Western Europe by Quality Resources, White Plains, New York.

1098765432

ISBN 0-87389-153-8

Acquisitions Assistant: Deborah Dunlap
Production Editor: Mary Beth Nilles
Marketing Administrator: Susan Westergard
Set in Janson Text by Zahn-Klicka-Hill. Cover design by Barbara Adams. Printed and bound by BookCrafters.

For a free copy of the ASQC Quality Press Publications Catalog, including ASQC membership information, call 800-248-1946.

Printed in the United States of America

Printed on recycled paper

ASQC
Quality Press
611 East Wisconsin Avenue
Milwaukee, Wisconsin 53202

Dedicated to my wife

Contents

Section II

Preface

This book is about managing organizations to become more competitive and successful. Business functions need to become more competitive; nonbusiness functions need to become more efficient *and* effective.

Humans have a need to believe that they are individually different, even superior. Witness the behavior of nations, ethnic groups, races, and organizations. It is a common expression of managers of organizations in one line of business to think that what they do, the problems they have, the markets they are in are different and unique and they have little to learn from others outside that market.

There are differences, but there are also fundamental similarities, particularly in how to make organizations function more effectively. The basic methodology of organizations of all types is similar. Organizations function by establishing processes to get tasks performed. Some use machines and some don't. All use people.

There is often resistance by managers to admit that their functions—managing processes—can be completely described. The difficulty arises largely because they have been trained, formally and on the job, to be oriented to task and organization functions.

Getting managers to recognize this difference—that all work is completed through the operation of processes and by functions, and that the success of the organization may be highly dependent on process management—is an important concept for success. It is important to appreciate that the quality improvement of these processes is the primary emphasis. It results in greater customer satisfaction as well as cost and schedule improvement. Quality assurance has been a specialized field of knowledge for many years. It has also been almost completely a manufacturing activity. It is now an activity for everyone in every organization. The old practices are still a part of managing, but they are modified, supplemented, redirected, and described as total quality management (TQM). Perhaps most significantly the responsibility for success lies primarily with management. The manager of quality is the chief executive officer.

The old tools are inspection, sampling, and statistical process control. Another, design of experiments, is not new but its applications in industry are. To these older tools, the Japanese have added quality function deployment and quality deployment. Benchmarking, another important new tool, has been developed by the Xerox Corporation. This book is organized to first discuss the various elements and philosophies of TQM: what it is, how it all fits together, and how it is applied. In the second section, there is a more detailed description of each of the major tools and techniques.

Special emphasis is placed on the importance of human relations issues. Implementing TQM requires the understanding and commitment of all organization members to succeed. Management has to set objectives differently from those in the past, it has to play a new role, use a different style, and plan how it will be done. In short, this is a new way to manage. The intent of this book is to provide a single source for a description of what TQM is, its principles and practices, and how they fit together. It is intended to be used as a basic textbook on the subject as well as for managers and others to understand the thrust and scope of TQM. It includes references describing the elements of TQM with a bibliography for the reader to pursue more tutorial aspects.

Although the most comprehensive approach is required for industry, all of the principles and most of the tools and techniques are applicable and are being successfully implemented in all types of organizations in all sectors of business and government. Nonindustrial organizations can achieve an adequate understanding of TQM for their activities by reading Chapters 1 through 4, Chapter 6, Chapters 8 through 13, and Chapters 16 and 18. The other chapters, although more oriented toward industry, may stimulate useful analogies.

The book is a result of the author's experience in a class with the same name and subject matter as this book title in a master's degree program in quality assurance at the California State University—Dominguez Hills.

Introduction

Business management has always operated using hard quantitative goals for cost and schedule. But goals for quality were only vaguely expressed. They were expressed in terms of slogans or exhortations like, "Do it right the first time," "Be quality-minded," or "Reduce scrap and rework." There were occasional efforts to reduce scrap, but total organization quality improvement, with quantitative objectives, were uncommon. The concept of quality improvement for nonproduction activities simply didn't exist, at least not in any organized form.

The traditional cost and schedule emphasis evolved from the work of Fredrick W. Taylor into what became industrial engineering. In the late 1940s the specialty of quality engineering took form. The emphasis was inspection, and in a few cases, from the work of Walter A. Shewhart, statistical quality control. Economic inspection using sampling was common and dependent on the tables prepared by Harold Dodge and Harry Romig.

In American business, quality engineering became part of a specialized organization called quality control or quality assurance. It was typically responsible for inspection of produced and procured products and the measurement of quality. The practice was that industrial engineering focused on process efficiency and quality engineering focused on what was called quality control. Its emphasis was on inspecting what processes produced. This left the responsibility for product quality ambiguous. Until the advent and application of total quality control, the ambiguity was not resolved. So it is not surprising that with little understanding of what quality was and how to manage it, management grew to hold the quality organization responsible for the quality of other organizations' work. The quality organizations, with limited success, went along with it. The emphasis was on inspection: Catch bad quality. From this grew the belief that high quality was costly because it was equated with higher inspection costs. Tighter tolerances were also equated with higher quality costs because, lacking the understanding of statistical thinking and process capability, it resulted in increased scrap.

One factor behind the evolution of the dependence on inspection was that quality was directed by the buyer. Requirements were defined by the buyer (this was initiated first by the military). The producer designed the process and quality system to meet those requirements. The simplest response was to set up control points and inspect everything to the buyer's specifications. If the quality system needs had developed from a producer goal to produce the highest quality, the focus would more likely have been on the production process. This fundamentally different objective is a source of the difference between the Western and Japanese quality systems and between traditional quality assurance and total quality management (TQM).

In the 1950s, the Japanese developed a different model. They studied quality systematically. They realized that quality was an important attribute to penetrate the American-controlled markets. From these studies emerged the recognition that high quality was the result of the efforts of the entire organization. It was a management responsibility and could only be achieved if planned. Everyone's role had to be planned and integrated. This led to total quality control, sometimes referred to as the "Big-Q." In developing this approach the Japanese integrated the activities of many of the specialized U.S. quality functions into all or at least their key organizations. They adapted the existing tools and techniques, developed new ones, and applied them to improving the quality of every activity and product. They focused on customer satisfaction and continuous improvement as a business policy. In their model, higher quality resulted in lower costs. They became a world-class competitor.

The period of the 1980s and 1990s has been a painful transition in the business world because business ownership and markets have become worldwide. Competition of every kind has become more intense. One common denominator, however, is the demand for higher quality in products and services. Since it is now realized that it can be achieved with no increase in cost, quality has become a competitive weapon, even a survival issue.

It will become evident that TQM is a way to manage any organization. It is being successfully adopted in industry, government, and services. But it is not a collection of tools that can merely be plugged in to produce results. Some tools used alone can produce improvement, but only adoption of the fundamental principles will result in the maximum benefits.

Comparing the new way to manage with the old is analogous to the difference between the Old and New Testaments. The new way requires a change in beliefs in the role of management and employees. It is a change from directing the organization to leading and having everyone participate in meeting its goals. Getting organization members, particularly managers, to believe that the new way is better, if not required, is one of the most difficult aspects of TQM implementation. Lacking knowledge and insight as to their critical role, managers and employers frequently think it's another fad.

Another valuable result of implementing TQM, which is not obvious initially, is that by its very objective and methodology—reducing waste and variation—it reduces cycle time. Cycle time is the time elapsed between the beginning and completion of a task or series of tasks. (This is a primary objective of just-in-time, also a popular theme.) A cycle can be the completion of an order sequence by purchasing or the total time from taking an order to delivering a product. It should be obvious that reduction of this time reduces cost and better satisfies the customer (quicker delivery).

TQM is also for everyone and for every organization. The only prerequisite is a willingness to change. Even leading companies, like Boeing, that at this writing has a 10-year backlog of orders for its airplanes, have adopted TQM. Why should they change? The leaders of these companies have recognized that, in the long run, they must also help their customers by delivering higher quality at lower prices in a shorter time.

This book describes the principles and practices to use in adopting TQM as the management model.

Important terms in TQM and in this book:

- Process: This term includes any sequence of organizational activities, or tasks, whether in the manufacturing process or the office.
- Continuous improvement: Improving the quality of every process; reducing the variation in output of a process; driving defects and errors to zero; completing tasks in a shorter time; and, in the case of industrial processes, driving process variation toward zero.

SECTION I

Chapter 1

Quality–Markets–Management

QUALITY

The major new element in world-market competition is quality. During the 1970s and 1980s, the Japanese and their U.S. companies demonstrated that high quality is achievable at lower costs with greater customer satisfaction. It was the result of using the management principles of total quality management (TQM).

More and more U.S. companies have demonstrated that such achievements are possible using TQM as a new way to manage. Such companies also found that they were reenergized with everyone pulling in the same direction. Improvement had become a way of life.

In a speech summarizing the accomplishments of the 1989 Malcolm Baldrige National Quality Award winners, Joseph M. Juran said he was "astounded" that after only a few years' effort, the winners' customers experienced half the number of defects and half the costs. Most improvements were the result of team efforts within the organizations. The Milliken Company reported a ten-fold quality improvement in four years. Xerox reported a four-fold improvement in reliability and a 12-month reduction in the product development cycle. These improvements were all the result of implementing TQM.

The focus on quality, using TQM, is also appropriate in the service sector, the largest sector of the U.S. economy. Service can also include the many support groups within industry, such as finance, human resources, field service, sales, and marketing that are not directly involved in product design or production. The Wallace Company won the 1990 Baldrige Award in the service category, and Florida Power and Light won the prestigious Japanese Deming Prize. A review of the subjects presented in various TQM conferences indicates the growing diversity of TQM applications in government, hospitals, banks, insurance companies, and the like. This is discussed further in Chapter 2.

MANAGEMENT

Improving competitive position and profits has always been the responsibility of management. Before the 1980s, U.S. management was broadly successful. Until then the dominant management model was that of the autocrat. Management, primarily senior management, decided how the business was to operate, including what the policies and objectives were; how it was organized; what jobs were established; and how they should be done. Senior management delegated to lower management the responsibility to implement these upper-management decisions. It was an unquestioned axiom that if everyone did what upper management required, the business would be successful.

Organizations are composed of the people in them and the managers who lead them. People respond strongly to leadership expectations and rewards. If they are given little power over their jobs, they have little interest in improving them. If leaders exhort the members for better output but reward (promotions, bonuses, recognition) for mostly higher output, they get the behavior they reward. Quantity over quality has been a common management philosophy in the United States. This philosophy is no longer viable.

The first step in implementing TQM requires an upper-management change in philosophy and behavior. Managers must adopt the objective of customer satisfaction and continuous improvement. They must implement the change to achieve these objectives through their personal and continuous involvement and in the reeducation of everyone in the organization in TQM principles and practices. They must convince everyone that there is little choice. TQM principles and practices provide the method for success and survival. This is discussed further in Chapter 4.

MARKETS

This past philosophy of management can work reasonably well if a company dominates world markets. When markets become complex and worldwide with more and stronger competitors, however, a new model is needed. Asian companies and recently some in the United States have demonstrated that there is a more effective way to manage, quite different from the autocratic model: It is employee involvement in quality improvement. These companies also introduced high quality at lower cost as a competitive element, thereby changing the competitive equation for everyone.

The principles of TQM are the major components of that new way. The primary principles are:

1. Focusing on satisfying the needs and expectations of the customer.
2. Operating to continuously improve the quality of all the activities and processes in an organization.

There are additional tools and techniques involved in using TQM, but the two principles just mentioned are the essence of the approach and reflect the difference from past practices. For the external customer, businesses have generally concentrated on what sells in the marketplace and what their competitors were doing. Businesses did not normally determine *from the customers* what they wanted, expected, or needed. The Japanese have used the latter approach to produce products with world-wide demand. In addition, TQM introduces the idea of the internal customer defined as the recipient of the work output of another activity. With the recognition of the value of process management for all activities, process outputs are designed to satisfy their recipient, internal or external. This leads to the establishment of only those activities that are needed and add value.

Two examples of the results of the old versus the new customer satisfaction emphasis are the automobile and television markets. In the automobile market, U.S. business decided not to fill the consumers' desires for good, small cars. In the television market, only marginally reliable televisions were provided. Many televisions were sold with defects or developed them shortly after use.

The Japanese provided good small cars, gained a solid foothold in the U.S. automobile market, built a reputation for quality, and expanded by selling larger cars. In the case of televisions, the higher quality of Japanese-manufactured televisions took over the market and, as with Sony, were not even the cheapest. Subsequent analysis showed that the application of the principles of what is now called TQM was mostly responsible.

RESULTS

The success of the Japanese changed the rules of business competition. As General Motors now teaches its suppliers, the model used to be:

$$\text{Cost} + \text{Desired Profits} = \text{Price}$$

It is now:

$$\text{Existing Market Price} - \text{Costs} = \text{Profits}$$

"Thus, to remain competitive in today's market, a company must focus on satisfying the customer to remain in the market, improving its processes, and developing its employees to control cost. To do this, top management sets goals based on feedback from continuing operations and provides resources to departments to improve, the primary business goals of quality, cost, schedule."[1] This describes the application of the principle of TQM in terms of management actions to compete. It reflects the management support of the focus on quality through process improvement in all important activities.

The TQM principle of continuous improvement also means a profound change in operating philosophy. It means that no activity or process is good enough. Every activity and process in the company is constantly improved as long as it is economically feasible. Improvement also means quality improvement. All errors and defects must be driven out and variation minimized. They all contribute to higher costs and lower quality.

Chapter 2

The Evolution of Quality

It is not surprising that high quality has been so inconsistently achieved when it is so inconsistently defined, loosely applied, and poorly understood. Even in industry, where quality has been a term commonly applied, its definition has been ambiguous.

Table 2.1 lists the most common definitions by authoritative sources. It is significant to note that the sources of these definitions are primarily quality professionals. Production management didn't much care, concentrating on meeting the requirements given to production by the designers. With the development of TQM principles, the narrow industry definitions are inadequate.

PROCESS QUALITY

A key principle of TQM is the continuous improvement of process quality. What does this mean? Most simply stated it means the reduction in process variation and process completion time. The most common measurements of these are error reduction and cycle time. These basic measures can be applied to any process in any type of organization. For example, in an office activity a defect chart might be used in tracking performance over time (Figure 2.1). These are explained in more detail in Chapter 19. The quality target is zero with no defects or errors. This can be approached or achieved using tools and techniques like the seven quality control tools and benchmarking. Frequently, however, zero defects is only a part of the improvement objective. Cycle-time improvement is also of great value. Improvement as shown in Figure 2.2 is obtained by using process analysis and other techniques discussed later.

Table 2.1 Common Definitions of Quality

Definitions	Source
Quality	
"The totality of features and characteristics of a product or service that bear on its ability to satisfy given needs."	1, 4, 5
"Fitness for use."	2
"Conformance to requirements."	3
"The degree to which product characteristics conform to the requirements placed upon that product, including reliability, maintainability, and safety."	6
"The degree to which a product or service is fit for the specified use."	7
Quality Assurance	
"A planned and systematic pattern of all means and actions designed to provide adequate confidence that items or services meet contractual and jurisdictional requirements and will perform satisfactorily in service. Quality Assurance includes Quality Control."	8
"All those planned or systematic actions necessary to provide adequate confidence that a product or service will satisfy given needs."	1
"Meet expectations of the customer."	9

1. *ANSI/ASQC Standard*, "Quality System Terminology," A3-1978, prepared jointly by the American National Standards Institute (ANSI) and the American Society for Quality Control (ASQC).
2. Juran, J. M. *Quality Control Handbook.* 3d ed. New York: McGraw-Hill, 1974.
3. Crosby, P. B. *Quality Is Free.* New York: McGraw-Hill, 1979.
4. DIN-53350, of Deutsches Institute fuer Normung, Teil 11, Beuth-Verlag, Berlin.
5. EOQC, "Glossary of Terms Used in Quality Control," 5th ed. European Organization for Quality Control, 1981.
6. QS-Norm Draft of Swiss Standard Association, 1981.
7. Seghezzi, H. D. "What Is Quality: Conformance With Requirements or Fitness for the Intended Use." *EOQC Journal* 4 (1981): 3.
8. Canadian Standard Association Standard, Z299.1-1978, "Quality Assurance Program Requirements."
9. Feigenbaum, A. V. *Total Quality Control.* New York: McGraw-Hill, 1991.

Audit Results of an Office Process Improvement Efforts

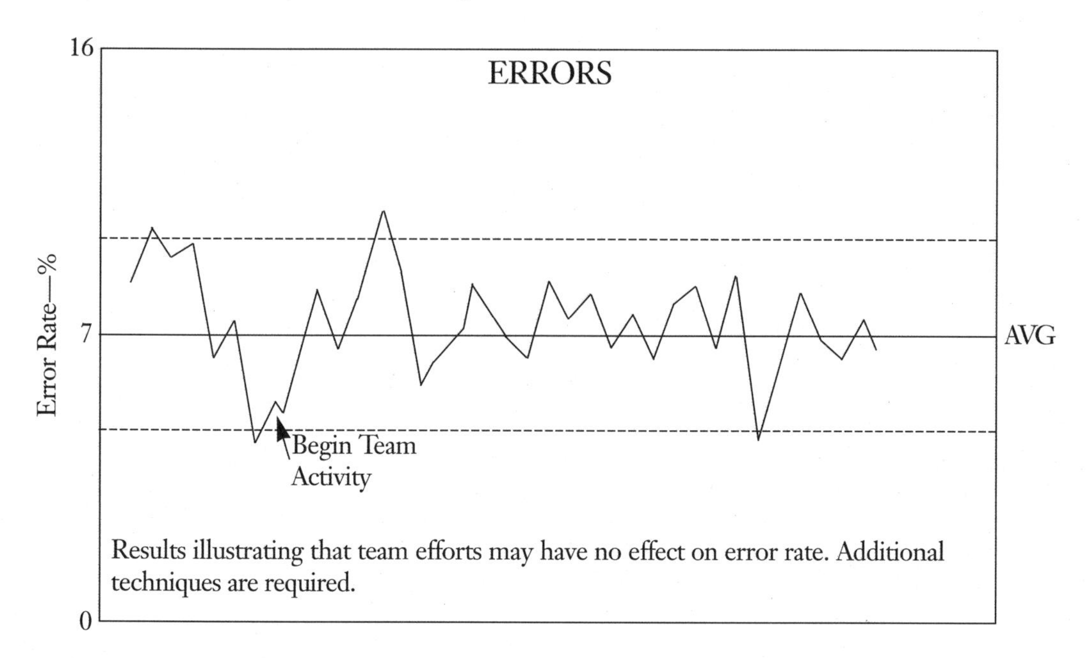

Figure 2.1 Defect Chart Used for Tracking Performance

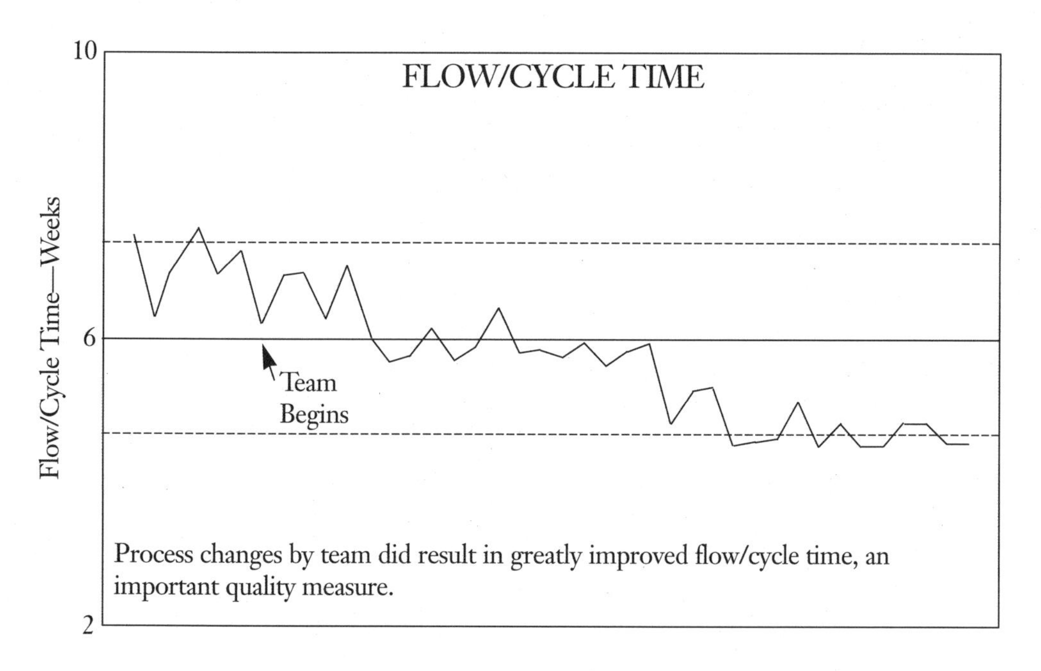

Figure 2.2 Chart Used for Tracking Improvement

INDUSTRIAL QUALITY

Quality in industry has been used in reference to the attributes of a product and its parts during production. It is in this context that the "meets requirements" quality definition developed. This definition has had several important ramifications that have limited industry's ability to meet new market quality standards for a variety of products. Figures 2.3 and 2.4 illustrate this point. Engineering specifications identify the dimensions of a product using a center value, or nominal, with upper and lower limits that define the acceptable range—in other words, a tolerance on the ideal. This recognizes that no process can produce everything at the nominal value. All processes, and therefore their outputs, vary.

In Figure 2.3, if following the meets requirements doctrine, a product measuring at point B, although almost out of tolerance, would be accepted. The same product measuring at point A would be unacceptable. If the two points represented something like the speed at which an auto transmission shifted, a customer would probably not recognize the difference between operating points A and B but would likely be more satisfied and notice the difference between A and B compared to C. In other words, if everything measures close to nominal, less variation has occurred in the process of making parts and it is customer satisfaction that is the measure of acceptance and not just tolerance specifications.

It is the recognition of this concept that supports the value of the principle of continuous process improvement. This is illustrated in Figure 2.4. The three curves represent the distributions of the output of three similar processes. The output under A is producing mostly within the tolerance but with a little waste outside the limits. Curve B is a process producing widely but within the tolerance extremes. C is the process with much less variation producing higher quality than A or B. Almost all the output is close to nominal.

The definition of quality is important in obtaining improvement. This concept is explained in Chapter 7. Until the principles and practices of TQM were defined as the way to manage for higher quality and lower cost, management did not have the tools or skills to be effective. This has been demonstrated by applying the appropriate techniques to existing processes considered to provide the highest yields known. Yields were further raised and output variation reduced to provide greater homogeneity.

Another factor in the U.S. approach to achieving product quality is that it has not been systematic. It is based on the performance of different organizational activities. Engineering designed and set tolerances. Manufacturing developed processes to try to stay within those tolerances. A quality organization measured the success of these processes. When they couldn't or didn't stay within tolerance, scrap and rework resulted. Also, a large percentage of product costs are for materials purchased from other companies and incorporated into the final product. Quality of purchased material was defined the same way—the supplier only had to meet drawing and

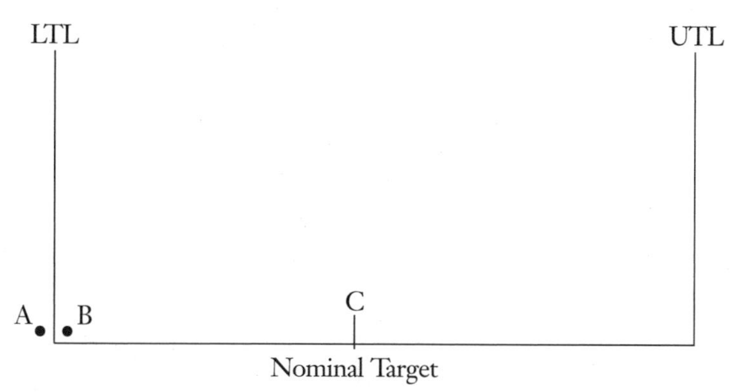

Customer would not likely consider operation at point A much different than B, but would notice the difference between A and B compared to C.

***Figure 2.3** Following the "meets requirements" definition results in accepting a part anywhere within upper tolerance limits (UTL) and lower tolerance limits (LTL) and rejecting anything outside a limit (measurement A).*

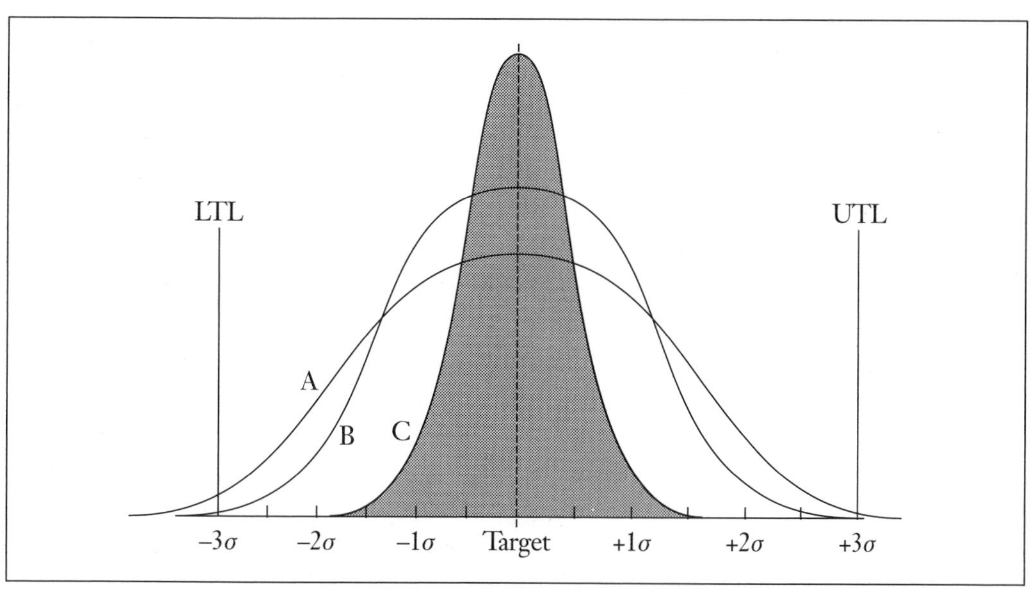

Products A or B could be the outputs of processes anywhere in their distributions as shown. Better product performance and customer satisfaction would be achieved if all process variation was as close to the target as C.

***Figure 2.4** These curves represent the idea of comparing the variation in the outputs of the same product from three different processes. The width of each curve represents the total variation of each process.*

specification tolerance requirements. Variation within those tolerances was uncontrolled. (See Chapter 13.)

The "requirements" definition and its resultant methods of managing and manufacturing produced products with widely varying quality in internal operations and widely varying quality to the customer. This meant a significant cost of poor quality to the producer and customer at every step in the production chain. Quality varied widely primarily because the focus was not on managing processes, and because there was little consideration given to the effects of process variation on product quality.

The Japanese demonstrated that if process variation was narrowed, costs were lower and customers were more satisfied. They achieved these results using a total approach to managing for quality. Everyone and every organization systematically improved themselves and their products—their outputs. Quality was more than merely a given product attribute. It is the level of excellence achieved by every activity and every process. It was also dynamic, to be improved continuously. The results are seen in the marketplace.

J. D. Powers and Associates conducts an annual quality survey of new car owners to determine their satisfaction in the first 90 days of ownership.[2] Automobile manufacturers consider the results an important strategic marketing tool. Buick was the only U.S. manufacturer to make the top 10 in either 1989 or 1990. From one year to the next, it cut the defect rate 8 percent; this would have put it into first place in 1989. Toyota and Mercedes, however, improved by 34 percent, and Lexus, which wasn't on the list in 1989, introduced new cars and took the lead. The survey is conducted for manufacturers, but sales of the leaders jumped dramatically after the results were published. The highest rank the United States achieved was for a Japanese car, 85 percent of which is built in the United States.

VARIATION REDUCTION

Broadly speaking, the evolution of quality has been from just meeting engineering requirements to variation reduction. The idea of variation reduction is reflected in a quality definition by Genichi Taguchi: Quality is the degree of variation from the target (nominal) value.

The greater the variation from target, the lower the quality. Figure 2.5 shows a measurement and its upper and lower tolerance limits. Taguchi selected a parabola to describe the loss function that exists as a produced dimension deviates from the target (nominal). Performance or customer acceptance, or both, decrease as an increasing continuous function. It usually doesn't occur suddenly as a dimension passes through a tolerance limit. Taguchi's concept represents the customer's interest rather than that of the production line. But there can be an impact on production costs if there isn't customer acceptance. Narrowing the tolerance to use only parts nearer the nominal is a possible alternative, but it isn't a good fix. This raises costs because meeting this

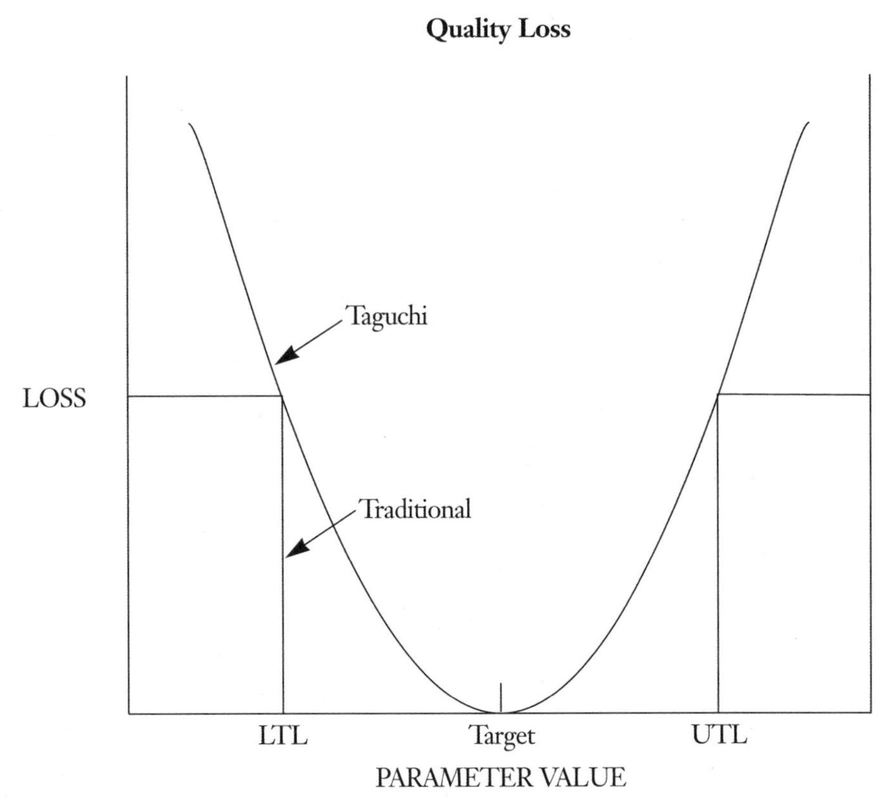

In the traditional understanding of quality, everything between the upper tolerance limit (UTL) and lower tolerance limit (LTL) was good. In the Taguchi concept, quality deteriorates at an exponential rate as it varies from the target nominal value.

Figure 2.5 Quality, Variation, and the Loss Concept

new tighter requirement produces even more out-of-tolerance products unless the process capability is greatly improved. This is the focus of TQM.

An example of quality being a continuous function is the experience of Ford Motor Company with a transmission. It was being manufactured to the same drawings and specification in the United States and also in Japan by Mazda Motors. Evaluating customer complaints, Ford found that there were few for the Mazda unit. There were a significant number of complaints for the Ford manufactured units concerning the speed at which they shifted. The variation was greater in the Ford units, and some customers didn't like the shift point in the one they got. Analysis showed that Mazda manufactured the parts closer to nominal (less variation); Ford manufactured to stay anywhere within tolerance. The variation in performance of Ford transmissions was greater because only the tolerance requirements on its parts were met. This also illustrates the incompatibility of a "meets requirements" philosophy with customer expectations. All the Ford transmission parts were within design tolerance limits. But when machine processes are not operated to produce parts not only within tolerance but close to nominal, those parts may all be near one tolerance extreme and assembled to a matching part at the other extreme. The transmission functions but not near the optimum. The customer doesn't like it, and the service manager can't adjust it out. Telling the customer that there is nothing wrong or that it's a "normal" condition does not remove customer anxiety. The customer may very well select a different car manufacturer next time.

This example also illustrates another of Taguchi's definitions of quality: Quality is the loss imparted to society. This is a startling and perhaps confounding definition compared to those previously presented. It is philosophically incomparable but well worth understanding.

Taguchi is stating that any variation from nominal creates a loss and that the loss increases with the degree of deviation. The loss can be expressed in monetary value. It can be composed of the lost business from customer dissatisfaction, the loss to the producer for warranty costs, or the customer from repair costs. Reduction in variation reduces these losses.

Application

Adopting the "target value" definition also makes it appropriate for all kinds of organizational activities, wherein the goal is to reduce variation around a target value, which itself should be constantly improved. This target value definition also assists in implanting in everyone's mind the principle of continuous improvement.

TQM DEFINED

Total quality management, or its equivalent, total quality control, is the present quality philosophy incorporating all the elements of what has been discussed.

Total is an appropriate term because this management process involves everyone in the organization—every function and activity. It is a systematic approach to achieving excellence. Total involvement is recognizing that every activity contributes or detracts from quality and productivity, and that the people working in those activities (processes) are in the best position to know what needs improvement and to identify and implement the change using TQM techniques. It leads to a more motivated membership unified in working toward common goals.

Quality is the dimension by which the value of this management method is measured. It focuses on improving the quality of all functions, systems, and processes. This includes not only the elimination of undesirable output but provides output closer to the ideal. The result is a more satisfied customer receiving higher quality products and services. The lower costs for this higher efficiency improve a company's competitive position.

Management in this context is not people with titles. It is the actions involved in applying TQM principles and techniques to all activities. There are old and new techniques. They are assembled and applied in a combination more effective than in the past. It is actually the first truly scientific management method in that it relies on older proven principles and methodologies as well as some that are new. The old principles are that employees want to do high quality work and that known tools like statistical process control (SPC) are important aids in its achievement. The new principles are related to management philosophy, that is, continuous process improvement and internal/external customer satisfaction.

TQM can also be represented as a model and its key elements, discussed in detail in later chapters, are represented in Figure 2.6.

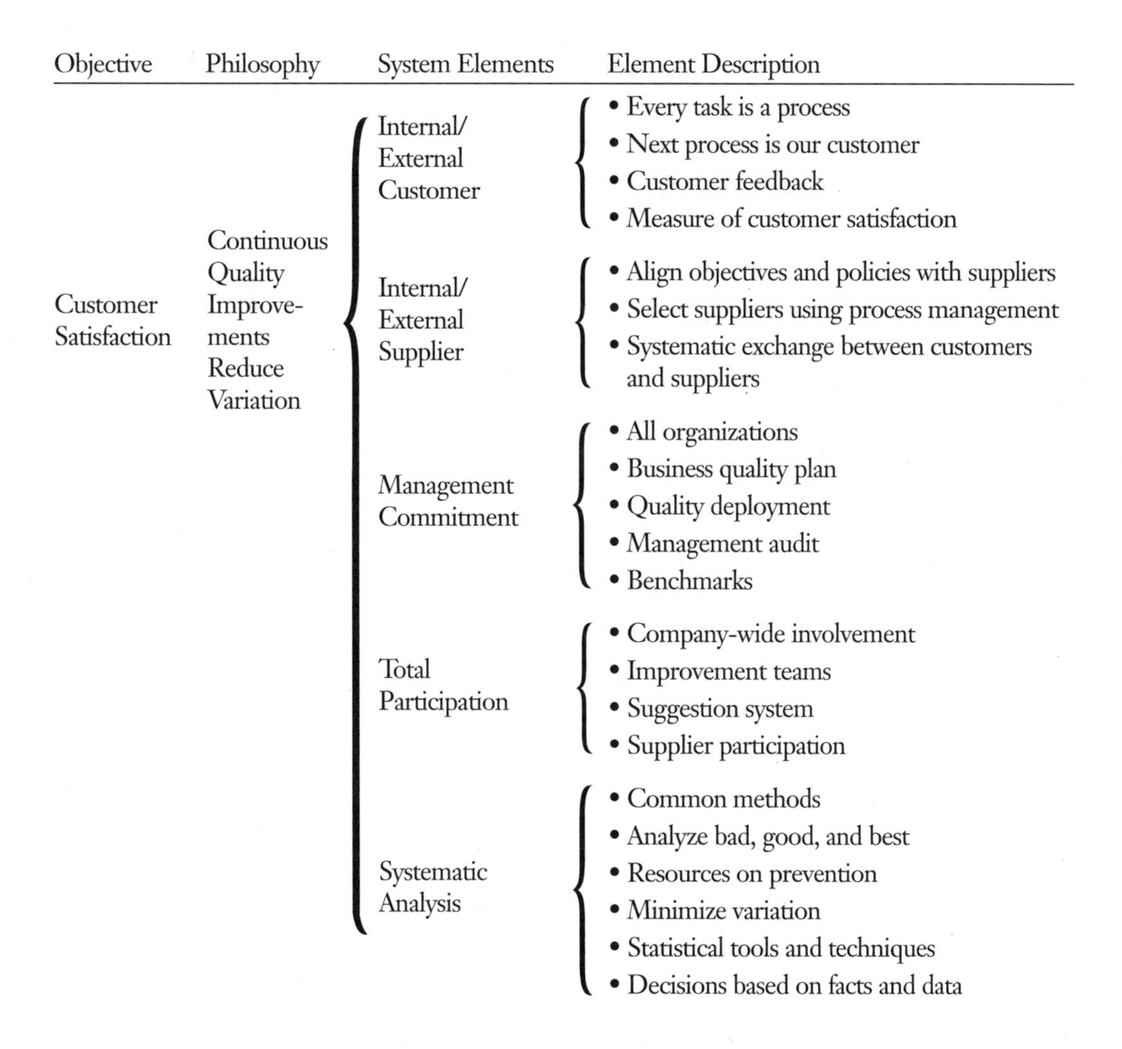

Figure 2.6 Total Quality Management Model

A COMPARISON OF TQM AND CLASSICAL MANAGEMENT

The elements of TQM, when first encountered, seem foreign to the traditional functions of management, such as planning, organizing, operating/directing, and controlling. They are different but related. TQM language and activities have a different emphasis—people, customer satisfaction, and continuous improvement—but they are all related to the traditional factors as shown in Table 2.2.

Table 2.2 TQM and the Classical Factors in Management

Common Management Factors	Related TQM Factors	TQM Tools
Planning	Strategic: • Satisfy customer needs and expectations • More competitive (cost, development time, quality) • Policy deployment Operational: • Employee empowerment • Error/waste prevention • Process variation reduction	Quality function deployment (QFD) 7 management tools Benchmarking Baldrige Award Teams Design of experiments (DOE) 7 Quality Control (QC) tools
Organizing	• Process definition and ownership • Multifunctional teams • TQM council • Less management	7 QC tools Input/output analysis Team facilitation
Operating/ Directing	• Concurrent engineering • Continuous process improvement • Supplier improvement	7 QC tools DOE QFD Benchmarking Just-in-time (JIT)
Controlling	• Data-based decisions • Reduce process variability • Cost of variation from objectives	SPC QFD Activity-based accounting

Although this relationship can be shown, the table does not express that these different activities provide a profoundly different outcome for the enterprise, and that outcome is what must be achieved to compete in today's marketplace. Note that:

- Instead of only planning for some improvement, better prices, and increased market share in the traditional way (such as, "Let's get __ percent better."), TQM factors reflect more specific objectives, such as satisfying the customer's expectations, needs, and wants. Using all the TQM factors to do this requires the organization to operate differently.
- With employee teams trained and empowered to manage and improve their own activities, the organization can be simpler; not as many layers of management are needed.
- Operating and directing still have to result in being successful in such things as meeting schedules. But operating and directing also have to satisfy the planning strategy of satisfying all the internal and external customer wants. This means higher quality, lower costs, and faster deliveries. Thus, continuous process improvement and waste elimination are the major emphases.
- Controls are still necessary. Quality control inspection, however, is not the mainstay to sort good from bad after the work is completed. Now controls rely on process control to prevent waste and reduce nonvalue-added activities.
- These objectives, and the activities to reach them, are sought by all the organizational functions, not only production. This is in recognition of the fact that errors anywhere create losses and waste.
- The old prorated or allocated cost data are no longer adequate. Cost data based on the resources used in a process must be available for improvement decision making. This requires activity-based cost accounting as discussed in Chapter 12.

The table also identifies tools used to meet these new TQM objectives. Their complexity varies widely, but they have proven to be effective in achieving TQM objectives as well as in fulfilling the traditional management responsibilities.

Chapter 3

Productivity and Quality

It has been a widely accepted axiom in industrial management that there was a fixed relationship between cost, schedule, and quality. It could be represented by the equilateral triangle shown in Figure 3.1.

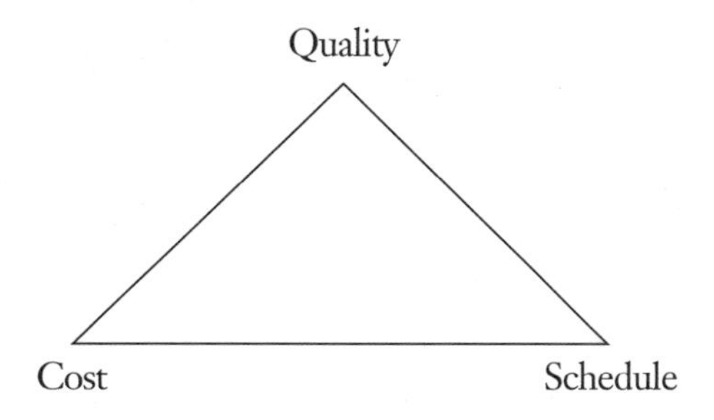

Figure 3.1 Fixed Relationships

The belief was that the three factors had to be kept in balance. It was believed that if one went up they all went up. This idea contributed to the lack of improvement in quality as a specific effort. Management liked to present this neat concept when preaching to others even though it frequently took actions to reduce schedule and cost regardless of the effect on quality.

This idea is categorically wrong because an increase in quality lowers cost and improves schedule. What that equality assumed was that higher quality costs more. This was not questioned because quality had an inexact definition. Higher quality was also equated with tighter tolerances. It was also thought that to achieve it workers would have to take more time or much more costly inspection was required to inspect for perfection: inspecting quality in. There was truth behind these beliefs in that the output variation of tolerance was not known or controlled so tightening tolerances would result in higher costs—scrap.

The ignorance of both production and quality management regarding quality was often demonstrated by managers in both activities who argued about the attitude of inspectors. In the author's 30 years of industrial experience, it was not unusual for production (and other) managers to argue emotionally that some inspector had too much interest in finding defects. Another expression of this was to argue that quality control should inspect to accept, not reject. This of course was the expression of the frustration in not understanding what quality is and how to control it and, more fundamentally, not knowing what processes were capable of producing.

These ideas also persisted in spite of Walter A. Shewhart's work in SPC in the late 1920s. Shewhart demonstrated that quality is controlled through process control and developed SPC to do it.

Why, when all this information was available, did industrial managers pay so little attention to it? Perhaps for these reasons:

1. They weren't educated to understand process management or to use SPC.
2. Their role models didn't use it. It wasn't visible.
3. It wasn't necessary for promotions. You got ahead by meeting schedules and time standards. Some level of defects was considered normal.
4. They did what they had always done and that was good enough. Before the 1980s, they pretty much sold everything they made anyway.
5. Management was strongly directed by accounting practices and its structure, and accounting had not been measuring nondirect labor productivity or process element costs. How accounting measured and reported organizational performance was the basis for rewarding management.
6. Quality was not a significant competitive factor.

Now the standards for quality in the marketplace have changed. High quality is a requirement to compete. Also, the true relationship between quality, cost, and schedule has been accepted. Higher quality raises productivity.

For any activity, in any organization, the following is true:

$$\text{Productivity } (P) = \frac{\text{Output (goods or services)}}{\text{Input (cost of output)}}$$

Productivity is the result of an effort. It can be measured at any level, macro or micro.

Here is a production example:

$$P = \frac{\text{Number of items}}{\text{Cost to produce}}$$

$$P = \frac{\text{Number of items}}{\text{Labor} + \text{Material} + \text{Capital} + \text{Expenses}}$$

Industrial productivity is a measure of the items produced versus the resources required.

Quality is a factor in productivity since errors and defects anywhere in an organization expend extra labor and, frequently, material. When extra labor and material are used, invariably capital and expenses are also required. These costs would not be incurred if there were zero defects. Therefore, the presence of defects adds cost to the output and lowers productivity. (Quality costs are discussed in Chapter 15.)

In symbolic terms:

$$\text{Total output} = \text{Output with quality } (Q_o) + \text{Output nonquality } (q_o)$$

$$O = Q_o + q_o$$

$$\text{Input} = \text{Resource } (R) = \text{Labor, Materials, Capital, Expenses}$$

$$P = \frac{Q_o + q_o}{R}$$

$$P_{max} = \frac{Q_o}{R} \text{ (No error or defect cost)}$$

Also, with no q_o, schedule capability is increased since the resources that were used to produce $(Q + q)$ are now available to make more conforming output, Q_o. These same principles of productivity apply to industrial suppliers of goods and services. Lower quality costs improve both the supplier's and buyer's competitive positions.

Productivity measures have traditionally been applied to manufacturing labor, capital, and material. The evolution of industry toward lower total labor content necessitates improving quality in *all* business functions and organizations.

Total productivity is becoming less a product of human ingenuity and technological breakthroughs to save factory labor. In the United States, 17 percent of labor is direct factory work. It is projected to decline to about 10 percent by the year 2000. This has already happened in agriculture now where less than 5 percent of the labor force produces our food versus 40 percent many years ago. About 25 percent of the industrial labor force is professional, technical, and managerial; the rest comprises other support jobs. This is a fertile area for productivity improvement through process quality improvement methods. Quality improvement in the work of all employees would reduce total cost and the cost of production since support worker errors contribute to production process variation and product defects.

Chapter 4

The New Quality Assurance

Implementing TQM has a significant impact on traditional industrial quality organizations. The new organization differs from the old in size, scope, and responsibility.

The largest and most comprehensive quality organizations existed within industries doing business with the Department of Defense (DOD). This was a result of the way the DOD used comprehensive military specifications for quality programs when contracting for equipment.[3] All quality activities a contractor had to initiate were defined. The military specifications described not only what had to be done but often gave strong direction on how to do it. It was also a required practice to have a contractor quality organization. In addition, the DOD used its quality personnel to confirm that the contractor's quality organization was effective in ensuring that all contract requirements were fulfilled. It was a redundant and expensive approach. It was directed toward merely meeting minimum requirements not toward improving quality. Quality organizations grew to be large and expensive adjuncts to contracting with the DOD. This had a strong influence on how quality assurance (QA) developed throughout all industry. The emphasis was on inspection.

Military specifications didn't require that quality activities be the responsibility of a separate quality organization. It just evolved that way. There was, however, some justification for it in the mind of the military customer. Without the presence of the quality police, the military received considerable defective material. (Actually, studies showed that they just received less defective material *with* that approach.) Until top management in both industry and the DOD accepted the principles and benefits of applying TQM (circa 1988), both parties lived with the situation and absorbed the cost. The customer occasionally resorted to a "get tough" action, but that did little more than raise costs through more inspections, scrap, and rework.

It is interesting to note that during the period from the 1950s onward, when industry in general was concentrating quality efforts on an inspection approach, the Japanese were listening to the counsel of W. Edwards Deming on how to use existing techniques to improve quality by concentrating on process improvement and statistical analysis, the genesis of TQM.

The thrust of TQM is to control and improve processes using structured problem-solving and statistical techniques. This improvement objective is the basic difference between TQM and military specifications (MIL-SPEC) thinking. Military specifications don't prohibit process control and improvement. In the evolution of the contractual relationship between contractors and the military, however, both parties came to accept the condition that meeting engineering specifications was all that was legally required, and that was "good enough."

Both parties accepted the fact that some level of scrap and rework was normal. But no one knew what the normal level was. In addition, all industry had an activity called material review. This was a quality activity that devised ways to "rework" or "use as is" material that didn't meet specification. This practice was recognized by the DOD, and its representatives participated in the procedure. The government had the authority to require a discount for nonconforming material, but it was rarely enforced.

All this isn't meant to suggest that management wasn't cost conscious but that its focus was on increasing production rates at lower cost: make more products faster with less labor. Making more products correctly was not in the equation. If a defect rate was 10 percent before a rate improvement, and it was no worse after, the change was acceptable.

Applying TQM changes all this. In government work the contractual requirements are the same. It's the management philosophy that changes. Process control and improvement result in higher quality products at comparatively lower costs. The only inspection necessary is that done by the process operator on samples to obtain data for process measurement. Inspection of purchased material can be virtually eliminated when suppliers implement process control and improvement. The entire production sequence costs less.

This new direction and philosophy impacts the QA organization. Much of it—its policing activities—is not needed. Quality is being controlled and improved where it should be: at the source, within the process.

Table 4.1 compares the differences the old quality organization was responsible for and how it changes under TQM. This reflects not only major shifts in responsibilities, and a much smaller QA function, but a change in the working relationships between other organizations and quality.

Table 4.1 Quality Organization Functions Before and After TQM

Old Testament	New Testament
Definition—conformance to requirements	Degree of variation from target value
Quality planning	Quality function deployment
Design to specification	Design for robustness (Taguchi) and customer expectations
Acceptable quality level	Continuous improvement
Manufacturing emphasis	All employees involved
Statistical process controls in manufacturing	SPS and SPC for all employees and organization activities
Build to specifications (specs)	Target value and satisfy internal and external customer
Quality costs—prevention, appraisal, failure	Reduce all process variations ($) everywhere
Inspection by quality organization	Control of processes by producer; quality just audit
Quality-operated corrective action	Producer problem solving and improvement of their process
Quality training—workmanship	Quality training every manager and employee in problem solving and process control/improvement
Quality organization responsible for quality	All organizations responsible for their quality, top down—quality organization to audit, train, and educate
Supplier quality—receiving and source inspection	Suppliers adhere to new testament—process control

Source: Cartin, T. J.; 1989; Quality: The Old and New Testament; AIAA/ADPA/NSIA First National TQM Symposium, AIAA Washington, D.C.

NEW SCOPE OF QA RESPONSIBILITIES

Figure 4.1 lists the QA functions before and after adopting TQM. The differences between the two parts are based on the following changes.

The functions of contract review, design review, and quality planning are performed by quality engineering in conjunction with design engineering and manufacturing engineering, preferably using concurrent engineering. Full responsibility for quality

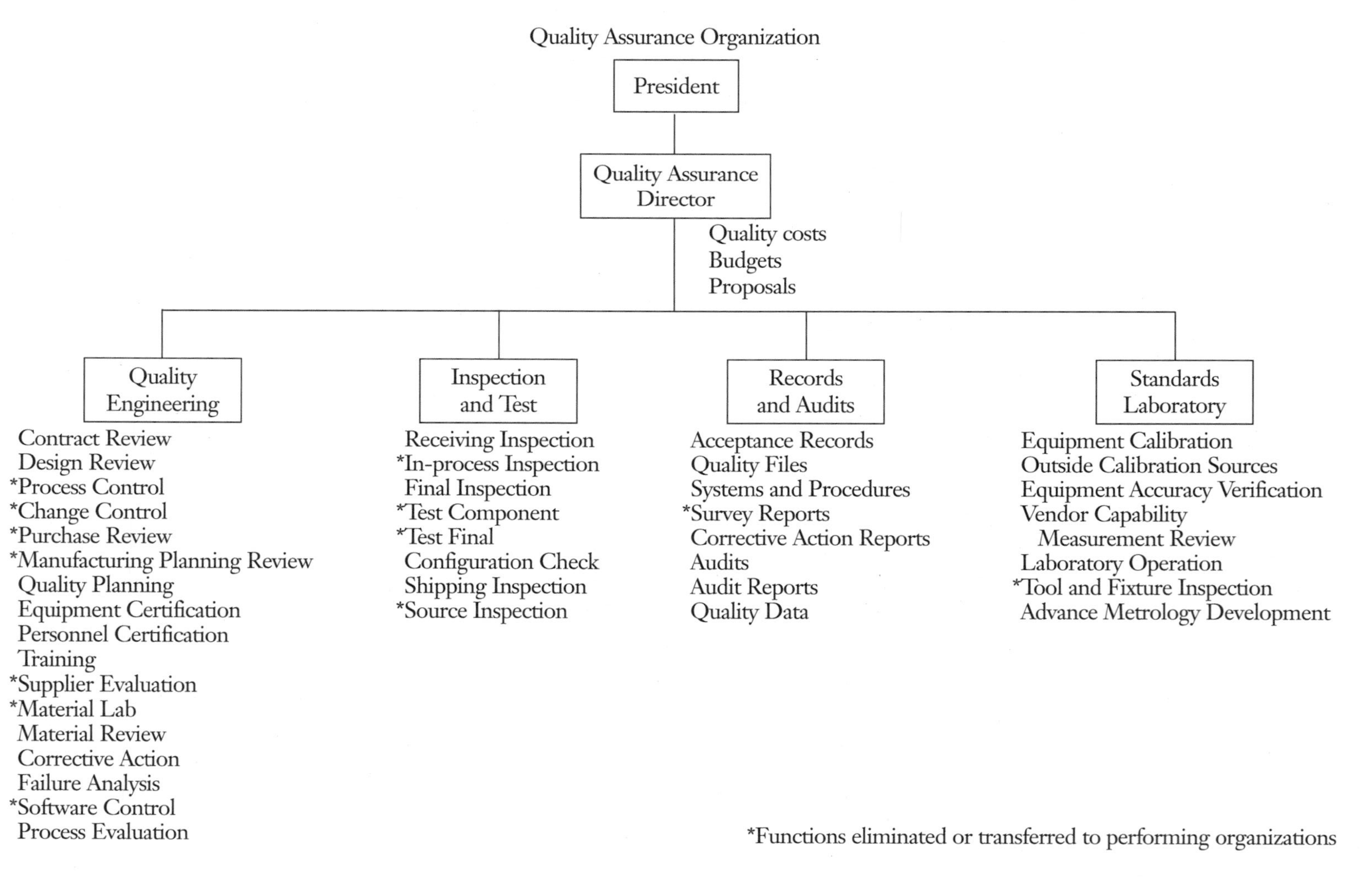

Figure 4.1 Typical Quality Organization Functions Before and After TQM Implementation

purchasing is assigned to the procurement function. Following Deming's policies the emphasis is on total procurement cost, not price. One approach to ensuring that purchasing personnel understand quality requirements was made by the Delco Division of General Motors Corporation. Its purchasing personnel became Certified Quality Engineers (CQEs). CQEs have to demonstrate their competence in a full body of knowledge in quality engineering by passing a written examination administered by ASQC.

The process control activities in which many quality organizations were involved are changed to process measurement and evaluation. The determination of a process' capability and improvements of that process are done in conjunction with the manufacturing engineers or design engineers using techniques like designed experiments. The process evaluation is performed as part of the expanded audit activity of QA.

In-process inspection or product testing or both becomes the responsibility of the manufacturing function.[4] QA would be achieved by means of the QA audit activity. Quality auditing takes on a new and more important role. It becomes an important arm of management. Audits determine whether the principles of TQM, namely customer satisfaction and continuous improvement, are maintained in all important organizational activities. These audits should monitor more than status and compliance; they should determine and measure effectiveness. Effectiveness is measured by determining whether the principles of TQM are being satisfied: continuous improvement in all the processes that affect customer satisfaction.

The reporting level of the QA manager has been a controversial issue in the past because of the emphasis of Western management on schedule and cost (over quality), and because QA was delegated to a specialized organization. The high reporting level was equated with the perceived need for authority to make other organizations comply. High-level QA management reporting may still be necessary during the beginning years of TQM implementation. When TQM is well entrenched (that is, institutionalized), its reporting level can then be changed. However, the quality audit function must continue to report to top management since this is a key to its continued involvement and knowledge of TQM progress.

SUMMARY

The significantly different role of QA in a TQM organization can be summarized using an excerpt from a report on the subject.[5]

The new role of QA can be summarized in terms of the following tasks:

- Support managerial leadership of quality improvement by performing detailed quality/performance auditing within each function to identify
  - the quality of the informational products and services being generated and the principal remaining sources of quality shortfalls as they affect external and internal customer satisfaction.

– the status and cost-effectiveness of quality control and improvement work being conducted.

– the quality of inputs to the function from other functions within the company and by any external sources.

– priorities for improvement in each of these areas.

This quality/performance auditing would have a more detailed diagnostic emphasis in office and technical (O&T) functions than in production and materials management, because quality-related skills are incompletely developed in the O&T functions.

- Provide internal consulting on day-to-day operations control and improvement efforts in each function, particularly the O&T functions. Consulting would include assistance in estimating the costs of imperfect quality (the costs of coping with errors and defects and the costs of detecting and preventing them) and associated process performance measures; identifying and organizing potential improvement projects; bringing to bear the diagnostic tools of improvement, such as process flow analysis and cause-and-effect analysis; developing and confirming potential solutions; and measuring and tracking performance improvement (see the seven QC tools in Chapter 18).
- Identify, acquire, or develop (or acquire and develop) new methods and tools for performance or new applications of existing tools.
- Design and conduct training and other mechanisms (newsletters, conferences, and so forth) for disseminating the methods and tools for performance improvement.

Chapter 5

The Critical Role of Management

STRATEGY AND QUALITY

A primary role of management is to lead an organization in its daily operation and to maintain it as a viable entity into the future. Quality has become an important factor to success in this latter, strategic responsibility.

Although ostensibly always an objective of business, customer satisfaction, *in customer terms*, became a specific goal in the late 1980s. Providing high quality was recognized as a key element for success. Most large corporations taking that path have documented their success. First, they survived the strong overseas competition that had set the high quality levels and now have regained some of their former markets. Smaller companies are also adopting similar goals. The Xerox Corporation filled 85 percent of the copier market up to about 1979, when its share dropped to 15 percent. Its Japanese competitors could *sell* an equivalent but higher quality machine for the Xerox *manufacturing* costs. Xerox was close to losing it all. Through its subsidiary in Japan it determined that the Japanese application of TQM made the biggest difference. Xerox also implemented TQM and after years of hard work regained 60 percent of the copier market. Management, with a new approach, has played the critical role. The new approach is reflected first in the expressed changes in policy. The Ford Motor Company *Operating Philosophy* is a good example:

"The operating philosophy of Ford Motor Company is to meet customer needs and expectations by establishing and maintaining an environment which encourages all employees to pursue never-ending improvement in the quality and productivity of products and services throughout the corporation, its supply base, and its dealer organization."[6]

Douglas Danforth, chairman and chief executive officer (CEO) of Westinghouse Electric Corporation, contended that quality is the key to American business success in the world markets in the 1980s and thereafter. According to David Garvin, associate professor of business at Harvard Business School, the perspective toward quality taken by top management of many organizations has shifted. CEOs have begun linking quality more closely with profitability thereby causing quality to be viewed as an important competitive weapon.

U.S. industrial management has been aware of quality in the context of a product characteristic and in the identification of an organization function. However, it has only recently become aware of quality as an objective, a market strategy, a competitive weapon, and an enhancement to productivity. Management has always played a critical role in the success or failure of an enterprise. It sets the policies, procedures, prices, and wages. It selects products and markets and marketing strategy. It is responsible for the integrity of the organization. It sets the climate. The behavior of managers is more closely observed by employees than managers may realize, and it is their behavior and its direct result that determines to a great extent how the organization members behave.

Now management accepts a new role, a new paradigm for managers and their organizations. As management understands the value of TQM it must also accept the critical role it plays in inducing change.

At this stage, the early 1990s, there is considerable discussion in the media about the need for America to become more competitive and to provide higher quality goods and services. There is reported progress by companies who started a few years ago, but there is a long way to go. A critical factor is still what employees think is being said versus what they believe is still going on. *Fortune* magazine published the results of an ASQC poll on the subject (Figure 5.1) in May 1991. Participants in the poll saw the same inconsistency between what management says and how it acts. Only management can reduce that gap by making its actions and its daily business decisions consistent with what it says.

This is the critical role of managers. They must understand the TQM philosophy, tools, and techniques, and regularly participate in their application at every level. They must change if the organization is to change. The old analogy of a company leader being the captain of the ship is no longer appropriate. The leader of a company can't just set the course and bark orders when corrections are needed. He or she must set the objectives but solicit the crew on the best and lowest cost way to get there and let ongoing correction come from the crew. This analogy suggests a radical change in behavior and roles for everyone. That is exactly what it is, and it will occur only if the change in leadership is demonstrated by those in charge.

Most important in adopting TQM, measurable quality improvement in every product, process, and service must be established as a prime organizational operating principle and never made subservient to schedule and cost. It will be a long time before management will be trusted to be fully committed to TQM. Managers have the opportunity, but they have many, many years of double-talk to overcome.

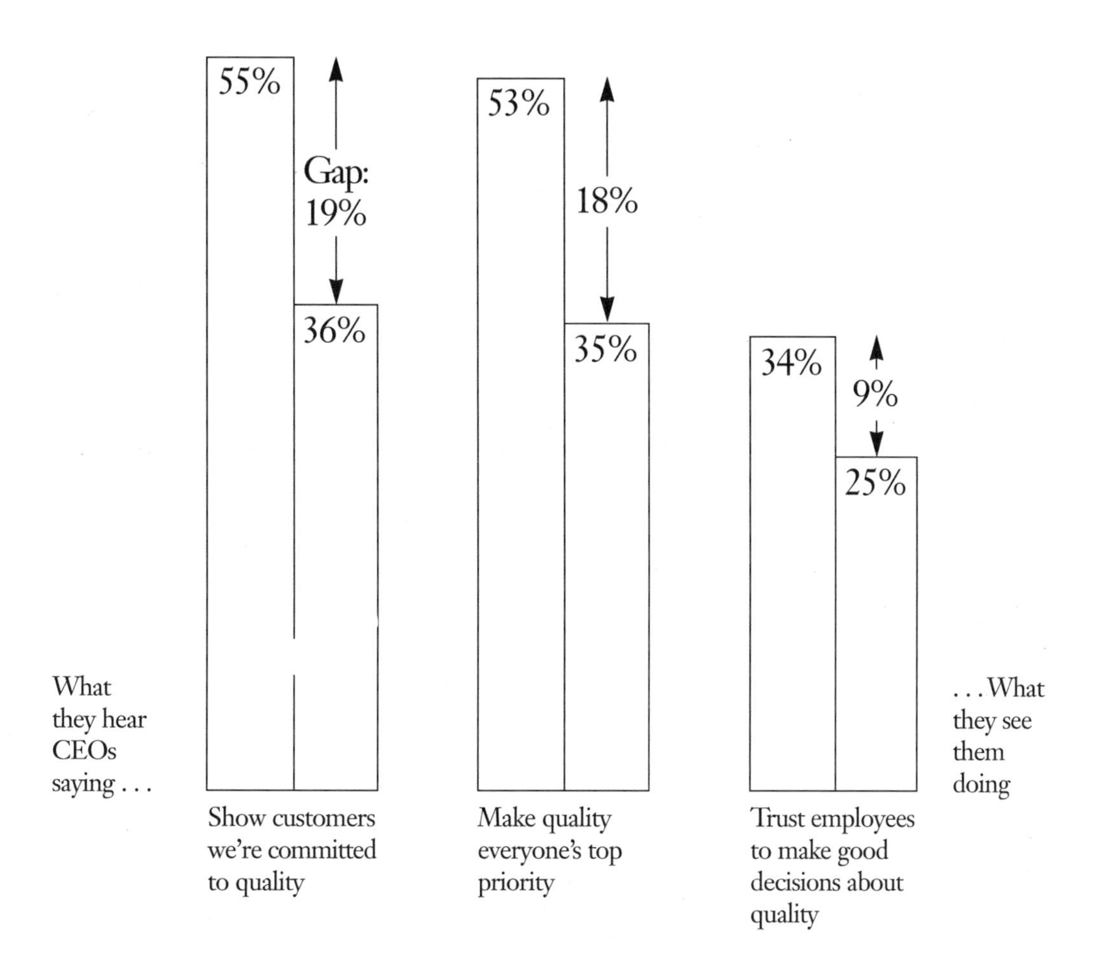

Talk is free but quality takes work: There's still a gap, employees think, between what top executives say about the subject and what their companies actually do.

Figure 5.1 Employees' View of the Quality Commitment

Chapter 6

TQM–Management by Objective–Management by Exception

Deming has been a major critic of American management practices. Of course, he has the experience and credentials to do so. Using his management philosophy as their guide, the Japanese have given him most of the credit for their adoption of the quality imperative. His ideas conflict directly and philosophically with the dominant American model that is best represented by management by objectives (MBO) and management by exception (MBE).

Peter Drucker is credited with coining the term management by objectives. It is defined as "a process whereby the superior and subordinate managers of an organization jointly identify its common goals, define each individual's major area of responsibility in terms of the results expected of him/her, and use these measures as guides for operating the unit and assessing the contribution of each of its members."[7]

The key is that subordinates play a major role in setting their own objectives and not in merely receiving objectives from above. MBO has been practiced more successfully at upper levels than at lower levels mainly because the activities at the lower levels are much more dynamic. Objectives agreed to one month might be inappropriate a month later because some unforeseen event affects an operation. This is not too surprising, in hindsight, when it is recognized that, without the ability to manage and control the work processes, unpredicted destructive events were assured.

MBO also emphasizes functional performance measurements under the control of individual managers. This is not always related to and may work against multifunction process performance—the activities that have the greatest impact on total organization performance. The MBO concept does not conflict with TQM if it is modified to fit TQM objectives. The same goal-setting process can be followed except that the goals *must* emphasize continuous process improvements, the team process *must* be the foundation of how results are obtained, and the performance measures *must* be in terms of measured process improvement and customer satisfaction. MBO used in this manner would be close to what the Japanese call quality deployment or hoshin planning. (See Chapter 17.)

MBE is another common American management method. This is one of the oldest techniques for identifying targets for management attention and action. For MBE, reporting systems are established to identify variables (cost, quality, or volume) that are performing outside forecasts or budgets. By definition such items are problems to correct. It's a simple concept, but it doesn't produce the long-term results required for survival because:

1. Performance outside of arbitrarily set limits is usually a symptom rather than the problem.
2. Performance limits are not set based on the capability of the process. (They are frequently set as a result of MBO.)
3. As described in Chapter 7, all processes vary. So-called corrective action may be taken on a process already operating within its best capability. If objectives cannot be met by these processes, capability improvement is the appropriate corrective action. If the manager responsible doesn't know this, the wrong action is likely to be taken. A manager under pressure often forces results. Good results will be short-lived.
4. It is likely that corrective action will not be taken when a favorable variance suddenly occurs, yet this may indicate the existence of a special cause of variation that needs to be identified. It may be a valuable clue for permanent performance improvement.

The principle of MBE would be appropriate if it were based on reacting to variation outside the measured capability of a process. Otherwise it may do more harm than good.

Chapter 7

Managing Variation and Statistical Control

Everyone responsible for an organization, activity, or process makes performance decisions based on some kind of data. It may be qualitative (such as on-time, late, or too many errors), or it may be quantitative (such as 15 percent over budget, 75 percent yield, or 10 percent improved). Decisions are also made on such things as whether commitments are met, people are performing, or costs are acceptable. Typically all those conclusions are reached using one-dimensional data. The data may be very accurate, but it is integrated in relation to standards or objectives based mostly on experience, practices, and what managers have been trained to do. The critical missing information for intelligent decision making is simply what, in quantitative terms, activities and processes are actually capable of achieving as they operate day-by-day. Without the understanding and introduction of the *statistical* concept of variation applied to operating business processes, the wrong—even counterproductive—decisions may be made. One of Deming's key points is to manage using statistical thinking. This means recognizing that everything varies, including industrial and office processes and individual and combined human actions. To manage effectively and competitively the nature of this variation must be measured and understood. Fortunately, there are ways to organize data to depict performance reflecting activity/process variation to provide the basis for proper management.

VARIATION

Systems and processes are devised to accomplish a task. If acceptable, they are allowed to continue. If not, measured against some arbitrary standard, a correction is made. This methodology, which is the most commonly used, is essentially open-ended. The corrective action is event-oriented. In activities and processes with many variables—common in those that are important—their interactions are rarely understood so corrective actions are approached with ignorance and hope. No one is sure that the fix will work. It reflects a "do something" attitude. This approach is an admission that the task output is unpredictable and leads to a fire-fighting reaction. Adjusting a process might or might not lead to improvement. In either case, no one will quite understand why the adjustment succeeded or failed. Historically, this practice of managing has not resulted in stable processes with low error and defect rates or predictable output.

What is needed is a way to know the amount of variation to *expect* in activities and processes so that correction can be made if the variation is too large. The principles and practices of TQM are focused on achieving just that. There are some fairly simple, proven statistical tools and techniques to do it. They are key in managing continuous process improvements.

TQM emphasizes managing the variations in processes. That is very different from managing organization functions. It focuses on identifying processes, measuring their variation, and determining whether the variation is normal or abnormal and correcting it if necessary, then further improving it. It uses proven tools to do this and involves everyone in the activity. The recognition and understanding of variation is a prerequisite for reaping the benefits of TQM.

STATISTICAL THINKING

The fundamental factor in this concept is understanding that variation in *every* process is a normal condition and that the state of this normal pattern should be the basis for making decisions. If it isn't known the process output can't be managed. This applies to what is commonly known as an industrial production process but also to any series of tasks in any kind of organization. Activities of this nature have not commonly been recognized or managed as processes but are when using TQM. An example of these is given later in the chapter.

It is also critical to understand that every process has an inherent capability. A process operating within its inherent capability is doing the best it ever will do unless something in the process itself (such as the way tasks are done) is changed. Countless resources are wasted trying to fix a problem with a process output, not realizing that the process is doing its best. It isn't recognized that it simply doesn't have the capability to meet requirements consistently.

Before anyone can understand what variation means and how to control it, one must understand the basic statistical concepts involved in how things vary. It isn't very complicated and provides a quantum increase in the power to manage for higher productivity. Deming stresses that management must address the problems in processes (systems). The people in these processes are victims of management ignorance not the cause of the poor output.

Failure to understand the concept of variation leads to what often occurs now. People are blamed for failure to perform as a result of their inability to control a process for which they (and management) have inadequate understanding and authority to change. This leads to common erroneous business decisions. For example:

- Purchasing new equipment when it isn't needed. *Process* analysis and then improvement is often all that is necessary.
- Making changes assuming that something has gone wrong when it hasn't. A process may already be doing its best.
- Tampering with processes when no action was the correct action. Overreaction to events is a common mistake. If a process is understood its behavior is predictable.
- Causing organizational demotivation by looking for scapegoats. The process may be inadequate, but individuals should not be blamed.
- Establishing improperly based reward programs. Performance rewards should be based on improving process variation, not on exceeding some arbitrary goal.

These improper actions are a result of not understanding when a process is acting normally (doing the best it can do) and when it isn't, and that frequently the process variation must be reduced to meet requirements and objectives.

Normal and Abnormal Variation

A fact that has been tested and proven thousands of times since Shewhart's proof in the 1930s is that all processes have an inherent variation in their performance. He referred to this as operating with only common causes present. For example, a brand new high-precision machine, perfectly set up, repetitively cutting a diameter on the same size raw stock, does not cut exactly the same diameter on every piece. It varies, if ever so minutely, over time, around some average dimension. This is its inherent capability. It would be impossible for every finished diameter to meet a tolerance tighter than the span of that inherent variation.

A nonindustrial example is the time-based variation of product sales in one territory. Another would be the monthly variation in the accounts payable activity. If plotted over time, they would display a pattern of variation around some average value that would represent the normal process behavior, its capability.

Control

Another way to describe processes varying within their inherent capability (only common causes present) is to refer to them as operating in statistical control, that is, variation around the average is random and within calculated limits. Unless something new enters the process (some factor changes in an unexpected and negative manner), then the cost and quality output of a process in statistical control is predictable. The range of its variation (limits) can be calculated using simple mathematics. If it goes outside this range, some special cause is at work and can be removed.

A dramatic example of special causes occurred in the testing of the Salk polio vaccine in 1955 on two million children. The Salk vaccine was a killed polio virus that still worked to build immunity to the live virus. One small amount of inadequately inactivated virus vaccine was distributed. It led to 204 cases of polio and 11 deaths among vaccinated children. Some special cause occurred that was not detected and drove the process out of control.

The value and power of this knowledge is clear. When in control, you know whether the process will operate within the limits you need and whether it will continue to do so. On the other hand, if you don't know if a process is in statistical control, it probably isn't, and its output is therefore unpredictable. Taking action to "improve" its output may or may not work. The important beneficial action to take is to put it in statistical control. Remove the special causes.

GETTING STATISTICAL CONTROL

When the process is not varying in a random manner, the inherent capability is being affected by something that is causing the "nonrandomness." It is said that a special (assignable) cause is present. These are causes of variation that are not present all the time and are not an inherent part of the process. If, in the example of the cutting machine, a bearing lubricant leaked out, the machine variation would change because an assignable cause occurred. Maintaining processes in statistical control is what SPC is about.

The tool for measuring processes to gain statistical control is the control chart. This is a chart that displays the process performance, using sample measurements of a process output at fixed time periods, from which the expected statistical range of variation can be calculated. The chart is useful because it signals when to take action and when to leave the process alone. It also indicates the process capability. Figure 7.1 shows control charts for sales figures. It shows the upper and lower control limits for sales processes. There are three limits even though upper management acts as though there is only one. This is a common failure when statistical thinking is missing.

In Figure 7.1, upper charts reflect a single bonus level for what is actually three independent processes. Lower charts reflect performance in each. The bonus awards would be very different.

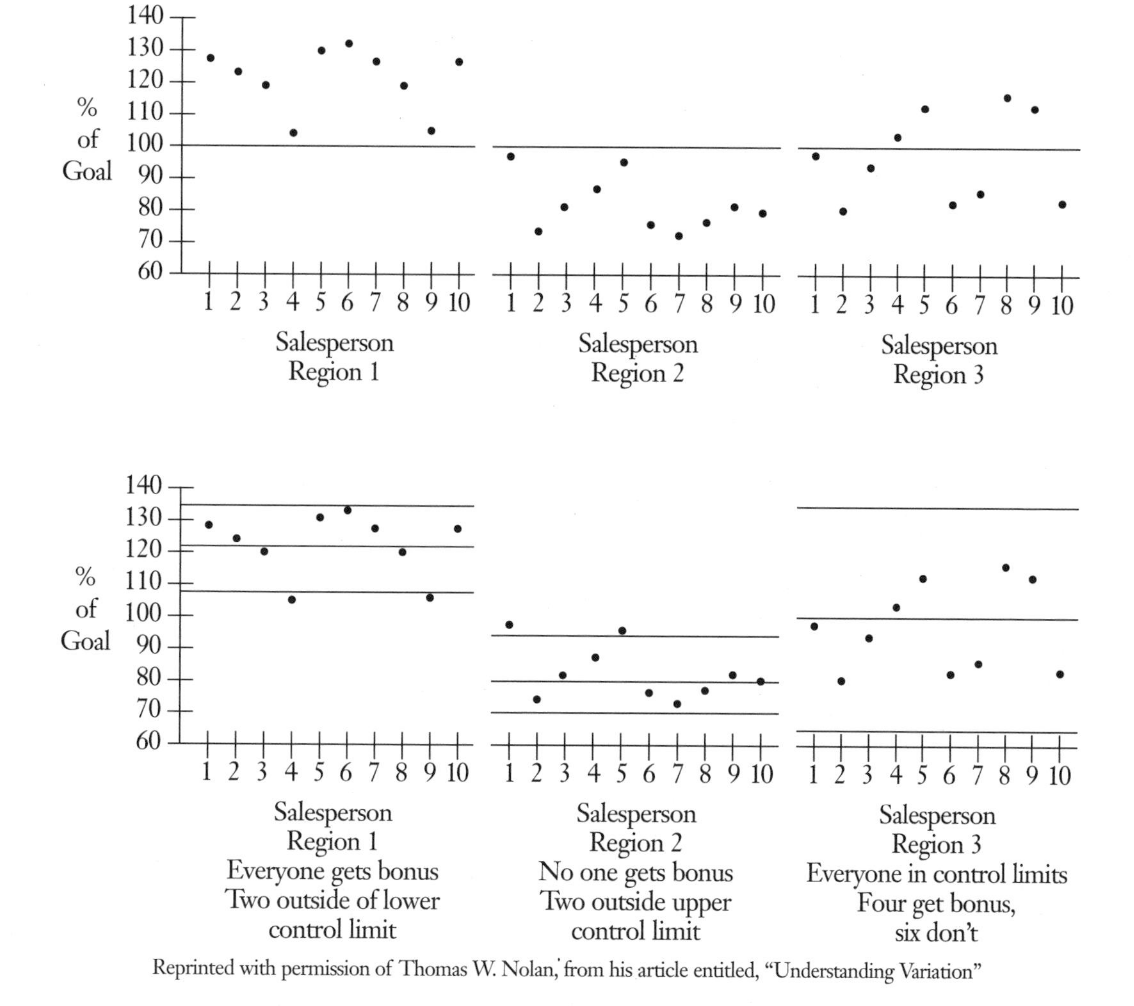

Reprinted with permission of Thomas W. Nolan, from his article entitled, "Understanding Variation"

Figure 7.1 Application of Control Charts to Sales Data

CONTROL CHARTS

Control charts are powerful tools for management decision-making because:

1. They indicate when a process is operating in statistical control (only common causes present).
2. They indicate when action should be taken (operating outside limits or demonstrating patterns that indicate a special cause is present).
3. They indicate the capability of a process (the scale between limits).
4. They provide feedback to managers of a process on the effect of actions taken to improve the process.

5. They communicate clearly to those operating a process by showing how well they are performing.

Control charts are also misused. They are not a panacea; they must be constructed and interpreted accurately. When using control charts, the following limitations must be considered:

1. They indicate when a process is out of control and needs correction. They don't indicate the assignable cause. Other tools are used to do that, particularly the seven QC tools discussed later (Chapter 18).
2. They do not indicate whether an in-control process is good or bad, capable or incapable. Capability can be determined using the charts of an in-control process by comparing the expected (calculated) operating range with the specified or desired range.
3. A process capability that is not compatible with requirements needs either the requirements expanded or the process changed to reduce its variation by removing *common* causes. Methods to manage this are discussed in Chapter 9.
4. The achievement of statistical control is the beginning of the improvement process. All of the causes of variation (common causes) must be identified and removed or reduced based on the costs involved.
5. The results of the application of the mathematics of statistics is based on sample measurements. Therefore the results are estimates. However, careful adherence to the procedures developed for their use will result in very good approximations. Another factor that requires care in the use of calculated data is that process variation is dynamic, constantly shifting over time.

SUMMARY

Statistics can contribute broadly to management activities, both as a method of thinking about management problems and as a set of tools for more effective management. The key to success is blending ideas about organizational behavior and process behavior with quality control statistics.

The performance of every process varies. All variation has a cause. Variation should be reduced based on customer requirements or the cost of improvement. TQM is largely managing processes for improvement. Process variation, common and special, must be understood to make the appropriate management decisions. Process performance measurement requires the understanding and use of statistical analysis. The most useful tool to depict process performance is the control chart. It describes the capability of a process to meet requirements. It indicates the effect of process improvement actions and normal or abnormal operation of a process. It should be the basis for process management decisions. From this we get a new management philosophy for achieving greater customer satisfaction by improving quality through reduced process variation.

Chapter 8

Setting Quality Goals—6-Sigma Capability—Parts Per Million—Cycle Time

Organizations need goals to focus their energies and resources on common values; goals are important for unifying efforts. At the same time, it is also difficult to set single meaningful goals for the entire organization. They tend to become so broad that organizational elements and individuals fail to see the connection between their efforts and some generalized goal. The following discussion identifies some successful approaches that make goal setting more meaningful.

QUALITY DEPLOYMENT—MANAGEMENT BY PLANNING

The Japanese have for many years used a unique form of planning to deploy quality throughout a company. It is commonly called hoshin kanri.

Hoshin kanri is different because, although there is organizational goal setting involved, the focus is on the planning process itself. The objective is to improve the planning process continuously. The emphasis is not on meeting goals because they were set but to learn how to set them better. The result is that targets normally are exceeded.

The process begins with the setting of a few key goals for the company by top management. Then down through the organization managers and employees establish goals that correlate with those of the company. Peers then meet to make sure that their plans are complementary. The final plans are posted in the work area.

After developing their targets, individuals document a monthly self-assessment that is given to their supervisors who combine it with their own and send it to their supervisors and so on up to the top. Everyone in the chain knows what is going on.

Flexibility and continuous improvement are reflected in the procedure whereby measured gains become the new standard, from which further progress is planned. The new standard becomes the level for daily control. There are then two activities involved: meeting standards and making improvements. Other unique features include the monthly audit to analyze what was learned. Also important is an annual presidential audit to assess progress to determine how the planning process is improving and how the president can assist.

QUALITY GOALS

There is one belief that the only real goal of quality is zero defects. This was the goal of a nation-wide movement around 1960. It had a short life. One reason is that the process to achieve it contained an emotional component that was not sustainable. Another is that seeking perfection seems too difficult and beyond human achievement. Perhaps most important, managers themselves did not participate; they believed zero defects was for everyone else.

Another opinion is that the policy of continuous process improvement itself is a goal. Quantitative goals, although desirable, may not be necessary. An argument for this is that setting quantitative goals is frequently arbitrary. On the positive side, though, there can be a sense of achievement and of winning if the goals are met. Not meeting them is often considered failure. However, is coming to within 90 percent a failure? There is also the disadvantage, as mentioned in the discussion on MBO, that long-term benefits tend to be sacrificed for short-term gains. In comparison, just using continuous improvement as a goal and measuring the trend is a simple concept and can be a motivation to continued improvement. Adding a quantitative measure of *how* good is ideal. A simple approach is particularly useful in the early stages of TQM implementation when people are learning the philosophy and methodology. The complexity of measurement can be added after the data are collected and understood.

Benchmarking (Chapter 16) is an excellent goal-setting technique that is being used more frequently. If an organization discovers that another company can operate a similar process at a lower cost and higher quality output, this establishes an improvement goal. It is frequently found that benchmark goals are more difficult than an organization would normally set, but since they have been proven achievable they are accepted.

A different idea has been initiated by the Motorola Corporation and adopted by others like IBM. It sets quantitative goals for all organizations and processes. A goal to achieve 6-sigma capability sets a quantitative goal, difficult but achievable for the company, its elements, and its suppliers. It is also a rather sophisticated statement. It requires an understanding of basic statistics and statistical thinking about process management. If TQM is to be successfully introduced, however, statistics have to be learned anyway. Even though setting a goal in this form is fraught with measurement problems and misinterpretations, strict rules must be established for measuring and reporting results.

VARIATION[8]

Sigma (σ) is a statistical measure of variation.[9] It indicates the amount that a controlled process can be expected to vary from its average performance. Figure 8.1 shows this measurement. The curve, the normal distribution, represents the output variation of a process in control. The horizontal scale is sigma. The characteristics of a normal distribution is such that 99.73 percent of it is contained within the range from -3σ to $+3\sigma$. The normal distribution and its characteristics are the foundation of statistical thinking and managing in TQM.

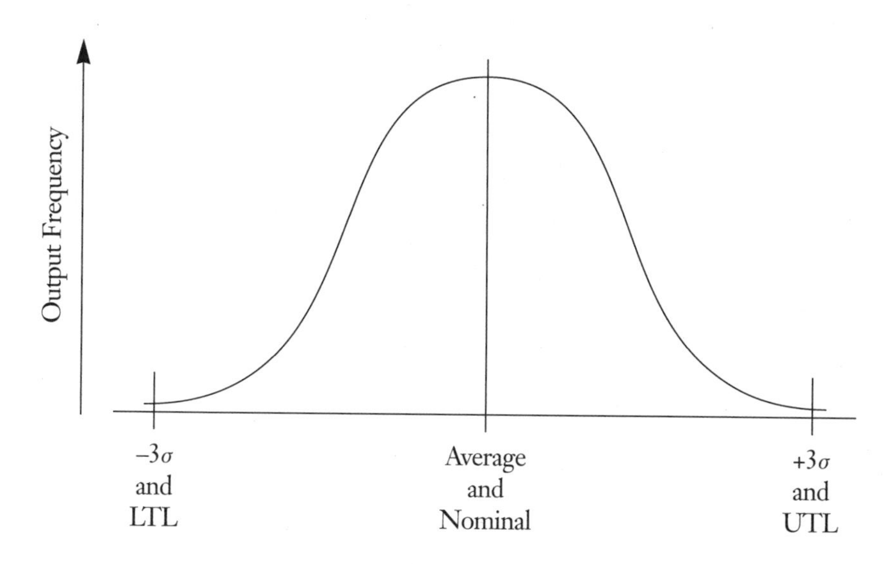

Figure 8.1 The Normal Distribution
The output of a controlled process is represented by the normal distribution. Most of the output is near the average of the process output. The output spread is measured in sigma.

If a process operation displays the distribution as shown in Figure 8.1 and the product design specification tolerance limits coincide with the $\pm 3\sigma$ limits, the process is said to have a 3σ capability.

If the specification limits were $\pm 6\sigma$ away from the specification nominal, it would have a 6σ capability (Figure 8.2). Initially, establishing a 3σ capability goal is a valuable step. It makes a process minimally capable, and it leads the organization to understand and control process variation.

This, in turn, leads to a change in organizational management philosophy and

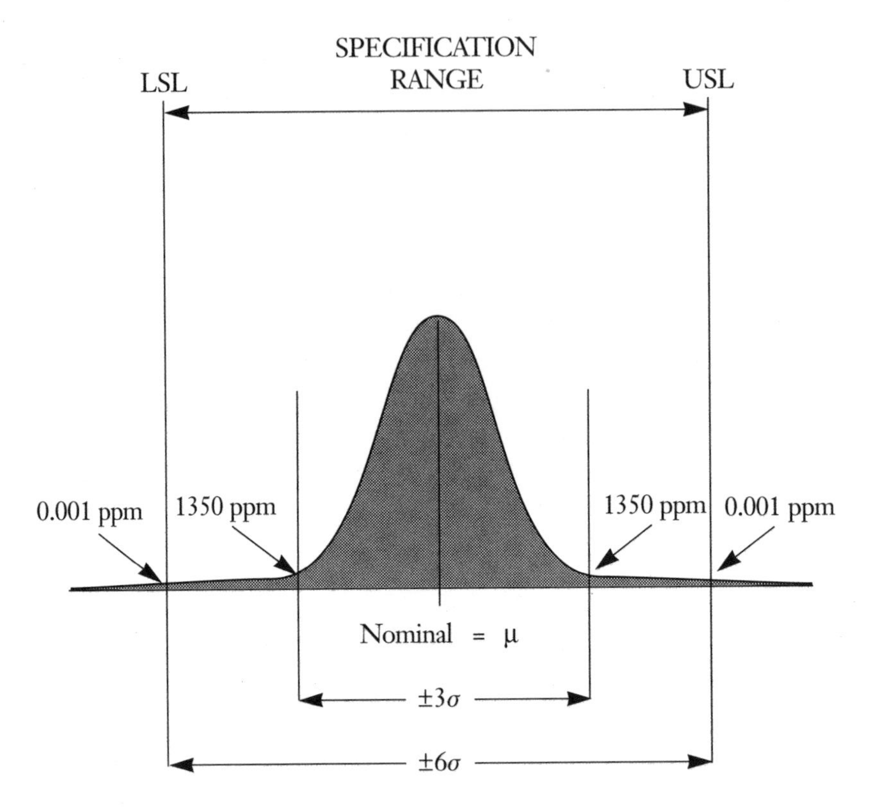

Figure 8.2 This distribution is a comparison of a ±3σ and ±6σ process capability compared to specification tolerance limits. Also shown are the probable error rates (parts per million) in a 3σ and 6σ process.

culture change. Management becomes more process-oriented and less function-oriented. After reaching the 3σ level, higher goals, such as 6σ, can be set for continuous improvement.

PROCESS DYNAMICS

The previous discussion represents the ideal. For operating processes, the 3σ limits rarely correspond to the specification tolerance range. The factors at work in a process are dynamic and, even while remaining in statistical control, cause some shift in the average with respect to the product tolerance nominal. In that case, the $\pm 3\sigma$ limits would sometimes fall outside the tolerance limits and the number of non-conformances would probably increase.

To allow for this shift, the $\pm 3\sigma$ operation of the process must be smaller than the tolerance allowance. The capability of the process must provide a safety margin with respect to requirements. Another reason to have a margin is that the sigma calculations are estimates. They are based on samples and the assumption is that their distribution is normal. A common goal is to establish $\pm 4\sigma$ as a minimum process capability initially and $\pm 6\sigma$ as the ultimate for the long term. If the tolerance limits remain fixed the only way to improve the capability from $\pm 3\sigma$, $\pm 4\sigma$, or $\pm 6\sigma$ is to make improvements that reduce sigma.

PARTS PER MILLION

Parts per million (ppm) is another way to express a goal equivalent to a sigma capability. It means defects or errors per million operations or products produced in the operation of a process, office, or industry. It is also based on normal distribution characteristics. In a process with a 3σ capability as previously described, only 0.27 percent of the output will be outside 3σ. That equates to 2,700 defective items produced or operations performed in every million. With a 6σ capability it is 3.4 ppm. This illustrates the relationship between a 3σ and 6σ capability with respect to customer satisfaction. The 6σ would result in an almost insignificant 3.4 versus 2,700 delivered defective products. Figure 8.3 lists the ppm for different sigma capabilities for common activities. It shows the high capability required to approach zero defects.

The best-in-class notation is made in comparison to the average company performance. The best-in-class notation is the benchmark process to equal or exceed.

CYCLE TIME

Another TQM-related goal is cycle time reduction. From a macro viewpoint, cycle time is the time between the receipt of an order to the delivery of a product or service. This is an important measure of company performance in satisfying the customer. It is also a key issue in the just-in-time (JIT) concept. This macro measure is of course made up and determined by the many internal cycles, and it is these that are the targets for improvement. Cycle times for new product development to market time are of growing importance and can provide a major strategic advantage. The company first to market with a high quality product or service will reap the highest profit before competition drives prices down. It can also be a factor in retaining market share. Eastman Kodak Company has retained the world market share lead by supplying ever-improving products that have kept the customers satisfied.

Cycle time reduction is an appropriate objective for any organization.

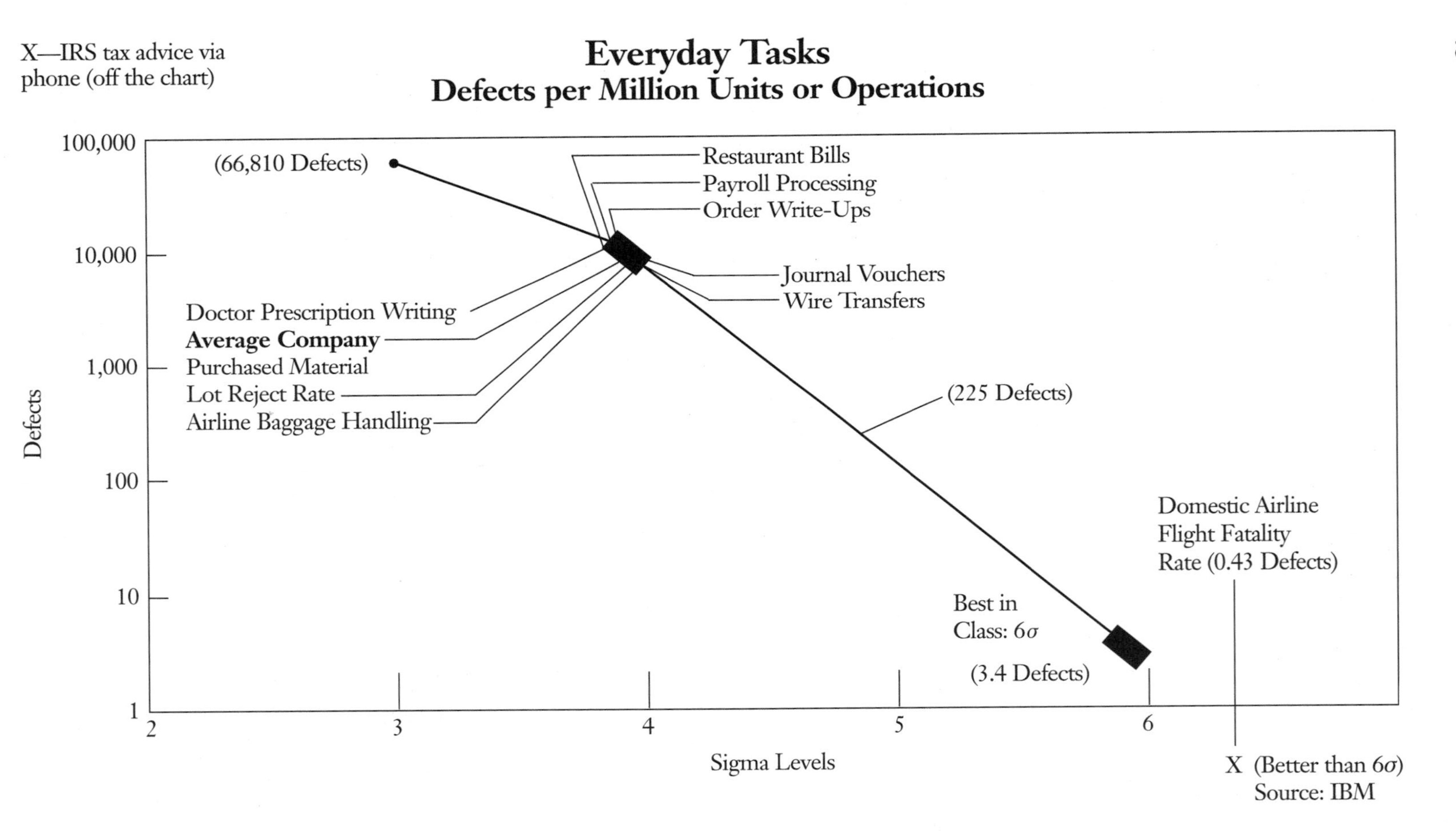

Figure 8.3 Some Common Performance Capabilities

Chapter 9

The Systems Approach to Improvement

The most common approach to business problem solving and to making improvement has been to use a piecemeal instead of a systematic approach. One reason for this was the practices that evolved in American business toward using organizational structure and specialization to manage.[10]

Historically, as hiring workers became more complex, industry went from the foreman doing his own hiring to a personnel office, to industrial relations, then to human resources. As quality requirements became more complex, inspection became the quality control, then quality assurance or product assurance. When productivity was highlighted, a leader was appointed. Now that TQM is a popular objective, it is common to have a TQM leader.

Unfortunately, operational barriers grew as ornaments were added to the organizational tree. This led functional organizations to solve problems within the scope of their responsibilities even though the causes of many problems were interfunctional. The root causes were not addressed. In addition, system problems were not resolved because no one was responsible for the performance of the true multifunctional system or for its improvement.

As the United States emphasized function, the Japanese went in another direction. They simplified and flattened the organizational structure. This brought upper management in better contact with the lower echelons and improved two-way communication.

The Japanese introduced TQM. This systematic approach to managing across functions provided the framework for continuous improvement. Organizational barriers were reduced and the productivity of the entire enterprise was increased.

This methodology is powerful because all factors that relate to a process must be identified: how it works, how well it works, and, from that, how it can be improved. The value is multiplied by using knowledgeable teams. Those teams often call on functional specialists so that the best knowledge is used. It leads to decisions that are best for improving the entire process not merely one function.

Figure 9.1 shows a process model. It's the basic building block used in system/process analysis. Figure 9.2 illustrates the application of the process model to an organization. This represents everything from the total organization down to even one individual. *It is the basis* of the total quality improvement process.

The measurement points (*M*) shown in Figure 9.2 are intended to show that to manage a process its performance must be known (measured). Measurement at the key points shown will indicate status, the best targets for improvement, and the result of improvements implemented. To be most useful, these pulse points are not just places to measure status of events but must provide quality performance indicators. These measure the health of the processes.

PROCESS MANAGEMENT AND IMPROVEMENT: CHARACTERISTICS

A process is a sequence of activities or tasks completed by a person, group, or set of equipment. It consists of any combination of people, methods, machines, materials, or environment.

As Figure 9.2 shows, outputs are generally inputs to another process. All processes vary:

- No two process outputs are exactly alike.
- The sources of variation vary.
- Some randomly occurring variation is normal.
- Some variation is due to assignable, removable causes.

Reducing the variation in a process provides higher quality and customer satisfaction. A sequence of related processes is a system. Processes and systems have attributes of efficiency and effectiveness in terms of their performance.

Interrelated processes act as both a supplier and customer. In providing requirements to a supplier, a customer becomes a supplier. In receiving the output of another process, a supplier becomes a customer. Every process displays these characteristics. That is what makes the model truly representative of reality and to which TQM tools and techniques can be universally applied.

A high quality process:

1. Achieves intended results and satisfies the customer.
2. Uses resources efficiently.

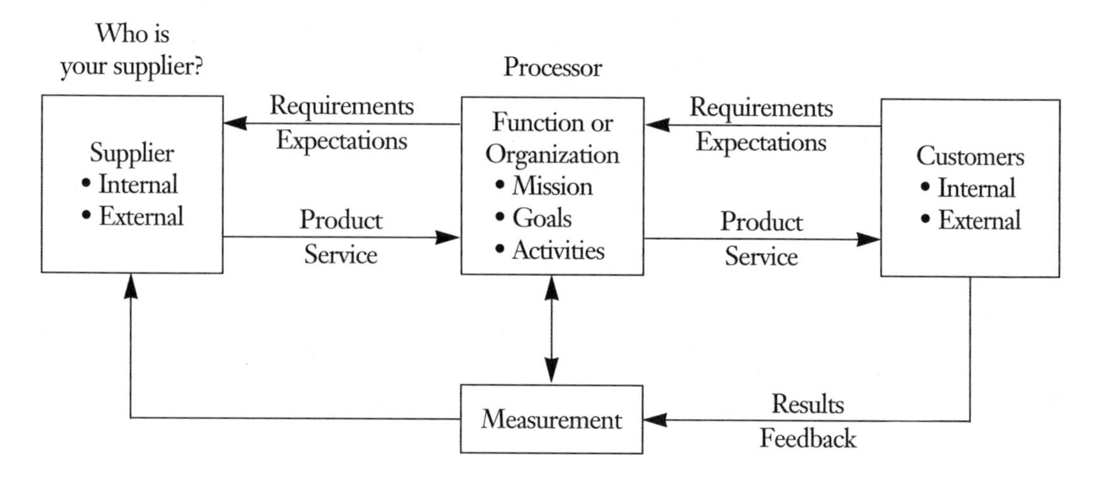

Figure 9.1 Organization relationships that form a process. Every function or activity plays all three roles at one time or another in its operation.

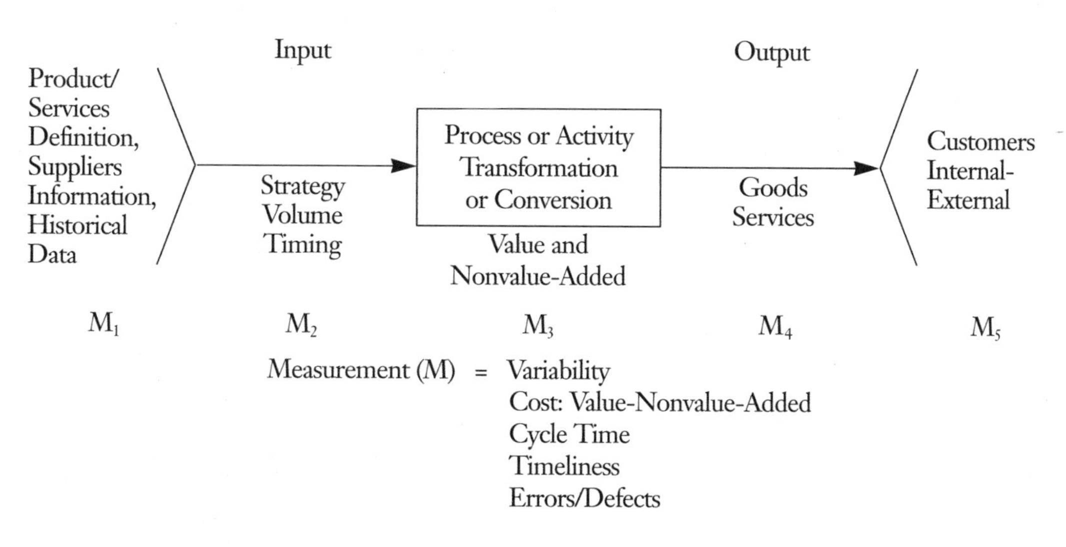

Total Quality Management and Measurement Points. Critical Performance Measurement Points for Enterprise, Division, Plant, or Function.

Figure 9.2 Process Performance

3. Displays variability at the lowest economically achievable level.
4. Uses key point quality measures to assess performance.
5. Adds value to the enterprise objectives.

PROCESS ANALYSIS AND MANAGEMENT

Managing a process involves simple principles that are important in achieving the highest efficiency and effectiveness. These principles are:

1. Establish ownership. Most important business processes are usually cross-functional. Therefore, pieces are managed by different functions. The result is that organizational barriers limit performance and improvement.

   Recognition of the need for ownership led the Xerox Corporation, after identifying the 62 key business processes for successful operation (Figure 9.3), to identify a senior manager for each process who is responsible for its performance and improvement.[11] In this case it also indicates the evolution to using process management to manage the company. This illustrates the significant difference involved in managing processes as well as organization functions.
2. Verify and describe the purpose of the process. Are all of its elements necessary?
3. Define the process, boundaries, and interfaces. Successful management depends on defining boundaries and interfaces. This is important to establish the limits of the process owner and to ensure that every element of all processes has been identified and assigned. Interfaces are critical and must be managed by interrelated process managers in their roles as both supplier and customer.
4. Organize and train the process improvement teams. Fundamental for all teams is training in operating rules and the seven QC tools (Chapter 18). Other appropriate tools and techniques should be taught to the specific need and application.
5. Define and document the process. Defining a process is a fundamental and highly valuable step. Without a written description in some form—like a flow chart—on which an analysis team agrees, the most effective improvements cannot be made.

   In fact, the wrong action may be taken. It is common to begin at the highest level and break tasks into subprocesses as needed. This maintains the integrity of the whole. In complex organizations, however, this can become overwhelming. In these cases it may be more understandable to start at the lowest level. Build the total by identifying and describing each element then the interconnection of elements.

Xerox Business Area/Process List

1. Market Management (7)
   - Market Selection and Analysis
   - Segments and Customer Requirements Understanding
   - Customer Requirements Management
   - Market Planning
   - Marketing Support
   - Marketing Communications
   - Market Tracking
2. Customer Engagement (6)
   - Sales Territory Planning
   - Prospecting Management
   - Enterprise Management
   - Agreement Development
   - Agreement Management
   - Customer Support
3. Order Fulfillment (7)
   - Order Processing
   - Scheduling
   - Customer Preparation
   - Staging and Pre-installation
   - Delivery/Removal
   - Installation/Deinstallation
   - Product Production
4. Product Maintenance (8)
   - Service Call Management
   - Service Dispatching
   - Product Servicing
   - Service Call Closure
   - Product Maintenance Planning
   - Product Performance Monitoring
   - Technical Information Provision
   - Service Coverage Planning
5. Billing and Collection (5)
   - Invoicing
   - Banking Operations
   - Cash Application
   - Collection
   - Third-Party Leasing Administration
6. Financial Management (10)
   - Financial Planning
   - Financial Analysis and Reporting
   - Financial Outlooking
   - Tax Planning and Management
   - Accounting Operations
   - Financial Auditing
   - Disbursements
   - Financial Asset/Cash Planning
   - Financial Asset Control
   - Security
7. Inventory Management and Logistics (5)
   - Inventory Planning
   - Logistics and Physical Distribution Planning
   - Logistics Operations and Material Control
   - Delivery Management and Order Satisfaction
   - Supplier Management
8. Business Management (3)
   - Business Strategy Development
   - Business Planning
   - Business Process and Operations Management
     - Process Specification
     - Coordination and Integration
     - Inspection
     - Benchmarking
     - Process Improvement
9. Information Technology Management (5)
   - Information Strategy Planning
   - Business Solution Development
   - Technical Environment Management
   - Information Integration Management
   - Technology Management
10. Human Resource Management (6)
    - Manpower Requirements Planning
    - Hiring and Assignment
    - Benefits and Compensation Management
    - Personnel Management
    - Work Force Preparedness
    - Employee Communications

Memo: Total Processes—62

Information furnished by Xerox Corp.

Figure 9.3 Xerox Business Area/Process Management List

A common methodology should be developed for process definition throughout the organization. Otherwise connecting interrelated activities will be difficult.

6. Define and control at points of control. It is not necessary or desirable to establish controls for every task or step in a process. There are points in a process, however, where performance measurement indicates the level of performance and provides a logical place to introduce control actions. Control points can be significantly influenced by the next factor—measurements.
7. Establish process measurements. Process performance (vitality) must be measured before intelligent decisions can be made toward improving it. The measurement's dimensions should be the important indicator for organizational success and meaningful process improvement. Measuring cost alone is often not a useful index. Costs are a result of the variation in other factors. If the TQM emphasis on process improvement (variation reduction) is to be maintained, important characteristics, such as cycle time, quality, and productivity should be measured. Every process can be measured in terms of its output and the resources used. It is also important that measurements be tracked over time so that characteristics, such as trend and capability, can be determined.

   Process measures should be customer driven—measures that when improved provide greater satisfaction. It is less important to use the traditional type used for control. Figure 9.4 demonstrates that there are performance measures for every kind of activity.
8. Improve the process. Identify all causes of variation and determine the cost to reduce them. Improve those that are economically justified, and make improvements to make the process capable of meeting requirements all the time.

Effective process management means to review performance periodically so that it meets the preceding criteria, is modified to accommodate new business needs and requirements as they occur, and ensures that improvement continues.

Production

$\frac{\text{Direct hours}}{\text{Standard hours}}$	$\frac{\text{Scrap costs}}{\text{LBM additions}}$	$\frac{\text{Inventory shortage}}{\text{Inventory additions}}$
$\frac{\text{Earned hours}}{\text{Direct hours}}$	$\frac{\text{LBM and support costs}}{\text{No. of units produced}}$	$\frac{\text{Total production hours}}{\text{Direct earned hours}}$
$\frac{\text{Indirect hours}}{\text{Direct hours}}$	$\frac{\text{Fixed price cost of sales}}{\text{Gross net inventory}}$	$\frac{\text{Delinquent units} \times \text{selling price}}{\text{Average daily sales}}$
$\frac{\text{Salvage hours}}{\text{Direct hours}}$	$\frac{\text{Sales/VA sales}}{\text{Direct headcount}}$	$\frac{\text{Production support costs}}{\text{Production LBM costs}}$
$\frac{\text{Set-up hours}}{\text{Earned hours}}$	$\frac{\text{Sales/VA sales}}{\text{Total headcount}}$	$\frac{\text{Indirect headcount}}{\text{Direct headcount}}$
$\frac{\text{Direct labor \\$}}{\text{Standard hours}}$	$\frac{\text{Product build and support hours}}{\text{Equivalent units produced}}$	$\frac{\text{Production hourly headcount}}{\text{Production control headcount}}$
$\frac{\text{No. of units accepted}}{\text{No. of units inspected}}$	$\frac{\text{Customer accepted lots}}{\text{Lots submitted}}$	$\frac{\text{Production hourly headcount}}{\text{Production engineering headcount}}$
$\frac{\text{Wait time hours}}{\text{Direct labor hours}}$	$\frac{\text{Warranty repair costs}}{\text{Sales}}$	$\frac{\text{No. of defects}}{\text{No. of units inspected}}$
$\frac{\text{Units scheduled}}{\text{Units produced}}$	$\frac{\text{Sales/VA sales}}{\text{Indirect headcount}}$	$\frac{\text{Hrs. on labor ticket rejects}}{\text{Total hours reported}}$
$\frac{\text{Complete kits issued}}{\text{Total kits issued}}$	$\frac{\text{Cost of quality}}{\text{Cost of sales}}$	$\frac{\text{Actual burden rate}}{\text{Planned burden rate}}$
$\frac{\text{Cost of sales}}{\text{Gross inventory}}$	$\frac{\text{PBIT}}{\text{Employees}}$	$\frac{\text{No. of personnel transfers}}{\text{Headcount}}$

LBM = Labor and bill of material
VA = Value added
PBIT = Profit before income tax

Figure 9.4 Common Performance Measures

(Continued on next page)

Engineering

$\frac{\text{Direct labor}}{\text{Total time reporting labor}}$	$\frac{\text{No. personnel transfers}}{\text{Headcount}}$	$\frac{\text{Milestones completed}}{\text{Milestones scheduled}}$
$\frac{\text{Sales/VA sales}}{\text{Time reporting headcount}}$	$\frac{\text{Projected unit build. cost}}{\text{Target unit build. cost}}$	$\frac{\text{No. of key performance specs met}}{\text{Total no. of key performance specs}}$
$\frac{\text{Sales/VA sales}}{\text{Indirect headcount}}$	$\frac{\text{Production support costs}}{\text{Production LBM costs}}$	$\frac{\text{No. of programs where PVWA > actual}}{\text{No. of programs}}$
$\frac{\text{Sales/VA sales}}{\text{Total headcount}}$	$\frac{\text{No. of ECOs}}{\text{No. of drawings}}$	$\frac{\text{No. of drawings}}{\text{Drafting headcount}}$
$\frac{\text{No. of software instructions}}{\text{No. of software engineers}}$	$\frac{\text{Hrs. on rejected time reports}}{\text{Total hours reported}}$	$\frac{\text{No. of ECOs}}{\text{No. of engineers}}$
$\frac{\text{Cost to prepare drawings}}{\text{No. of drawings produced}}$	$\frac{\text{Projects with plans}}{\text{Total projects}}$	$\frac{\text{Bid hours}}{\text{Estimated hours}}$
$\frac{\text{Prod. build. hrs. on layouts}}{\text{Prod. build. hours}}$	$\frac{\text{Projects overrun \$}}{\text{Total projects \$}}$	$\frac{\text{Negotiated hours}}{\text{Bid hours}}$
$\frac{\text{PBIT}}{\text{Employees}}$	$\frac{\text{CAD hours usage}}{\text{CAD hours available}}$	$\frac{\text{Planned cost all programs}}{\text{Actual cost all programs}}$
$\frac{\text{Actual burden rate}}{\text{Planned burden rate}}$		$\frac{\text{Factory costs}}{\text{Production engineering costs}}$

ECO = Engineering change orders
PVWA = Planned value of work authorized
MPR = Material purchase requisitions

(Continued on next page)

Quality

$$\frac{\text{Quality dept. hours}}{\text{Production hours}}$$

$$\frac{\text{Quality indirect hours}}{\text{Total quality hours}}$$

$$\frac{\text{Earned hours}}{\text{Direct hours}}$$

$$\frac{\text{Cost of quality}}{\text{Cost of sales}}$$

$$\frac{\text{Sales/VA sales}}{\text{Product assurance headcount}}$$

$$\frac{\text{Total receiving insp. hours}}{\text{Lots received}}$$

$$\frac{\text{Material lots inspected}}{\text{Receiving inspection headcount}}$$

$$\frac{\text{Total operating headcount}}{\text{Quality dept. headcount}}$$

$$\frac{\text{Operations budget}}{\text{Quality dept. budget}}$$

$$\frac{\text{Production earned hours}}{\text{Quality eng. support hours}}$$

$$\frac{\text{QE support costs}}{\text{Production LBM costs}}$$

$$\frac{\text{Errors on inspection procedures}}{\text{Inspection procedures issued}}$$

$$\frac{\text{Errors in data collection}}{\text{Volume of data collected}}$$

$$\frac{\text{Actual burden rate}}{\text{Planned burden rate}}$$

$$\frac{\text{Prevention costs}}{\text{Cost of quality}}$$

$$\frac{\text{Appraisal costs}}{\text{Cost of quality}}$$

$$\frac{\text{Failure costs}}{\text{Cost of quality}}$$

Procurement

$$\frac{\text{Purchase order errors}}{\text{Purchase orders audited}}$$

$$\frac{\text{Estimated savings on orders placed}}{\text{Dollar value of orders placed}}$$

$$\frac{\text{Material proposal records received}}{\text{Material proposal records completed}}$$

$$\frac{\text{Incoming material lots accepted}}{\text{Incoming material lots}}$$

$$\frac{\text{\$ amount of purchases}}{\text{Purchasing dept. headcount}}$$

$$\frac{\text{No. of POs placed}}{\text{Purchasing dept. headcount}}$$

$$\frac{\text{Total operations headcount}}{\text{Purchasing dept. headcount}}$$

$$\frac{\text{Sales/VA sales}}{\text{Procurement dept. headcount}}$$

$$\frac{\text{\$ amount of purchases}}{\text{Purchasing dept. budget}}$$

$$\frac{\text{No. of MPRs returned on time}}{\text{No. of MPRs returned}}$$

(Continued on next page)

Communications

$$\frac{\text{Reproduction costs}}{\text{No. of pages produced}}$$

$$\frac{\text{Sales/VA sales}}{\text{Communications dept. headcount}}$$

$$\frac{\text{Viewgraphs redone}}{\text{Total viewgraphs produced}}$$

$$\frac{\text{Operations headcount}}{\text{Communications dept. headcount}}$$

$$\frac{\text{Cost of viewgraph changes}}{\text{Total graphics cost}}$$

Service Engineering

$$\frac{\text{\$ orders received Y-T-D}}{\text{\$ orders planned Y-T-D}}$$

$$\frac{\text{No. of proposals}}{\text{No. of marketing reps}}$$

$$\frac{\text{\$ orders received month/year}}{\text{No. of markeeters/contract admin.}}$$

$$\frac{\text{\$ orders received}}{\text{Service eng. budget}}$$

$$\frac{\text{Total operations personnel}}{\text{Service engineering personnel}}$$

$$\frac{\text{No. of DD250 errors}}{\text{Total DD250s processed}}$$

$$\frac{\text{Sales/VA sales}}{\text{Service engineering headcount}}$$

$$\frac{\text{No. of active contracts}}{\text{No. of contract administrators}}$$

$$\frac{\text{Operations budget}}{\text{Service eng. budget}}$$

$$\frac{\text{FP orders with progress payments}}{\text{Total no. of FP orders}}$$

$$\frac{\text{\$ delinquent deliveries}}{\text{Average daily sales}}$$

$$\frac{\text{Sales proposal \$}}{\text{\$ orders received}}$$

$$\frac{\text{Service eng. budget}}{\text{Operations sales}}$$

(Continued on next page)

Employee Relations

$$\frac{\text{Change notices processed}}{\text{No. of compensation clericals}}$$

$$\frac{\text{Sales/VA sales}}{\text{Employee relations headcount}}$$

$$\frac{\text{Total operations headcount}}{\text{Employee relations headcount}}$$

$$\frac{\text{No. of change notice errors}}{\text{Total change notices}}$$

$$\frac{\text{No. of people interviewed and hired}}{\text{No. of people interviewed}}$$

$$\frac{\text{Operations support}}{\text{Employee relations budget}}$$

$$\frac{\text{Elapsed time of unprocessed ECRs}}{\text{No. of unprocessed ECRs}}$$

$$\frac{\text{Insurance claims processed}}{\text{No. of insurance claim clerks}}$$

$$\frac{\text{Lost time for injuries}}{\text{Total hours worked}}$$

$$\frac{\text{Workers compensation costs}}{\text{Total hours worked}}$$

$$\frac{\text{Offers made}}{\text{Offers accepted}}$$

$$\frac{\text{Employees terminating}}{\text{Total employees}}$$

Information Systems

$$\frac{\text{Output distributed on time}}{\text{Total output distributed}}$$

$$\frac{\text{Hardware uptime}}{\text{Total hardware time}}$$

$$\frac{\text{Out-of-service terminals}}{\text{Total no. of terminals}}$$

$$\frac{\text{Trouble calls received}}{\text{Unit of time (week, mo., etc.)}}$$

$$\frac{\text{Keypunch earned hours}}{\text{Keypunch actual hours}}$$

$$\frac{\text{Jobs completed}}{\text{Jobs scheduled}}$$

$$\frac{\text{Sales/VA sales}}{\text{IS0 headcount}}$$

$$\frac{\text{Total operations headcount}}{\text{IS headcount}}$$

$$\frac{\text{Operations budget}}{\text{IS budget}}$$

$$\frac{\text{User complaints}}{\text{Hours of usage}}$$

$$\frac{\text{Proj. estimated development cost}}{\text{Proj. actual development cost}}$$

$$\frac{\text{MRP/HMS performance/usage}}{\text{Various MRP/HMS criteria}}$$

(Continued on next page)

Finance

$$\frac{\text{Trade billed receivables}}{\text{Avg. trade billed sales/day}}$$

$$\frac{\text{Invoices processed} \times \text{standard}}{\text{Disbursement audit hours}}$$

$$\frac{\text{Total operations personnel}}{\text{Finance personnel}}$$

$$\frac{\text{Net assets}}{\text{Sales}}$$

$$\frac{\text{No. of pricing proposals}}{\text{No. of pricing people}}$$

$$\frac{\text{Operations budget}}{\text{Finance dept. budget}}$$

$$\frac{\text{Sales/VA sales}}{\text{Finance personnel}}$$

$$\frac{\text{No. of DD250 errors}}{\text{Total DD250s processed}}$$

$$\frac{\text{Receivables over 60 days}}{\text{Total receivables}}$$

$$\frac{\text{Incomplete cost standard}}{\text{Total cost standards}}$$

$$\frac{\text{Finance dept. budget}}{\text{Sales}}$$

$$\frac{\text{\$ value of pricing proposals}}{\text{No. of pricing people}}$$

$$\frac{\text{Invoicing errors}}{\text{Invoices processed}}$$

Customer satisfaction index

Logistics

$$\frac{\text{No. of programs where PVWA > actuals}}{\text{No. of programs}}$$

$$\frac{\text{Average maintenance downtime of GVROS}}{\text{Selected repair target (days)}}$$

$$\frac{\text{Quantity of spares delivered}}{\text{Qnty. of spares to be delivered per contract}}$$

$$\frac{\text{Maintenance costs/FLT hr.}}{\text{Target cost}}$$

$$\frac{\text{Units in-house for repair}}{\text{Units installed}}$$

$$\frac{\text{Orders for logistics services}}{\text{Total orders}}$$

$$\frac{\text{Average grade level of FLD engrs.}}{\text{Average grade level of ideal work force}}$$

$$\frac{\text{Sales/VA sales}}{\text{Logistics headcount}}$$

$$\frac{\text{Specific prog. logistics orders}}{\text{Specific prog. non-logistics orders}}$$

(Continued on next page)

General/Miscellaneous

$$\frac{\text{Actual hours/\$}}{\text{Estimated hours/\$}}$$

$$\frac{\text{Backlog hrs. on maintenance work orders}}{\text{Maintenance headcount}}$$

$$\frac{\text{Direct headcount}}{\text{Indirect headcount}}$$

$$\frac{\text{Nonproductive time}}{\text{Total time available}}$$

$$\frac{\text{Operations headcount}}{\text{Department headcount}}$$

$$\frac{\text{Department costs}}{\text{Department budgeted costs}}$$

$$\frac{\text{Operations sales/VA sales}}{\text{Department headcount}}$$

$$\frac{\text{Headcount}}{\text{No. of secretaries}}$$

$$\frac{\text{Building square footage}}{\text{Maintenance cleaning personnel}}$$

$$\frac{\text{No. of people in QC teams}}{\text{Total employees}}$$

$$\frac{\text{Maintenance orders within estimate}}{\text{Total maintenance orders}}$$

$$\frac{\text{Sales}}{\text{Assets}}$$

$$\frac{\text{Unplanned absent hours}}{\text{Total hours}}$$

$$\frac{\text{Profit}}{\text{Employees}}$$

$$\frac{\text{Assets}}{\text{Employees}}$$

Chapter 10

Total Employee Involvement–Empowerment–Training

Western managers believe that they are "in charge." They set objectives, reap the greatest rewards, and sometimes pay the penalties for losses. Managers make all the decisions concerning the business and everyone else in it without involving nonmanagers (or even first-line managers) in meaningful decision making about improving their work. One of the principles of TQM (and a critical factor in its application) is the effective participation of all members of the organization in the continuous improvement of the processes and systems in which they work (the key processes as a minimum).

Involvement is most effective when organizational members are organized into teams. Teams are trained to use problem-solving and decision-making tools that are appropriate for the task. Empowering people to take control of their jobs in this manner is based on the simple premise that, by working in and being part of a system or process, they have the information needed to describe it and identify how it can be improved. In addition to the direct benefits of improvement by participation, people tend to become more loyal and satisfied when their ideas are used. In addition, people are more motivated to continue the improvement process. This concept has been described in the literature of the behavioral sciences for many years but rarely practiced on a large scale until the advent of TQM.

Beginning in the late 1970s, there was a sizeable movement to introduce quality circles (teams), but the number has dwindled far below its peak. One reason for this reduction is the limited scope of the activity of quality circles. These teams typically worked only at improving factors that directly affected how they did their work. They didn't resolve the important system problems. No one did.[12] TQM process improvement teams have a different mission. They are organized to improve the processes in which they work. This means among other things:

- Defining the process in detail.
- Eliminating unnecessary activities.
- Developing measures of performance.
- Establishing performance baselines.
- Setting improvement goals and changing the process to meet them (or describing the changes necessary).

To a great extent the people in the process become its owners and managers. Performance improvement includes not only saving money but satisfying the customer of the process (whatever activity receives its output). This logically means that the process teams define their needs in terms of improved inputs. The teams then determine needs and wants of the customers and work with their suppliers to obtain them. Getting this accomplished requires management support.

It should be obvious that as every process, beginning with the most important, is slowly worked on and improved, the total enterprise improves, often dramatically. It is this continuous improvement (kaizen) that has contributed so significantly to the Japanese success. Innovation is valuable but it will not cumulatively contribute as much as continuous, incremental improvement.

Establishing, training, and allowing teams to evolve into process managers is the core of TQM and its subset, JIT, and one of the most difficult things to achieve. It's difficult because it is a new way to manage. There is little precedence for it, and managers are reluctant to abdicate. But this is why a thorough understanding of TQM concepts is so critical. It's not abdication. It's developing people and facilitating their work instead of trying to direct everything they do. It's also important to understand that it's not based on theory. It works. It takes several years. However, many Western companies are now reaping the benefits of their investment. Those that are most conspicuous have won or were finalists in the Malcolm Baldrige National Quality Award. They all increased customer satisfaction, produced higher quality products, shortened lead and cycle times, and increased productivity.

TEAMS

The practice of using employees in problem-solving teams is a powerful way to manage. Properly trained, a team's value constantly exceeds the arithmetic of the numbers and provides benefits greater than the sum of the team members' individual contributions. Teams are not a new idea in American business. It has been common practice to form a team to solve a problem or bottleneck. The team often solved the problem but didn't fix the cause. The most common analogy used for teams is football. It's a familiar one but much too simplistic. Sports teams are highly regulated;

there's a rule for every situation and immediate penalties if the rules are broken. Specific behavior is developed for each player. Each player is evaluated and coached.

This isn't the situation in business. The business operating environment is far more complex, dynamic, and unpredictable. The only rules are laws set by government. Adversaries don't always play by rules. Competitors aren't all known until they appear in the market. So business teams need to be organized and operate differently. To be most effective, the teams must include all levels, reflect horizontal and vertical organizational structure (all the functions related to a process), and be trained in the proper use of the appropriate analytical tools and techniques. This training cannot be over-emphasized—not only because of its value but also because the kind of training required is different from what has been traditionally offered. It gives team members the ability to contribute to the team objectives. Without this training, teams are similar to committees composed of diverse interests that typically talk a lot and compromise on a problem solution.

As mentioned, teams should be organized at all levels. TQM implementation is most successful when initiated by teams at the upper levels. Those teams should lead the way. Their task is to identify the key business factors and the related critical systems and processes and their important performance measures. These factors are then further broken down to the organization(s) responsible for the process used to complete the tasks. They should also set the organization improvement objectives. Organizing teams at all levels has some benefits that exceed process improvement. In their first step of defining a process, teams often realize that responsibility for its operation is fragmented between functional organizations. No employee or organization has full responsibility. This alone is often a cause of poor performance. This process definition and assignment of accountability frequently leads to rapid improvement independent of other actions.

Team Makeup. The process under review is the major determinate of the team members. Basically, the core members should represent the key process activities and sometimes include the process supplier and process customer. (How teams perform their analyses is covered in Chapter 18.)

Teams of this construction are called cross- or multifunctional. Their makeup reflects all functions involved (connected to the activity). Teams may require temporary members, such as a design engineer, a statistician, or a customer representative (sometimes a customer) to provide special knowledge. This multifunction representation is extremely important. It provides a consideration of all the process variables needed for effective process management.

Team Training. Implementing and perpetuating TQM differs from other management systems in that it requires decision-making and problem-solving skills not normally found in the typical manager or employee. A logical, structural, and disciplined approach to problem solving, particularly when it involves the emotional components of a group of interacting people, is not intuitive. Untrained teams generally operate at a high emotional level; objectivity is difficult to achieve. The skills are rarely taught to anyone before he or she joins the work force. Thus, business and government must provide this training to its members if they are to be effective in process improvement teams.

One partial exception to this has been that people educated in technical processes (science and engineering) are familiar or use the scientific method, which is briefly:

- Problem definition.
- Possible solutions.
- Solution selection.
- Selected solution trial.
- Verification.

Solutions to technical problems based on data usually follow this approach. Problem solution methodology taught to process improvement teams follows this same structure but also provides several specific tools and techniques to use within that structure to resolve process problems or identify improvement actions. The complexity of the tools also varies considerably from simple flow charts, brainstorming, and cause-and-effect diagrams that anyone can learn to use, to more complex statistical tools or the seven management tools described in Chapter 18.

When to Train. There are two general approaches that identify when to train. One is to determine the kind of TQM training appropriate for the various classifications of employees and then to train all employees. Every employee is then equipped to be effective in the analysis of his or her own job and is prepared when he or she becomes a team member. This approach is somewhat mechanistic and, for large organizations, less effective. It has been the experience of companies who used this mass training approach that, if skills are not applied within a short time after training, they are rapidly lost. A more effective approach is what the Northrop Corporation calls just-in-time training. After each team is formed, it is trained in the skills needed to begin, and then during its operation, it is trained further as specific new skills are needed. The learning is then immediately reinforced through application.

What to Teach. A team needs to:

- Solve problems.
- Know the process.
- Know how to work together as a team—work to rules.
- Know how to plan.
- Conduct good meetings.

- Manage logistics and details.
- Gather useful data.
- Measure process performance.
- Analyze data.
- Implement change.
- Measure its effectiveness.

The ability to do these things effectively is called having the soft skills of decision making and problem solving. This is compared to the many hard skills of various job specialties which are traditionally all that is taught.

The tools and techniques commonly used in TQM (see Chapter 18) are:

- *Seven QC tools:* Flow charts, Pareto diagrams, run charts, histograms, scatter diagrams, check sheets, and control charts.
- *Seven management tools:* Affinity diagram, the matrix chart, the arrow diagram, the relationship diagram, the matrix data analysis chart, the tree diagram, and the process decision program chart.
- *Benchmarking.*
- *Quality function deployment.*
- *Design of experiments.*

These items are listed in a somewhat increasing order of complexity. The seven QC tools are really basic problem-solving techniques that should be used by everyone in an organization in the normal course of operations. They add significantly to the effectiveness and efficiency of solving any problem. Managers in particular are skill-deficient if they cannot apply these tools routinely.

Who to Train and in What Skills. Japanese leaders have stated that quality begins with education and ends with education. Implementing TQM involves a planned change from one management system to another that is quite different. It is a management process improvement. Its scope, direction, objectives, and methodologies must be understood by everyone in the organization from the top down. It requires extensive training. This training must be planned so that all the required skills are identified and scheduled. The plan must also identify the training resources required.

The simple matrix, shown in Figure 10.1, is one training approach. It identifies which employees should receive which training module. This matrix is representative of the training plans in some companies.

Boeing, like several large companies, has established central productivity or TQM functions responsible for communications, facilitation, and training. In addition, Boeing assigns several key middle managers to its center for periods of

Students	Consultant	Total quality seminar	Team leader training	Facili-tator	Leadership/ people skills	Advanced problem solving	Process control methods	Introduc-tion to design of experiments	Design of experiments	Data gathering	Imple-men-tation
Team leader	●	●	●	▲	▲	■	▲	■	■	■	●
Team member	■	■	■	■	◆	■	■	■	■	■	▲
Facilitator	●	●	●	●	▲	■	▲	▲	■	▲	▲
Statistician	●	●	●	●	▲	■	●	●	●	■	●
Improvement manager	●	●	●	●	●	●	●	●	■	■	●
Nonmanagement	■	■	■	■	◆	■	■	■	■	■	■
Other key members	■	■	■	▲	▲	▲	▲	▲	▲	▲	■
Manufacturing	■	■	■	■	▲	■	■	■	■	■	■
Engineering	■	■	■	■	▲	▲	▲	▲	▲	■	▲
Office/ administrative	■	■	■	■	▲	■	■	■	■	■	▲
Management	●	●	●	▲	●	▲	▲	▲	■	■	●

● Required ▲ Recommended ■ Optional ◆ Not required

Figure 10.1 Quality Improvement Education and Training Plan

up to a year. During that period, they become thoroughly steeped in the practices and principles of TQM. This will result in a staff of TQM-oriented upper managers.

Team Success. Planning is critical for the successful transition to employee improvement and process improvement teams. The plan should be developed by upper management (preferably operating as a team). Total employee involvement should be scheduled over a comfortable period of time. An enterprise of 100 members may have everyone trained and teams functioning within one year. In larger organizations it may take two or three years. Changing attitudes takes an unpredictable length of time.

Employee participation using teams can be successful only when they receive management support and the proper infrastructure. Walter and Roger Breisch have identified 10 major infrastructure characteristics an organization must provide, in proper form, if employee involvement is to become the management system (see Figure 10.2 on page 68).[13] Managers must define each of these parameters for their organizations. How are they determined? Do employees really understand them? Are they in consonance with TQM principles? Will they inhibit team operation?

Senior management involvement—Senior management must be involved in the process and incorporate the language of involvement into its vocabulary. In addition, senior management controls the other parameters.

Focus on strategic operation issues (SOIs)—Focusing participation on the business' SOIs makes the input valuable and reinforces participation through progress. This focus also provides an effective way for all employees to prioritize decision making.

Empowerment—Delegation does not mean that every decision must go to the lowest level in the organization. But employees below the level of the decision maker must be given the opportunity to influence decision making.

People—First, while not every employee wants to participate in decision making, it is a mistake to simply assume employees don't care. Second, there are managers who simply will not listen; they must be given every opportunity to learn new ways of managing.

Reward systems—Human resource professionals ensure that organizational reward structures support participation. Employees should be rewarded for suggesting change; managers should be rewarded for implementing change and fostering team building.

Suggestion handling—Few aspects of participation bring the process to a screeching halt faster than poor suggestion handling. There must be a well-conceived way to accept suggestions, direct them to the lowest possible level, prioritize and act on them, and communicate decisions to the employees rapidly.

Training—Management must understand that a commitment to training is essential to success. In addition to technical skills, employees must have training in the "soft skills" of decision making.

Communication of business information—Managers are seldom asked to make decisions without the necessary information. Senior managers must acknowledge that information once thought to be sacred will now be disseminated throughout the organization.

Time commitment—Training, problem solving, and suggestion handling require time. It is unreasonable to expect employees to commit their own time to these activities.

Other human resource management practices—Since employee involvement (EI) revolves around the company's human resources (HR), all HR practices should be designed to support participation. Those practices with an obvious influence on EI are:

- Selection hiring
- Compensation
- Promotion
- Job security
- Orientation
- Career development
- Benefits

Figure 10.2 The Parameters of Employee Involvement

Reprinted with permission from *Quality* (May, '90), a publication of Hitchcock Publishing, a Capital Cities/ABC, Inc., Company

Chapter 11

Change: Achieving Commitment

TQM is a new way to manage with different objectives and policies from the past. How do leaders get members at all levels of the organization to change? First, members must accept these new objectives as beneficial, and second, they must believe that management really means it.

Significant, permanent change will occur only when there is commitment by the affected parties to make necessary changes. Managers cannot be successful unless commitment is demonstrated and has progressed to a stage where it is adopted as the new norm. Therefore, management must understand the commitment process, its dynamics, and how it takes place.

In small organizations there are usually only two organization levels: the nonmanagerial (worker) and the managerial (leader). In a small business the leaders are typically the owners. Communication is short and direct. The leaders are highly visible and participate in day-to-day operations. When they want something done the same old way or a new way, they say so, and that's the way it happens. If such a leader say, attended a TQM seminar and decided it had some merit and wanted to try it, he or she would only have to hire a consultant, and together they would initiate the first steps. If benefits were found, that's the way they would continue to operate. The attitude of management is fairly clear. Commitment and change can take place quickly. As organizations become larger achieving the same thing becomes more complex. The organization leaders are farther removed from day-to-day operations, and the workers interface more with intermediate managers. With further growth managers interface with more managers. The leaders become even more removed from day-to-day operations. When trying to achieve change in organizations with layers of management, the job becomes much more complex. Change of any consequence—like TQM—must be sponsored by top management and the other level managers must be the agents of change. The implementors, the worker members, are the target of the change since they are the ones who have to change their behavior and attitude. Because each element in this chain has to be successful, how is the commitment to change secured under these conditions?

THE NATURE OF CHANGE

As described in previous chapters, the degree of change required to implement TQM is comprehensive and affects everyone. The breadth and nature of the changes can be gleaned from the profile presented in Figure 11.1. The question is how can top management get lower management and the targets, the members, to accept the change from inception to implementation without reservations? Half-hearted acceptance doing it because it is directed from higher authority—by a significant number of people in the chain will make permanent change very difficult and the value of what is accomplished very low. It is critical that the initiators, the sponsors, remain visibly committed over the time it takes and through the trial and error necessary to see the project through.

WHAT IS INVOLVED

Business organizations in particular are accustomed to innovative changes like automation and computerization. Their success depends mostly on skill training. TQM involves empowering the work force to manage its own work. This change is not merely a more innovative way to manage; it is a social change, not something that most managers are equipped to deal with either by education or experience. It is also not easy to prescribe what to do. Changing human behavior is a complex task with many variables that affect the outcome. Little is known or understood about which elements have the most effect on success.[14]

Obtaining commitment is also a poorly understood phenomenon even though it is recognized as necessary for change to occur. A committed person is one who pursues a specific outcome in a consistent manner. This sticking to a course, often at high personal cost, is the mark of commitment in all walks of life. It is often quite obvious and inspiring. Those attributes are the reason why it is required in a sizeable proportion of the membership if the goals of change are to be reached and made permanent.

Commitment is therefore a prerequisite for successfully implementing change. It isn't widely recognized that the process of becoming committed follows some recognizable stages. Managers are generally unfamiliar with the idea that preparation (planning) is necessary to determine how commitment is developed and how it can be lost. This is particularly true when trying to introduce a new way of managing

Element	Before	After
Definition of Quality	Product Specification	Total Customer Satisfaction
Scheduled Batch Production	Company-Driven Push	Customer-Driven Pull
Organizational Priorities	Financials	Quality—The Driver
Business Horizon	Short-Term—1 to 2 years	Long and Short—3 to 5 years
Emphasis	Fix Problems	Prevent Problems
Problems Result From	Individual's Mistakes	Management Practices/Systems
Quality Responsibility	Department	Everyone
Management Climate/Culture	Fear and Finger-Pointing, Laying Blame	Continuous Improvement, Innovation
Organizational Structure	Hierarchical Static	Flat, Fluid, Integrated
Problem Solving is Done By	Those in Authority	Empowered, Disciplined Teams
All function objectives are affected in achieving TQM.		

Element	Before	After
Management Style	Flurry of Activity	Disciplined Action
Rewards/Recognition	Results	Processes and Results
People Are	Managed and Controlled	Directed for Continuous Improvement
Management Responsibilities	Control and Pressure for Performance	Provide Direction/Means for People to Continually Improve
Employee Involvement	Very Little Reward Individuals	Very Much Reward Teams and Individuals
Profits	Goal	Result
Training and Education	Minimal, Sporadic	Ongoing and Highly Directed
Management Vision	Narrow, Limited Scope	Comprehensive, Provides Direction Rooted in Values
Communications	Top-Down, Infrequent	Iterative, Frequent

Figure 11.1 TQM Organizational Profile

that will deeply involve all members of the organization, and which, in addition, requires managers themselves to reject much of what they have learned and practiced.

Change requires the understanding and acceptance of the organization members if it is to be successful. It is surprising how frequently managers will decide to adopt new systems or projects on how they operate with little planning on how they will go about it. Managers would not think of behaving the same way if they were going to begin a new facility, product, or service. Managers assume that if a change is initiated from their authoritative position, everyone will accept it and work toward its success. The lack of understanding has already seriously impeded progress of companies introducing TQM. In particular, top managers of several corporations have admitted that they learned this through great difficulty. After *they* were committed to TQM, they made the mistake of going directly to the workers without first getting the commitment of middle managers. While the workers were enthusiastic about hearing directly from top management, middle managers felt left out, even threatened, by being bypassed.

The preparation and publication of a plan should accompany the initiation of the change to TQM. Organizations are familiar with this approach, so it is an expected first step in any important change. A milestone plan is also valuable in ensuring that all the necessary factors have been identified and understood. If top management understands the complexity involved, it will more likely set realistic time frames. It should be stressed, however, that a milestone plan is not a schedule. Dates should be targets. Most of those responsible are treading new ground. Behavior change through commitment cannot be neatly scheduled.

BUILDING COMMITMENT

One way to understand building commitment is to recognize that it is a process involving identifiable stages. Figure 11.2 shows one way to depict how commitment takes place or fails to take place. The vertical axis displays the degree of support; the horizontal axis displays the passage of time. There are three developmental phases represented as commitment progresses: preparation, acceptance, and commitment. Each stage represents a critical juncture where commitment may be threatened (down arrow) or facilitated (forward movement). Consider each stage with respect to the introduction and implementation of TQM in an organization with little understanding of what it is.

The following is a brief explanation of the stage shown in Figure 11.2:

Level I

Contact: Management has become aware that many companies have adopted TQM in order to improve and has decided to try it. Typically, at this point, management is not really fully committed. It doesn't recognize that management and all other levels must change. Just announcing that TQM is going to be implemented won't result

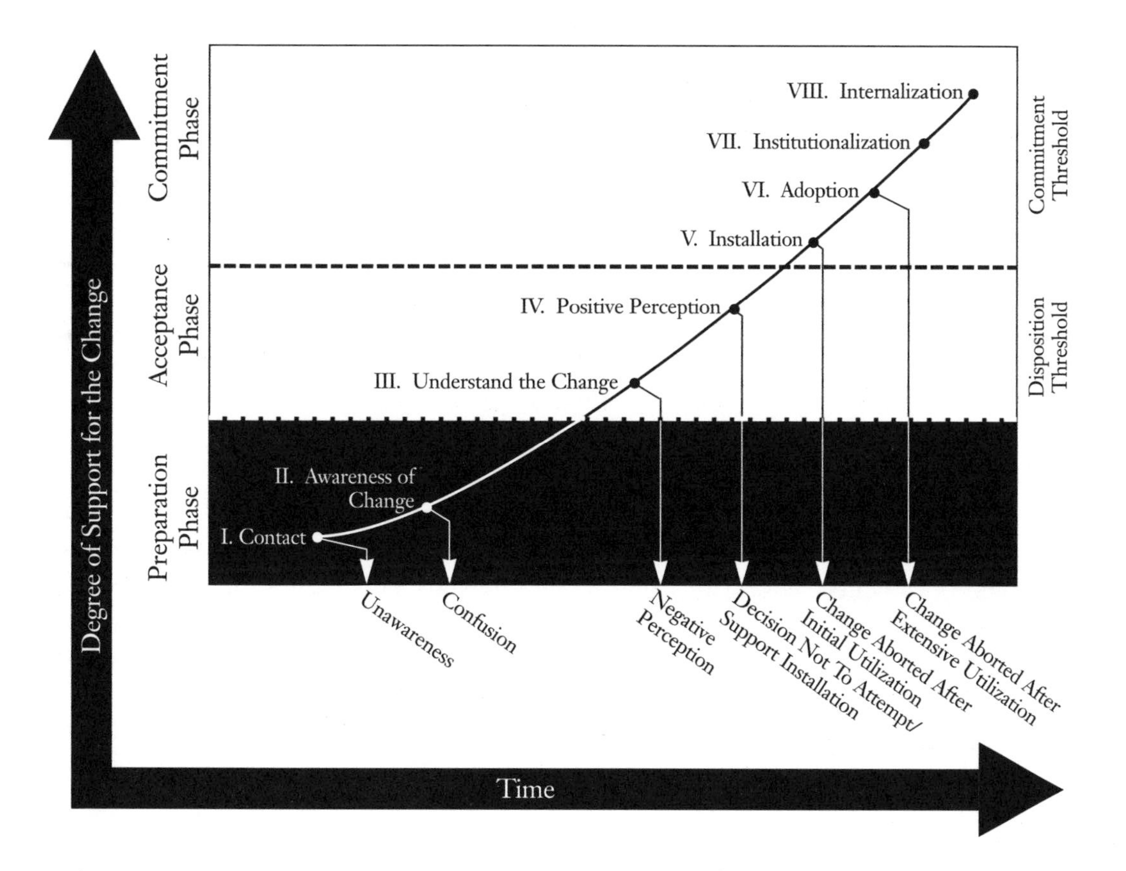

This illustration shows the stages organizations follow in achieving commitment to change. For organizations of 500 or fewer employees, a time period of five years should be considered to reach level VIII. For larger organizations, it will take longer.

Figure 11.2 Stages of Commitment to Organizational Change

in its acceptance, even if management has been warned by others or in seminars that it must lead the TQM initiative. At best there will be an awareness that a change may take place.

The most likely reaction by employees at other levels will be suspicion or cynicism. They have heard other management initiatives announced before that didn't survive.

Level II

Awareness of Change: Management and key people in the organization are studying TQM concepts, principles, and implications to the organization. Other employees are aware that some change may take place. During this phase clear, simple, frequent communication of what management is up to, and why, is crucial to future success. Without communication a lot of wrong information will fill the void and be time-consuming to overcome later.

This is identified as the preparation phase. The chart shows that more time should be spent here. Extra time in building a foundation will allow faster progress later. Management needs to develop the feedback network to learn how the information is being received at all levels. In small organizations the lines of communication are short and usually informal. This doesn't lessen the need to communicate plans, but the overall process should be concluded more quickly.

Level III

Understanding: An implementation plan has been prepared and the needs and benefits of change have been explained to all organizational members. Acceptance is based on personal evaluation and judgments and will vary. Members will react to the planned change and will express their opinions about it. They will behave positively or negatively toward it. It is critical that a generally positive perception be obtained before progressing. If negative reaction is detected, management should repeat the project benefits to all members.

Level IV

Positive Perception: Support for the acceptance of the changes implicit in using TQM are based on a positive perception of the proposal. Perception and acceptance depend not only on the reaction to the changes but to the climate in the organization. If the general perception is positive the members are ready to commit to action. This is a critical phase because a positive reaction is frequently mistaken for commitment. For example, it is a common experience in industry to use procedures to describe important operations. These procedures are often changed to resolve some perceived problem. The individuals involved in the solution, i.e., procedure change, believe that they have done the correct thing and issue the change. Often a related problem or an audit discloses that the change was ignored. The targets of the change never accepted it and didn't commit to observing it.

Level V

Implementation: The decision is to go forward with the plan and implement TQM. It is at this stage that true commitment to action is demonstrated. Managers at all levels demonstrate their willingness to expend the time and energy to achieve TQM goals. Teams are organized and trained then begin working.

Organizational changes are sometimes made to facilitate the process, that is, non-accepting managers are replaced. This demonstrates that management is serious about changing, and it facilitates the change as well.

Level VI

Adoption: In this stage the organizations become familiar with the TQM principle of continuous improvement. There are varying degrees of success and, therefore, varying degrees of commitment to continue to use the process. Management must maintain close surveillance of all implementation activities to remove roadblocks and provide support and resources.

Level VII

Institutionalization: The TQM processes and results have proven to be highly valuable intrinsically and extrinsically to the organizations and members, such that it becomes their method of operating and managements' principle for managing. The change has become the norm.

Level VIII

Internalization: Beliefs have changed or are congruent with personal interests, goals, or value systems. Members demonstrate ownership by accepting personal responsibility for the TQM process' success. Internalization is total commitment that is desirable but not necessary for all members to achieve. It may take some a considerable time to reach this stage. Commitment at this level is characterized by enthusiasm and persistence. This level must be reached if the TQM philosophy is to be sustained.

What is sought is also change in attitude toward the objectives of customer satisfaction and continuous improvement. As noted by the behavior psychologist, B.F. Skinner, management can't change someone's attitude.[15] However, if conditions are changed, the response will result in a change in attitude. The conditions in TQM that are a change from those that exist in the traditional, more autocratic environment, are that people understand the need to change and are given the skills to manage their own work process and then allowed to do so. Also, they believe that management really wants to improve quality. Schedule is not more important. Management has demonstrated that it shares power; there is trust between management and employees. This climate creates the positive, interested employees that management seeks.

What Works[16]

1. Create a vision of what the organization should evolve into and plan its achievement.
2. Mobilize energy for change. Convince employees change is needed. Get commitment. Share information on the company's competitive position and problems.

3. Articulate a theme for change. Quality is the one most used. Instill pride; this is essential to motivation. Traditional financial themes don't work. The connection between an individual's work and the organization profit or return on investment is too abstract to motivate.
4. Translate competitive need into clear, demanding goals.
5. Focus functionally organized organizations on business processes and use a participative multifunctional team approach.
6. Change the roles, responsibilities, relationship, and structure of managers and workers in performing their tasks. Approaches that concentrate only on change in attitude and knowledge will fail. Training supports change, it doesn't produce it.

   The principle is to change relationships (structure). This forces new behavior that leads to a change in attitude.
7. Decentralize authority to teams of workers, reduce supervisory levels, and change the role of supervisors. Their role is to support and facilitate the work of the teams.
8. Teach skills that are needed when they are needed. Education pays off in the later team action phases.
9. Lead by example. This is the most important factor in instituting change. Make improvements and changes at the top, and make them visible to everyone.
10. Select and promote leaders and managers who support culture change and whose values correspond to the new philosophy. This gives proof that upper management is serious. Leaving resistant managers in place hinders progress and makes top management commitment suspect.
11. Managers must develop the art of orchestrating not directing. They should not push a particular approach to organizing and managing. Create a context for change—articulate a theme and maintain a direction.

Pitfalls

1. Inconsistency. TQM is a way to manage, but management doesn't change. It continues to set the goals and gives the direction. It demonstrates that the changes are for everyone else and management is simply going through the motions.
2. Delegation of TQM to a staff function. There is a tendency, particularly in larger organizations, to delegate implementation as a staff function.
3. Inadequate training. Training is an investment to improve the skills of managers and all employees in the new and powerful tool for improvement.

Without new skills a TQM program will be words and slogans from the top, team activities at the bottom, and a lack of ability to achieve results.

This can lead to project failure for the following reasons:

1. TQM sets new kinds of objectives, internally and externally. These may not be aligned with each functional unit's needs and problems. Such imposed objectives cause conflict and resentment. A major change in organization philosophy, like TQM, requires personal management leadership.
2. The approach is not systemic. It usually covers only a few elements like skills and knowledge instead of all key elements, such as policies, organizational structure, the systems, and staffing.
3. Managers and nonmanagers learn best by doing not just by getting directions. Senior management must participate in the change process.
4. If a task or program is delegated, management has not clearly taken ownership. Without ownership there is no personal involvement. There is an understandable tendency for employees to judge tasks delegated to staff to be of secondary importance.
5. If the TQM implementation is perceived as just another staff-directed program, it will generate cynicism at all levels that will seriously delay success.

Chapter 12

Factors in Product Quality

Managing an industrial enterprise to achieve customer satisfaction requires an understanding of not only business principles but of the basic factors that affect product quality in the design production cycle. This is because these factors determine quality and, to a large degree, product cost. The factors included in this are design margin, reliability, complexity, producibility, and manufacturing capability. They are all interrelated and interdependent making the task complex and difficult. Customer satisfaction with a product is directly related to its quality and reliability. These are determined primarily by the design margin. This, in turn, has a direct correlation with such characteristics as failure rate for operating products or defects produced for others (including failures and defects during manufacture). The greater the design margin (that is, a product's capacity to withstand all the stresses of the manufacturing cycle and customer use) the lower the failure rate. An effort to increase a design margin then results in greater satisfaction and lower production costs (less rework). This supports the need for greater efforts in the design and development cycle as well as in production process improvement.

Highly capable processes (little variation) produce products closer to the design nominal. This allows products to approach their design reliability. Without high process capability, simply producing product parts anywhere within the tolerance limits increases the in-process failure rate and lowers the product reliability.

PROCESS CAPABILITY

Process capability from a total product perspective between the maximum range of product characteristics and the range of process variation is:

$$\text{Total Process Capability} = \frac{\text{Maximum Allowable Range of Product Characteristics}}{\text{Probable Range of Process Variations}}$$ [17]

If there is too much variation in the manufacturing processes, defective products are produced and the failure rate increases. If process variation is much less than the design range of characteristics, both the production failure rate (defects) and customer experienced rate are lower.

On an individual part basis, the process capability is:

$$\text{Process Capability} = \frac{\text{Part Tolerance Range}}{\text{Probable Process Variation}}$$

Using a crude analogy, the design characteristic range could be pictured as the width of a garage door opening. The car width is the process variation. If the car width is slightly less than the door width, the garage is capable of holding the car but both will become damaged with use. If the opening is much larger than the car width or a narrower car is used, the garage capability is increased. The car, moving in and out, could vary with less attention. Increasing the ratio of the door width to car width decreases the probability of damaging the car.

At the part level, the ratio shows that if the process variation was only equal to the part tolerance range, with the part dimension center and process center values equal, any increase in the process range, or its center shift, results in parts outside the tolerance. However, if a process was capable of consistently holding a range of one-half of the part tolerance (a process capability of two) most parts would measure near the nominal, and the process center could vary with little effect. Typically, major company processes in Japan have a capability of between three and four, and they are improving. Their product reliability is very high, cycle time is short, and costs are low. Process capability, C_p, is discussed further in Chapter 19.

Product complexity is another factor affecting failure rate. In fact, failure rate is inversely related to design complexity. Complexity means more opportunities for failures and defects. It results in a higher failure rate during manufacture and in use. Complexity also adds to product cost in labor and materials.

Latent defects, those occurring during customer ownership, are largely a result of inadequate design margin, complexity, and low process capability. They cannot be totally removed during production. The effort to increase the ratio of design margin to process capability is therefore critical to achieving customer satisfaction and reducing costs. TQM principles, tools, and techniques are capable of providing that increase.

QUALITY OF DESIGN

Product design determines cost, quality, reliability, and, ultimately, customer satisfaction. Manufacturing can affect these factors. It does not control them, however, and it cannot increase what the design has established. In fact, it takes careful planning and execution for manufacturing to *approach* its achievement. Therefore, the design-manufacturing sequence is critical to success in industry.

Product development is essentially a one-time event. If it is not done correctly and effectively (if it fails to meet the proper design goals) it results in less than the best. At the same time, to remain competitive, it is of strategic importance to reduce the development time to market a product. The result is a conflict between thoroughly designing and evaluating a product, and shortening the time to market. Too often this conflict is resolved in the direction of starting production too soon. The Japanese developed techniques such as quality function deployment (QFD) and applied older ones like design of experiments (DOE) in concurrent engineering to resolve this conflict. Development time and costs were reduced, and higher quality resulted.

Before companies began using these techniques, products typically entered production while still immature and not evaluated for producibility. The result was production delays and higher costs due to design changes to eliminate shortcomings. Such changes also frequently compromised the design to maintain production. In addition, the changes often caused secondary problems that were thought to be resolved but that had bred even more problems, resulting in a continuous fire-fighting cycle.

Much of this was caused by product designs in which requirements were poorly defined, characteristics and tolerances were not scientifically established, and design requirements were not compatible with manufacturing process capabilities. Tolerances were the best estimate of the designer. It was normal and expected that changes would be required in production. In many industries, it was common to include the cost of the number of expected changes (based on past experience with a similar product) in the product development cost estimate. No improvement was expected. Also, manufacturing processes were frequently not designed for a specific product; they were generic. It was expected that they could be adjusted to make the products being designed. The processes and the product would be debugged as production progressed. Inspection would sort good from bad, and the bad would be scrapped or reworked. This approach was the norm.

Figure 12.1 schematically depicts the way the typical design production process has worked. It is a sequential process with functional independence. Problems are fixed when they are found. Few integrated prevention activities take place.

THE DESIGN PROCESS

Product development is a sociotechnical activity. People in organized groups use various technologies to produce a detailed product description. Managing this is complex. All factors involved must be effectively integrated to succeed. One impediment in the design process is the organizational structure. Organizations are

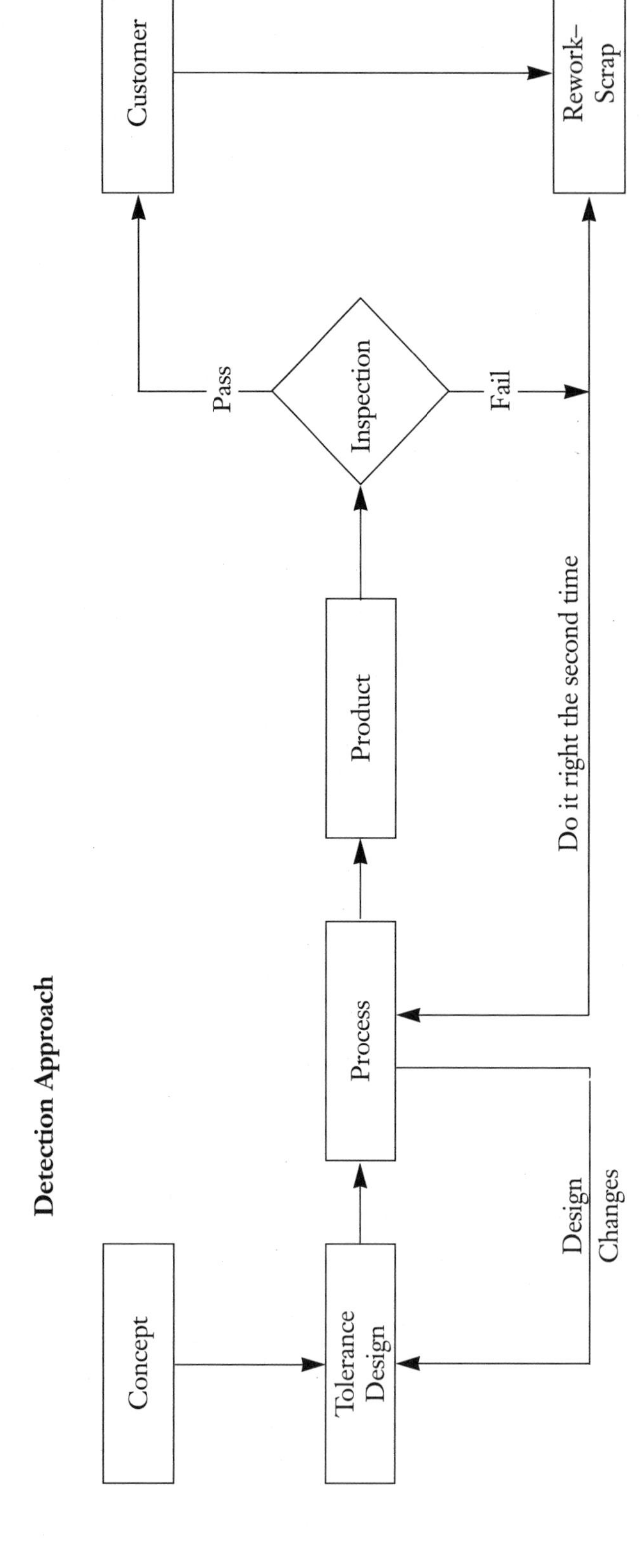

Figure 12.1 The Predominant Design–Production–Delivery Process Before TQM

structured vertically according to function: marketing, engineering, production, personnel, and so on. Most work and responsibility flows vertically; however, important information and communication flow horizontally through the boundaries between organizational functions. Communications and data bridging this barrier are often distorted, and employees don't always communicate well with organizations outside their own. Organizations tend to develop their own cultures and goals. The organizational boundaries are also perceived as the limits of responsibility. When engineering releases a product to manufacturing, there is less interest in the product because the engineers' work is done. Often the original designers are assigned to another project. After receiving the design package, manufacturing then begins the process design activity. Sometimes there is some early interaction between engineering and manufacturing, however, it is of limited value as practiced. Designs keep changing up to and after the turnover time.

One effective response to this has been to change organizational structure from the common vertical, military pyramid to a flatter organization with fewer layers. Combined with the multifunctional team concept for process management, this has simplified communications and has forced interorganizational cooperation because the teams have an interest in improving the quality of the design production cycles (the processes). The result is a product development process that contains all the work elements that affect the product with the members working to improve their outputs.

DESIGN CONTROL

The function of engineering is to interpret customer requirements and provide the detailed description of a product to manufacturing in a form—usually drawings and specifications (on paper or in using software)—sufficiently detailed so that the product can be produced at a competitive cost.

Typically, for products of some complexity, the design steps are an evolution from concept through development, preliminary design, pilot production, and release for manufacture. There are many terms used to describe this process, with variations in different industries. The complexity of the process can vary tremendously depending on the technological advances required and the nature of the product. There would obviously be a difference between developing an electric toothbrush and a communications satellite. There are, however, some factors in the process that are similar.

PRODUCT PLANNING

The purpose of a product is to satisfy customers' needs or desires. This satisfaction has several components. Some are obvious; some must be discovered. The latter might be in the nature of unexpressed customer expectations. For example, for many years U.S. consumers wanted more reliable and economical cars. If these factors, rather than style and higher profits had been more important to U.S. auto designers, that need would not have existed for the Japanese to fill (and consequently put them so heavily into that market). Not listening to the customer led to a major mistake in business strategy.

Product planning should thoroughly identify customer needs and expectations and ensure that all engineering and manufacturing decisions are based on filling those needs. It must be a thorough, disciplined, documented process that identifies customer needs, wants, and expectations and deploys them throughout the design and production cycles.

To ensure this, the Japanese developed QFD methodology. This technique, similar to task analysis, was first used in the 1960s and is now used widely in Japan. Its use is growing in the West. It requires a significant effort before the design is started or released to manufacturing. It results in a shorter design cycle and more reliable, producible designs with very few changes required after production begins. It also results in higher quality products and greater customer satisfaction. The products satisfy every definition of quality to a degree never before achieved on a large scale.

QFD is primarily comprehensive planning. It results in a series of interlinked, interdependent, detailed descriptions of design decisions, process identifications, and procedures, as well as process controls. The entire design production process is described, through to customer delivery. The quality to satisfy the customer is fully deployed through every activity and task. Figure 12.2 shows an overview of the QFD technique. It is more fully explained in Chapter 17.

CUSTOMER REQUIREMENTS

The first and most critical step is to identify customer wants, needs, and expectations. Extensive research is required to develop accurate definitions. Thoroughness is important because these factors determine the product cost, quality, and capability.

Figure 12.3 shows the relationship between various customer requirements. Customer satisfaction, measured vertically, is achieved by going beyond one-dimensional quality and discovering unexpressed customer expectations. It is also necessary to identify what would be new, exciting, and attractive to customers. The sloping line on the upper right shows that the relationship between factors is dynamic. Products, once considered a luxury, become a necessity when they are widely available. This trend has to be expected.

Following the research, the requirements must be translated into product characteristics. For example, a kitchen product must be dishwasher safe. This translation is commonly done between marketing and engineering. One knows customer requirements, the other has the technical knowledge to describe a design to fit the need.

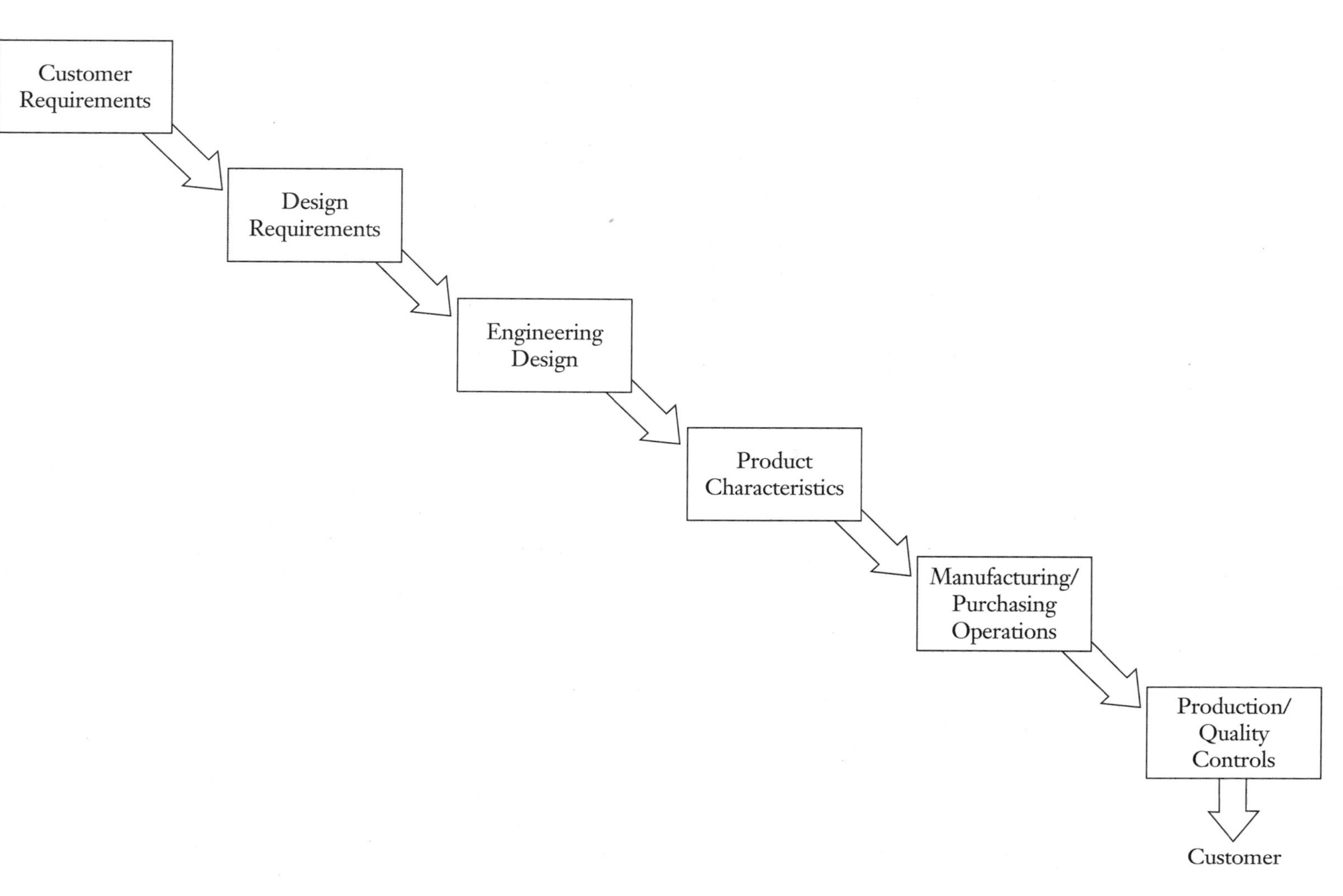

Figure 12.2 QFD Is Customer Requirements Deployed Through Interlinked Requirement Matrices in Every Activity

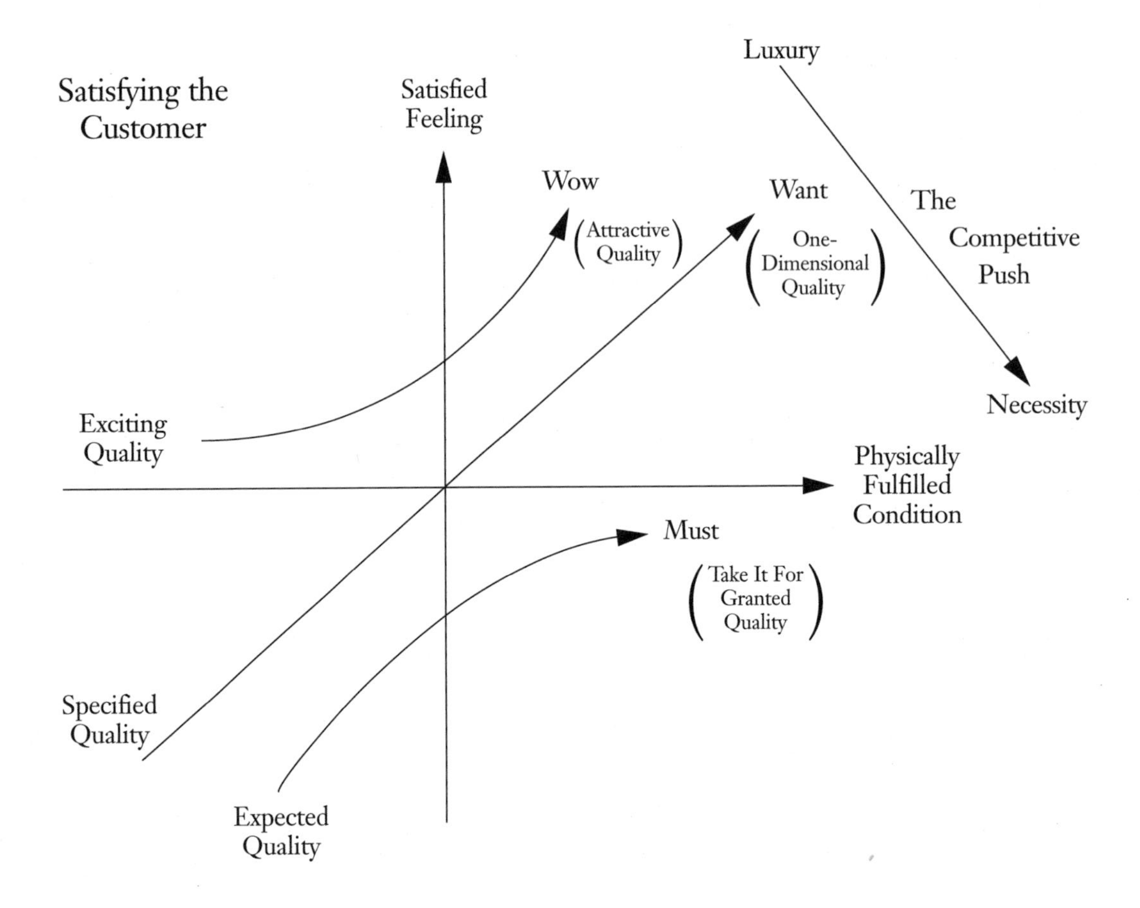

Figure 12.3 A Customer's Satisfied Feeling Versus Physically Fulfilled Condition

Frequently used tools for this translation process are the seven management tools:

- Affinity diagram
- Interrelationship chart
- Tree diagram
- Matrix chart
- Matrix data analysis
- Process decision program chart
- Arrow diagram

They are tools particularly appropriate for this activity, which is often complex and conceptual in nature. They are described in detail in Chapter 18.

DESIGN AND MANUFACTURING

Following the definition of the engineering approach to be used, the detailed design decisions are made followed by the manufacturing process descriptions. Also at this time, the critical control points are selected for process control. It is during these decision steps that the DOE techniques should be used to select the critical design and process parameters.

Forcing this process to a conclusion discloses many design and manufacturing problems to be resolved early on rather than when a product is in production or use. Correction at these later stages is more costly and even damaging to a company's reputation. In addition, late fixes often force a compromise in the product design integrity. Also, if subsequent product or process improvements are initiated the baseline QFD matrices are invaluable in maintaining the original customer requirements. The documents resulting from this effort represent an outstanding decision history and are a communication tool for everyone in the organization because they describe the basis for all decisions. They can also identify where their jobs fit into the process of satisfying the customer.

DESIGN OF EXPERIMENTS

It was not until in the late 1980s that U.S. industrial companies began to educate design and manufacturing engineers in the use of an experimental technique called DOE. One of DOE's greatest values is in determining how to reduce process variation and improve yield beyond what SPC can provide. It is the major tool in improving process capability.

The techniques were first developed by Ronald Fisher in England in the 1920s to evaluate agricultural experiments in the natural conditions while in the fields. The techniques determined which factors (sun, temperature, rainfall, soil, or fertilizer) had the most effect on growth, and determined the effect of different factor levels on results.

These are analogous questions that should be asked about a product. What effect do manufacturing process and customer use variables and stresses have on product performance and quality? The critical difference in this method over those in use is that it provides quantitative answers when the variables are applied or exist *together*, as they are in operating the processes of manufacturing and in customer use. One of its greatest values is that it provides the results (effects) of interactions between the variables. The typical one-dimensional testing (one variable at a time in the laboratory) cannot provide this. Yet it is frequently critical to know in order to optimize both the design and manufacturing process for maximum yield and lowest variability.

Applications of this method have been common in the chemical, textile, and pharmaceutical industries for some time but had not made the transition to other manufacturing industries to any extent. The work of Taguchi in the 1950s changed that. Adopted by the Japanese, DOE has a direct correlation with the high quality of

Japanese products. Taguchi made experimentation more practicable so that engineers would use it. His "cookbook" approach, using predesigned experiment set-up matrices (arrays) increased its acceptability and economy over the classical approach. Used by engineers experienced in design and production, like the approach of a chef versus a cook, and by running tests using the experimental results to confirm their values, the benefits of the Taguchi approach far outweigh the risks of a wrong selection. Anyone doing designed experiments should understand the principles involved and consult with a knowledgeable statistician about the design and risks. There is some controversy over Taguchi's simplification, particularly with more than two levels. (A level is, for example, a test temperature at which you want to examine several performance variables [factors]). Taguchi's fixed test matrices (arrays) with three or more levels can fail to indicate the interaction between variables and thereby lead to erroneous conclusion. However, there are ways to avoid this possibility and still realize the great benefits of DOE. They are beyond the purpose of this book but can be understood through the works of George E. P. Box and Dorian Shainan. See Chapter 20 for further details on DOE.

BENEFITS

Experimentation provides data that:

1. Allow engineers to optimize the design characteristics so that performance variation can be minimized in the manufacturing and customer-use environments.
2. Make products less sensitive to variations in their internal components.
3. Identify the best material, design, or method that provides adequate performance.
4. Produce the lowest cost design (avoid over-design).

It is important to understand that the method is an experiment and not simply a test. The experimenter must be alert to events as the experiment progresses. Sometimes the unexpected occurs with valuable results. An unplanned problem may be resolved. This is why experience and flexibility are important.

Benefits 1 and 2 relate to what Taguchi calls parameter design, which he describes as key steps to complete before tolerances are established. Setting parameters this way leads to robust design. Robust means, in this context, one that is insensitive to the environment. An advantage of robust design is that it is not necessary to control everything, such as the environmental factors like factory humidity.

A common management exhortation is to "work smarter." Other than waiting for an innovative idea to strike, the phrase has little meaning and management never described what they meant. DOE provides a way to work smarter in that it is a defined technique, and it is the best way to design products and processes that minimize variation—yielding higher quality.

APPLICATION

As discussed, DOE is a technique for making optimum design decisions. This is the Taguchi off-line quality engineering activity of process design and control functions in conjunction with new design experiments or with existing designs to reduce process variation.

For example, a common manufacturing process in the electronics industry is soldering parts onto printed circuit boards. The most common method is wave soldering, passing the assembled board over a bath of molten solder which solders all parts in one action. The key variables are solder temperature, speed through the bath, cleanliness, the solution's specific gravity, type of cleaner, assembly preheat temperature, and whether to preheat both sides. The success is typically measured in terms of the ratio between the number joints not soldered properly to the total number of joints required.

First, however, the process must be brought into control. SPC techniques should be used as the first action. These involve the following seven QC tools (also see Chapter 18) as described by Ishikawa:

- Flowcharts
- Pareto diagrams
- Histograms
- Check sheets
- Cause-and-effect diagrams
- Scatter diagrams
- Graphs and control charts

The result is to remove all special causes of variation in the process. This brings the process in statistical control. Only random factors are causing variation in its output. This usually results in a product with a few solder defects *per thousand* solder joints made. The process controls have been set based on experience.

Further improvement and further reduction in variation are achievable but can be attained only by changing the process variables. Without designed experimentation, this means tampering with the process variables settings and hoping for improvement. The economical action is to conduct designed experiments to identify which variables affect solder quality and determine the best settings. Controlling the process at these points can reduce defects to a few *per million.* The variation is reduced to the level that SPC may no longer be needed. Checking an occasional sample is sufficient. The cost and impact of undetected defects occurring at this low frequency would be insignificant even if they reached customers.

There are innumerable high value applications for statistical experimentation in any industry to give high payback. It is fundamental to producing higher quality products at the lowest cost.

What this indicates is the need for a thorough knowledge of how to set design parameters to match the manufacturing process and what the important variables are in the processes that affect the product quality. Established statistical techniques are the tools to fill these needs. Combined with a more systematic approach to product process design, they provide more stable, less varied products, higher production yields, shorter design to delivery cycle times, and lower costs.

DESIGN REVIEWS

Design reviews by specialists are intended to improve the design production process, but they haven't been successful. They fail because the review is done after design decisions are made; the scheduled time has been used and manufacturing is impatient to start production and meet the schedule. Too much has been expended to change anything by then, other than blatant errors. Culture and ego factors also limit the effectiveness of design reviews in the United States. Designers resent being second guessed by personnel from other organizations who were not involved in their design decisions. This was a common problem initially with U.S. engineers who worked for Japanese companies or U.S. companies taken over by the Japanese. The Japanese practice is to finalize designs through consensus. It is *expected* that designs will be reviewed and questions asked. Every engineer is not expected to know everything. Some studies have shown that American engineers in these companies first resented this peer review but came to understand its value and intent: to take advantage of the collective knowledge of the group objectively.

Fortunately, there are several interlinked and powerful tools that provide a better system for optimizing the design manufacturing process. They can produce high quality, shorter development cycles, and lower cost of Japanese products. They are all a part of the design development process commonly called concurrent engineering.

CONCURRENT ENGINEERING

Concurrent engineering (CE) involves the appropriate application of the tools and techniques of TQM with those of modern engineering like computer-aided engineering, design, and manufacturing. The key ingredient in CE is teamwork. Representatives from the key functional organizations—marketing, engineering, manufacturing, quality engineering, procurement, and frequently suppliers—collaborate over the life of a product—from concept to obsolescence—to ensure that the products fully satisfy customers' needs and expectations. It is a sustained effort to develop a functioning, reliable product that is highly producible with the minimum variation between product samples. The tools of success are not just the TQM tools mentioned previously but other modern tools like computer-aided design, engineering, and manufacturing. CE is a change from serial engineering, with organization functions contributing sequentially (Figure 12.4), to contributing as a team (Figure 12.5) with the emphasis in the product design phase. Design is not an end to itself. It must be done reflecting the other needs identified.

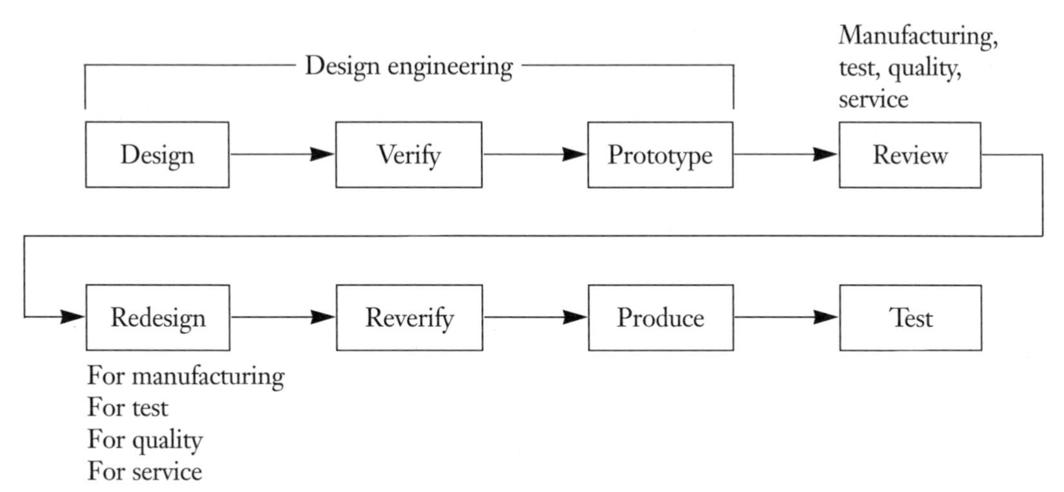

Serial engineering is characterized by departments supplying inputs to design only after a product has been designed, verified, and prototyped.

Figure 12.4 Serial Engineering

Performance
Testability
Manufacturability
Designs — Verify — Review — Produce — Test
Service
Cost
Quality

During product design, concurrent engineering draws on various disciplines to trade off parameters such as manufacturability, testability, and serviceability, along with the customary performance, size, weight, and cost.

Figure 12.5 Concurrent Engineering

The results, demonstrated by Japan and companies initiating CE in the West, are products more desired by the marketplace, more competitive, with lower engineering and manufacturing costs, and shorter design delivery cycle times. It should be a major element in every industrial TQM methodology. The Japanese, who pioneered CE, have, for example, reduced by one-half the labor expenditure to develop and deliver a new automobile, like the Lexus, in two-thirds the normal time. These factors alone provide a significant market advantage, but, in addition, the successful practitioner doesn't have its resources tied up in correcting errors and defects (serial engineering) but can apply them to the development of new and advanced products that it can also bring to market rapidly.

Some examples of using CE are as follows:[18]

1. ITEK Optical Systems Division of Litton Systems, Inc. found that Litton's adoption of TQM and CE created the changed atmosphere to greatly ensure that all the design and manufacturing factors were considered for one large project (astronomical telescopic glass segments) before beginning manufacturing.
2. John Deere and Co. used CE to cut 30 percent off the cost of developing new construction equipment and 60 percent off development time.
3. AT&T adopted CE and cut in half the time to make an electronic switching system.

CE is an expansion of the Taguchi "off-line and on-line quality control" methodology. Taguchi's particular emphasis was the introduction of a design step parameter design—to identify the nominal values of those parameters that determine product performance during manufacture and customer use. These are also the parameter values that manufacturing must control to ensure both product performance and high process yield. The key tool in this methodology is DOE. It is illustrated in Figure 12.6.

The role of SPC in manufacturing is to indicate how well the important parameters are controlled. All tools and techniques noted are described in various chapters of this book. CE is discussed in more detail in Chapter 21.

Expansion of the Taguchi approach into what is now CE could be depicted as shown in Figure 12.6. CE is an obvious reflection of the TQM philosophy applied to the product design manufacturing cycle. It is a different way to manage in that new products are not the sole domain of engineering. It is a joint venture of the total organization. For it to succeed, teamwork must be valued as highly as technical competence and innovation. The design goal must not be just superior performance but the best total quality.

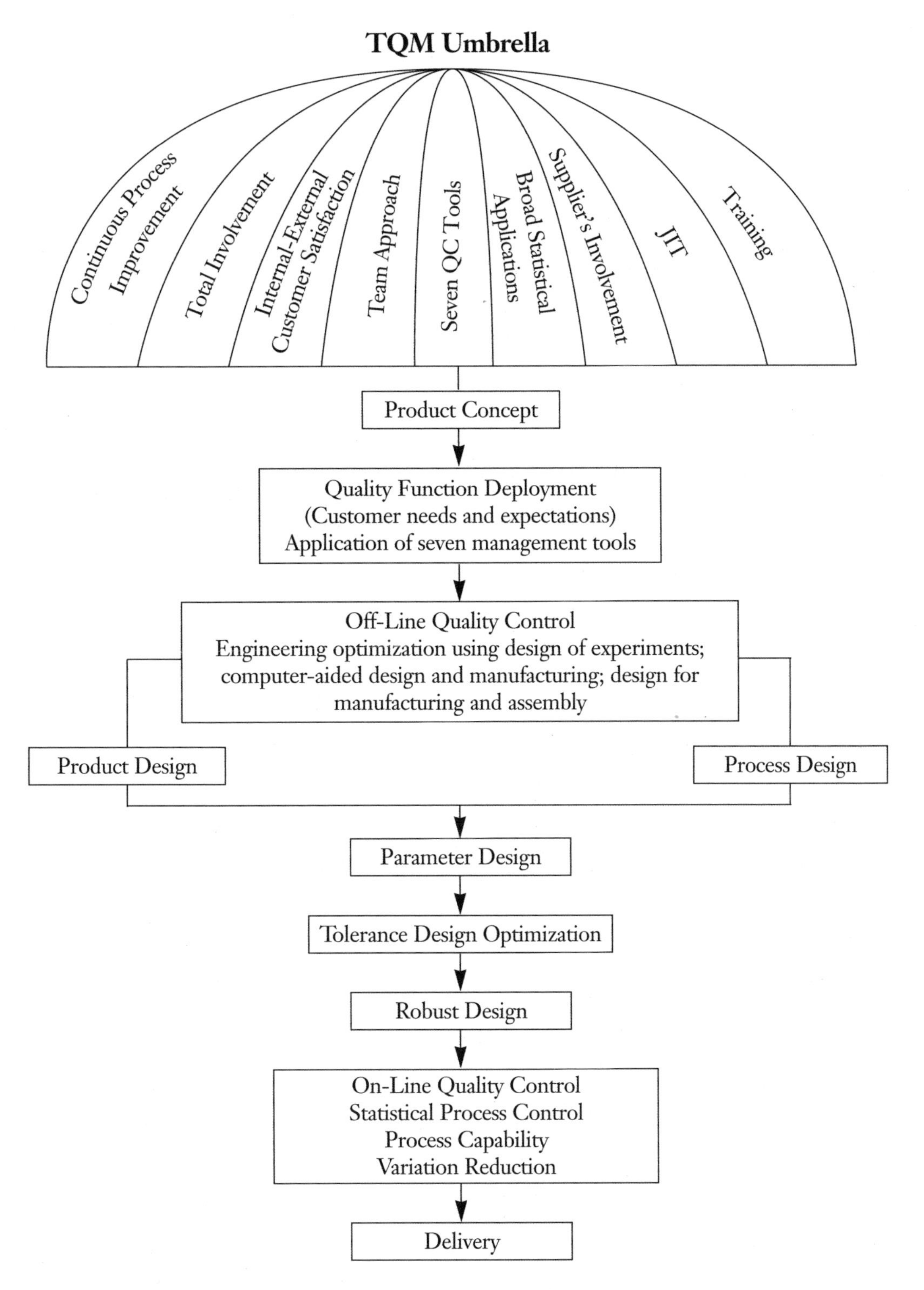

Figure 12.6 The Total Quality Management and Concurrent Engineering Process of Product and Process Design

Chapter 13

Supplier Quality Improvement

A product supplier that delivers within tolerance 99 percent of the time might be considered by many to be outstanding. With the advent of TQM that perspective changes. That supplier performance may or may not be adequate. The reason is that just knowing that specifications are met is insufficient. What is missing is the knowledge of the distribution of the performance of the delivered products with respect to the tolerances. Statistical thinking has to be brought into the evaluation. Another factor, unrelated to specifications, is also of critical importance in judging the value of a supplier: the operating philosophy of the supplier management. If it does not include a demonstrated policy of continuous process improvement, it is a supplier that will not deliver consistent quality at the most competitive price. This impacts the buyer's costs since the buyer pays for whatever the supplier makes—good or bad—over the long run.

These concepts can be depicted another way. If buyers specified that suppliers must deliver 97 percent of the product ordered to within ±2 sigma (2σ) of nominal for identified critical dimensions (assuming $\pm 3\sigma$ was within the specified tolerance) then:

1. Many suppliers would not understand the requirement.
2. Those who figured it out would charge more because they would have to select from the total produced.

However, this specification reflects a TQM goal of process performance measurement for suppliers' processes. Suppliers must think in terms of delivering products mostly near the nominal, not just anywhere within tolerance.

These ideas do not apply only to product suppliers. It is to a buyer's advantage to also contract with deliverers of a service to select those that practice continuous process improvement. They too will deliver the highest quality consistently and competitively. The desired situation is identified in Table 13.1.

PREFERRED PERFORMANCE

The principles behind the preceding discussion can be demonstrated by Figure 13.1. It shows the distribution of a critical factor for an ordered part measured outgoing from the suppliers.

Distribution 2 is the minimum desirable. Most parts will measure around the nominal and, if the process remains stable, all the parts *as made* will be within tolerance. As made versus selected through inspection means lower cost and better buyer product quality.

Distribution 4 depicts what would be most desirable. It would also meet the 97 percent, 2σ specification mentioned earlier. Here, more parts would measure

Table 13.1 Common Situation in Dealing with Suppliers Versus Desired and Achievable Situation

Common Situation	*Desired Situation*
Parts seldom arrive on time	Deliveries on time
Some parts defective	All parts good
Many parts require testing before use	No inspection needed
Part performance or dimensions vary widely between limits	Part performance measure symmetrically around nominal
Some parts found defective in production and require extra inspection and rework	Parts rarely found defective. No rework required
Safety stock required to cover part failures, unreliable receipts, unacceptable shipments	Little or no safety stock
Items require count and verification when received	No count required. Quantity shipped correct
Orders require purchasing follow up to ensure delivery	Orders arrive on time without confirmation

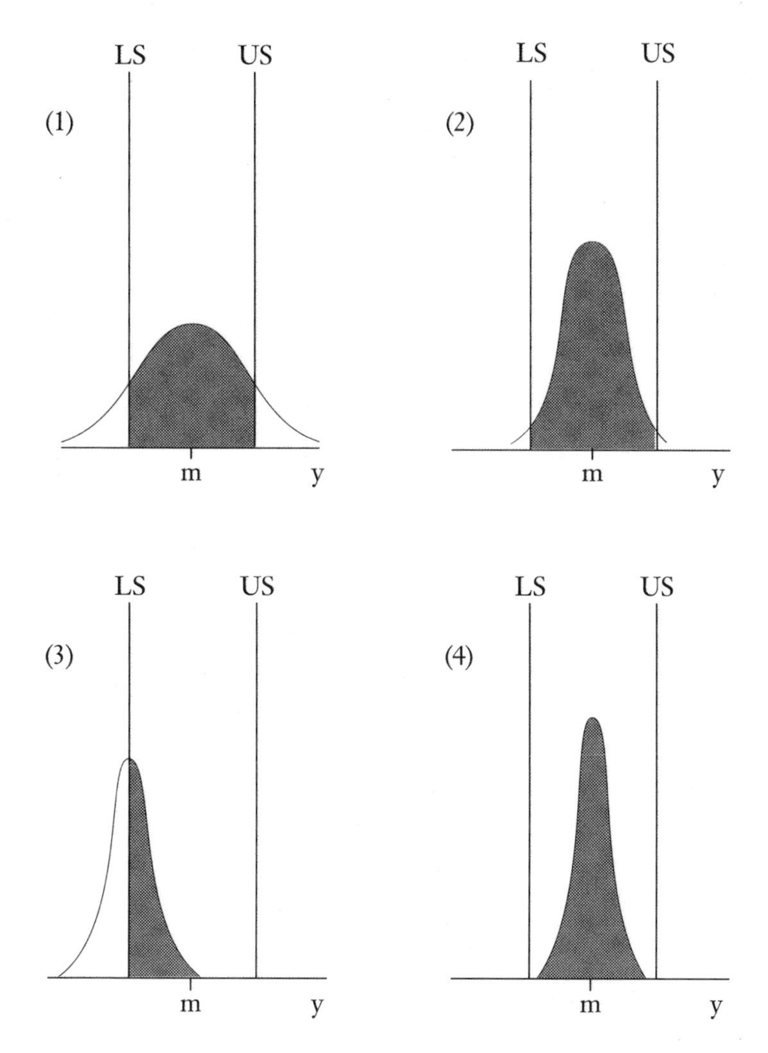

Figure 13.1 Output Distribution from Four Factors

closer to nominal and some process shift (which is highly probable) would not result in defective production.

Distributions 1 and 3 show that in the as-made condition the supplier would have to select parts that meet specifications. The balance would have to be scrapped or reworked if it could be used to fill an order. However, the customer would receive parts that would adversely affect the ability to produce products of high quality. Also, the supplier is less cost-competitive.

It is common for more than half of an industrial product to be composed of purchased material. It would be poor economy for a manufacturer to establish process controls in-house and use purchased parts from processes of uncontrolled variability.

It would have an unpredictable effect on final product quality and, thereby, customer satisfaction. Suppliers have to be approached and managed as direct extensions of in-house processes.

SUPPLIERS AND TQM

Suppliers should be considered a part of the overall manufacturing process. As such they should participate in the overall TQM process. They have strengths and value beyond what they deliver. Buyers should:

- Include suppliers in their design discussion and review process. The suppliers know their processes. They have experience and knowledge that can contribute significantly to product quality and cost.
- Require suppliers to adopt a management policy of continuous process improvement using the appropriate TQM practices to achieve it. Some TQM tools and techniques, like employee involvement and SPC, are useful in even very small businesses.

Suppliers must understand how to change from just meeting requirements to developing *at least* a capability such that *all* products produce measurements within the tolerance limits. They must also understand how to implement continuous improvement and process control.

Acceptable Quality Limits

Acceptable quality levels (AQLs) were established in the 1940s in conjunction with the use of sampling inspection plans. AQLs are related to economic consideration in sampling. An AQL is the percentage of defects allowed before rejecting a lot.

The use of AQL is a concept in contradiction to TQM because:

1. In essence, it contracts for some level of supplier defects.
2. It sets up a game whereby a supplier ships some level of defects and the buyer's inspection team tries to find them.
3. It involves statistics that allow for acceptance of some lots that are actually well outside specification limits. They end up in the product.
4. It does not use the TQM concept of process capability improvement in which the objective is zero variation.

As a result of these serious deficiencies and contradictions, AQLs are not used when adopting TQM. Zero defect sampling plans have been developed for high-volume acceptance inspection.

Supplier Cost and Quality

One of Deming's principles is to purchase on the basis of total cost versus lowest price and to reduce the number of suppliers to a minimum. This is also an important principle for using JIT.

Cost versus price means to consider the total cost experienced in dealing with a supplier instead of only the lowest bid price. The cost factors in addition to price are late deliveries and poor quality. Late delivery can increase buyer costs when it impacts production causing stoppages and workarounds. Poor quality raises cost as a result of extra handling, paperwork, problem analysis, inspection, and rework. It can also result in scrap, reorder, and delay. The negative impact of early deliveries is also discussed in relation to JIT.

Supplier Rating

Supplier selection should be based on performance history. The most common method of using historical information is through supplier rating systems. They vary from simple ratios of rejections based on total received to complex equations that include all cost factors resulting from processing rejections and late deliveries. Whatever rating process is used, it should provide the buyer with a comparison between like suppliers and commodities and, where possible, an indication of their process capabilities. Suppliers that demonstrate continuous process improvement should be rated higher than those that do not.

Certification and Inspection[20]

Inspection of purchased material on receipt has been a standard practice in American industry. Recognizing that it is an expensive nonvalue-added activity, there has been a trend toward certifying suppliers that demonstrate a continuous history of delivering conforming material. The material of certified suppliers is not inspected but goes directly to stock. Or often in the case of a JIT facility, directly to the point of use.

A common approach to certification is to require that a supplier deliver 10 consecutive acceptable lots, which are inspected; then there is a switch to skip lot inspection for 10 more lots. If all are still acceptable, the supplier is certified to ship that item to stock. Subsequent line rejections would cause the item to revert to lot inspection until continuous quality is again established. To achieve success, a certification program requires thorough preplanning and a full understanding of buyer requirements by a supplier.

The limitation in the preceding certification procedure is that the customer has no knowledge of how the supplier meets requirements, therefore, three unhealthy conditions may exist:

1. If the supplier is depending on its inspection to select parts out of the total made within specification, there will likely be an unbalanced distribution, that is, characteristics near one tolerance limit or another. This can easily affect customers' product and customer satisfaction.

2. The cost of parts made but rejected will affect the price paid by the customer.
3. Human inspection effectiveness has been measured many times and averages around 90 percent. Therefore, about 10 percent of the time, bad product is overlooked and delivered.

Certification and TQM

Certification mutually benefits suppliers and buyers. The supplier can plan on continued business because the buyer would have to incur all new lot inspection costs if a new supplier is chosen. The buyer benefits through the reduction of inspection costs and by having a dependable supplier. However, the conventional certification previously described is less effective, more hazardous, and more costly than one invoking a continuous improvement requirement that would require the supplier to adopt a proactive approach. A proactive approach better ensures the likelihood of process improvement and quality improvement and eventually would provide a more competitive position for both.

One method being used to overcome those disadvantages is to require suppliers to implement SPC, achieve statistical control, and demonstrate a policy of continuous process improvement. When a supplier process achieves control and is improved to the point where its control limits are consistently inside of the customer specification limits, then there is only a 0.27 percent probability that the operation it completes will be outside requirements. It is then a low risk to eliminate inspection and ship to stock. Evidence by the supplier of this achievement would be a copy of the control chart with the shipment.

Managing a supplier that is implementing the appropriate elements of SPC would not involve any significant product inspection. Process audits would ensure that continuous improvement was actually invoked.

Small Supplier TQM Implementation

Larger industries commonly depend on hundreds or thousands of small suppliers to provide a variety of materials and services. Some small businesses are in the process of implementing TQM as appropriate to their size, products, and processes but most have not. At this time, many are barely aware that it exists. TQM use will grow as buying companies adopt it themselves and reach the point where their suppliers must follow. If that does not occur, quality improvement will not reach the maximum, and foreign competition will continue to capture world markets.

Buyer Initiatives

One example of an approach to achieving TQM adoption by small suppliers is illustrated by California aerospace industries.

Several large aerospace contractors approached the State Department of Commerce with a concern that small businesses in the state were not conscious of the changing higher quality requirements and how to achieve them. As a result, they would likely become noncompetitive. Working with community colleges, the state developed the California Supplier Improvement Program (CALSIP) (Figure 13.2). It is applicable to any size organization of any kind.

The typical approach to initiating a program with a company would be:

1. Awareness: Supplier's top management is invited by its customers to participate in a one-day TQM orientation conducted by the community colleges, at a nominal fee. The objective is to describe the quality revolution and its advantages.
2. Self-assessment: At the end of the orientation, a self-assessment questionnaire is distributed to the participants. If they are interested, they may complete the questionnaire and review it with a state-paid, trained facilitator consultant.

   The questionnaire gives the manager and consultant insight into the present company culture and helps identify which of the predesigned training modules would be appropriate and of interest (Figure 13.2).
3. Training modules: The training modules (Table 13.2) are for TQM principles, statistical techniques, leadership, communication and team-building, and JIT.
4. Application: Immediately after training, the consultant works with the company in applying the skill.
5. Implementation: On-site training and implementation is offered through the college trainers. If a minimum of 100 employee work-hours is required, the employer is eligible for state payment for the trainer.

The objective is to have management take over the role of facilitator as quickly as possible. With this approach, the initiative to implement TQM is in the hands of management. As a methodology, this is a generic approach applicable anywhere. The incentive for change is strongly stimulated by the supplier's customers and the cost of the trainer is paid by the state.

One of the first companies to use the CALSIP approach, Continental Forge Company, a company of 225 employees, realized a 30 percent reduction in scrap, and continuous improvement thinking led to a reduction from 90 minutes to 15 minutes in die change.

Not surprisingly, the company owner started the change process with skepticism but became a major spokesman after experiencing the results. An interesting facet of this company's experience, probably not unusual among small business, was the early discovery that three-quarters of its shop personnel were illiterate in any language. This was overcome by hiring an educator to teach a basic competence. This was not only significant to the company's future but to the community as well.

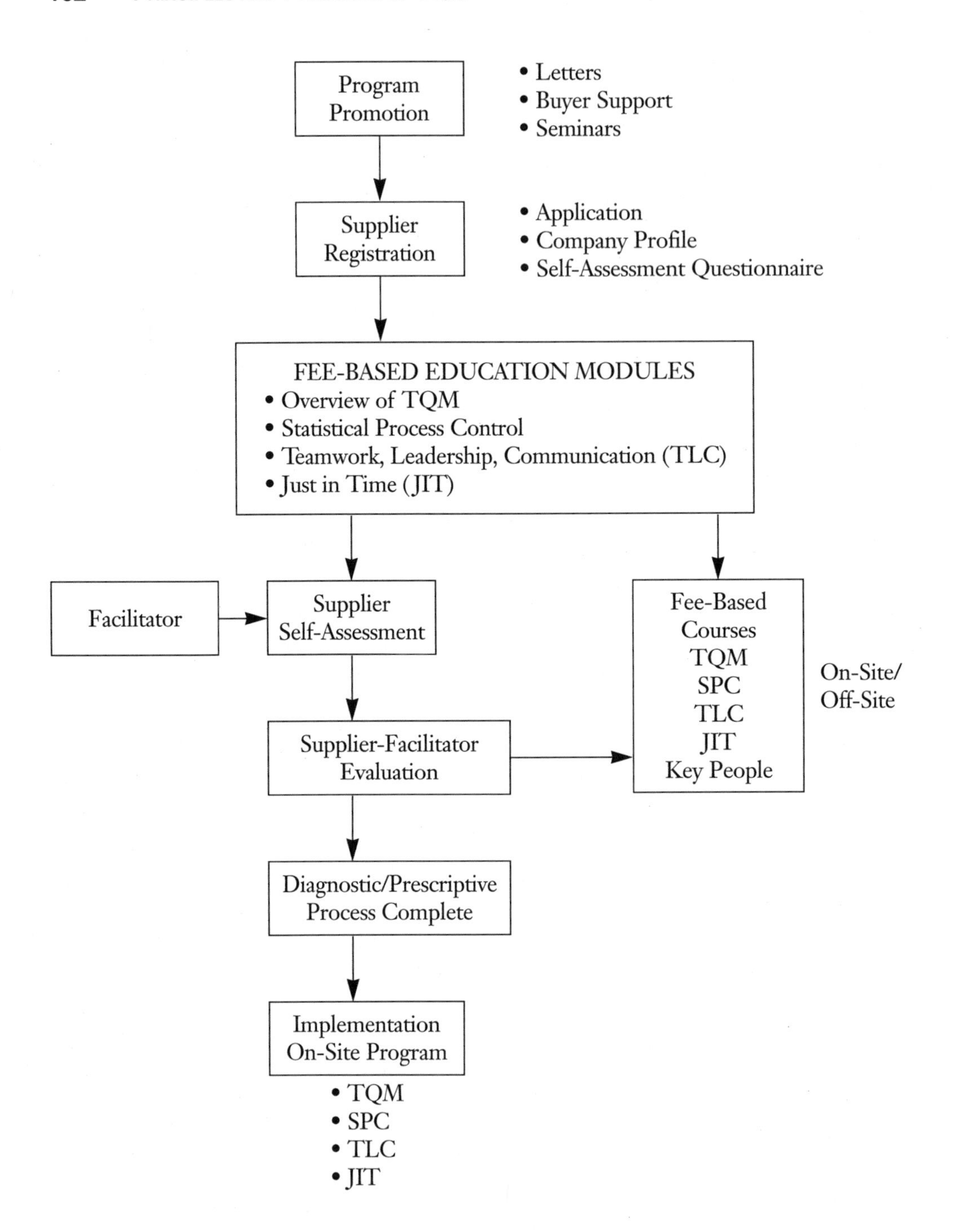

Figure 13.2 Basic Schematic Approach for Training Small Companies in TQM Principles and Applications

Table 13.2 CALSIP Curriculum Matrix. Elements of each of the four modules are selected based on each company need.

TQM	SPC	TLC	JIT
Introduction	Introduction/overview	Problem-solving process	What is JIT?
What is quality?	Organize for quality	Teamwork	People involvement/ total quality
What's in it for us?	Design for quality	Meetings	Methods for quality
Change	Ground work	Communication	JIT techniques
Leadership (management role)	Control chart—attribute	Leadership (required)	JIT production
Methodology adopt/structure	Control chart—variable	Leadership—normal versus TQM company	JIT interfaces
Tools and techniques	Analysis and interpretation		Implementing JIT
Final package presentation	Process control		
Prescription assessment	Improvement action		
	Process performance		

Chapter 14

Just in Time and TQM

JIT is a philosophy of manufacturing based on the elimination of waste and continuous improvement of *all* activities and processes in the enterprise. It includes the principles and practices of TQM. In addition, it includes the industrial engineering specialties of:

- Set-up time reduction.
- Lead time and inventory reduction.
- Cellular manufacturing and pull versus push production systems.
- Purchasing and materials management interfaces.
- Measurements.

In other words, it involves all critical operating systems and activities for every type of manufacturing. It is a goal-setting methodology as well because its ideals are never reached. It is never fully implemented because improvements are always possible. In this respect, it also parallels TQM in its objectives; in addition, it requires TQM adoption. In fact, JIT can be used as a theme for implementing TQM. Industrial management is traditionally so focused on production activities that it supports JIT objectives and accepts the additional requirement of adopting TQM to achieve them. Managers are comfortable with the production orientation of JIT with its focus on reducing cycle time, inventories, and waste. This speaks management's language even though JIT requires planning, operating, and measuring production differently than the traditional practices. However, once understood, its advantages are clear, and JIT is embraced. The need for TQM also becomes clear when management realizes that, if JIT is to succeed, poor quality in any activity is unacceptable.

APPLICATION

The use and success of JIT in Japan is common. It is not unusual for suppliers to deliver their products directly to the production line daily. The customer's personnel are practically not involved in the event. There is no inspection. The supplier quality is known and is near perfect. All this has been assured over the years taken to reach that level of performance. It is the result of full implementation of TQM and JIT by both the customer and supplier.

JIT began in the United States in the 1980s in conjunction with the development of TQM. Table 14.1 lists the benefits achieved by some companies.

Table 14.1 JIT Successes in North American Companies

Company	Reduced Inventory	Reduced Lead Times	Reduced Rework	Increased Inv. Turns	Reduced Space
Omark Industries	94%	95%	50%	–	40%
Hewlett-Packard	67-85%	80%	–	–	83%
Black and Decker	68%	65%	–	800%	65%
General Electric	82%	95%	51%	–	70%
Harley-Davidson	50%	–	52%	571%	62%
Westinghouse	75%	92%	–	372%	58%
Texas Instruments	60-94%	50-70%	75%	–	40%

Reprinted with permission of the American Production Inventory Control Society.

JIT THEMES AND CONCEPTS

The themes and concepts of JIT are identified in Figure 14.1. They are oriented to illustrate their interrelationships. All are integral parts of JIT's application. The outer circle identifies the major elements. The inner circle notes the three areas of focus. There is a certain redundancy in identifying the elements of continuous improvement, people development, *and* total quality control (TQC) since they are the basic principles of TQC but there is special focus on them for the production activities. Many dramatic improvements have been realized using these elements only in manufacturing functions without full TQC. However, the maximum benefit cannot be obtained if the entire company is not involved.

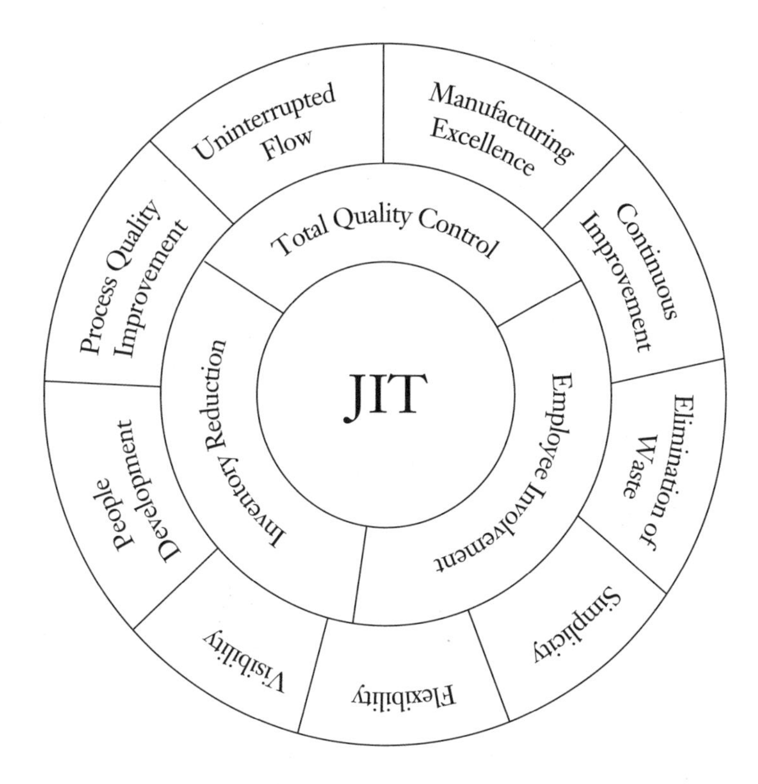

Figure 14.1 Elements of JIT and Their Interrelationships

It is not the intention of this discussion to describe JIT fully, but there are a few observations that further the understanding of TQM. TQM is not only a JIT theme but an equal partner in its achievement. Inventory reduction to the point of its elimination is another theme. Inventory is considered an evil. It subtracts from business success and consumes resources. Business has depended on it as a safety valve, to provide material because the internal processes were undependable and suppliers were unreliable. Total process management and improvement removes the need for inventory.

Figure 14.2 illustrates a technique for inventory reduction. It is the reduction of inventory in small increments to uncover process and system problems for resolution.

Some of the elements noted in Figure 14.1 are important because:

- Lead time (cycle time) reduction provides a sales advantage as well as a cost reduction. It provides flexibility to meet customer changes at lower cost.
- Productivity improvement is a major goal. With JIT, however, the emphasis is on overall company productivity improvement. The objective is to lower the total cost per sales dollar.

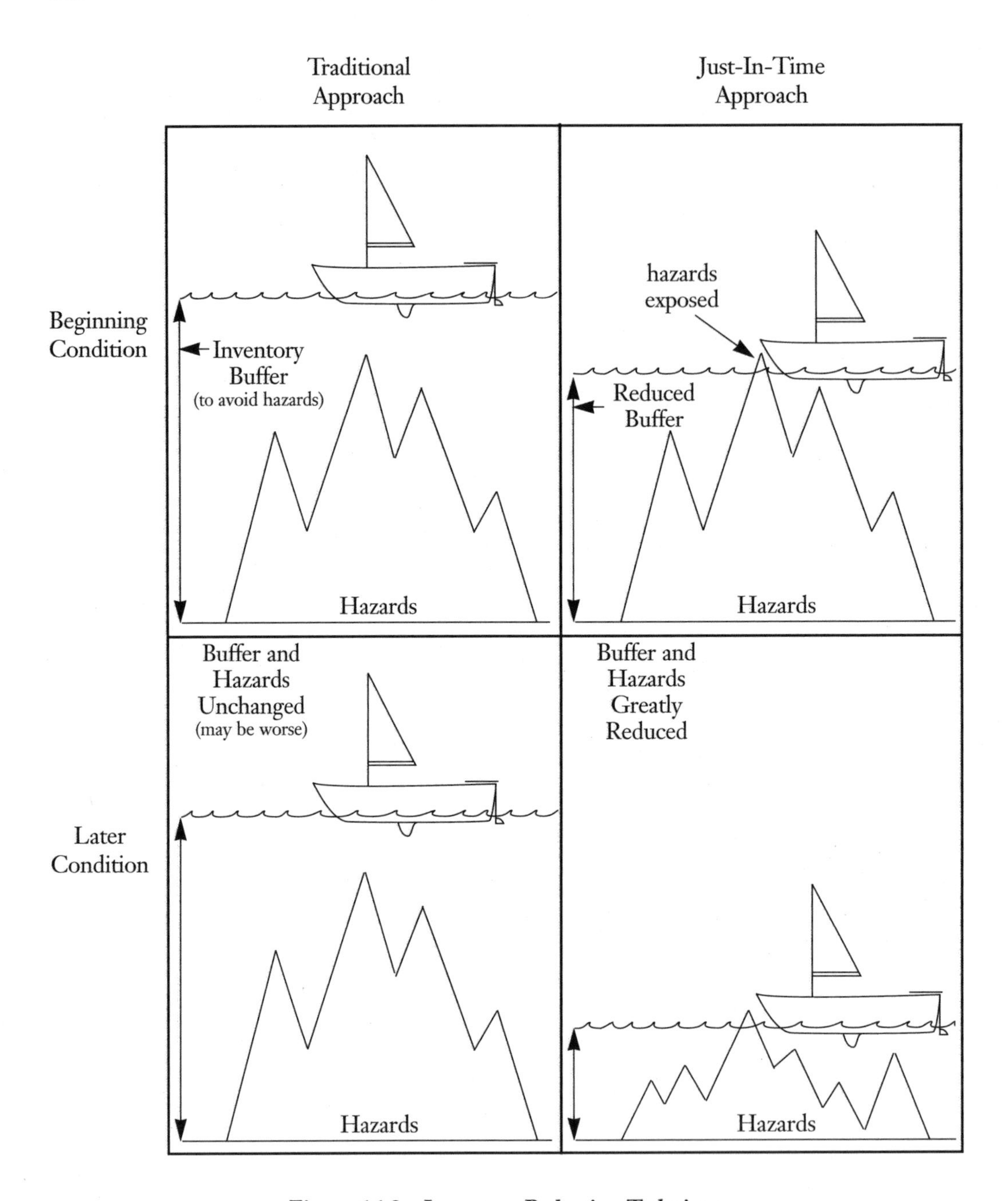

Figure 14.2 Inventory Reduction Technique

- Suppliers play a large role in product cost, quality, and customer satisfaction. Without their full participation JIT cannot be successful. They must adopt TQM (as discussed in Chapter 15). Uncontrolled variations in their product quality or deliveries could result in costly problems to their customers implementing JIT. Even early supplier delivery could precipitate a costly problem to a company operating a JIT system. It would cause a change in storage, manpower, and cash flow requirements.
- Manufacturing excellence refers to searching constantly for improvement—seeking to be the best. (See Benchmarking, Chapter 16.)
- The elimination of waste applies to striving to eliminate variation constantly in all activities so that there is no wasted effort by anyone in the company, no wasted material or facilities. It means that only value-added activities exist. It means total quality management.
- Simplification is an objective in both product design, manufacturing processes, and all organizational activities.
- Flexibility is the capability to react quickly to changing situations without loss or waste. Short cycle times and as little inventory as possible is basic to becoming flexible.
- Visibility is a key ingredient of JIT. It means exposing waste and complexity so that it may be removed.
- People involvement is also a fundamental requirement. In its best form, the people involved in the tasks of a process also manage it. They measure its performance and solve the problems related to improving it.

SUMMARY

There are many details not discussed, but the interrelationship of the JIT and TQM objectives should be clear. JIT is TQM but with special emphasis and techniques for production. In an industrial application both are required for customer satisfaction.

Chapter 15

Quality Costs—Old and New

One of the important precepts in implementing TQM and also one of Deming's 14 points is to make decisions based on data, not on precedent or opinion.

There are no data more fundamental in any organization in management decision making than cost data. Almost every organization has cost data. They vary from simple, all-inclusive accumulation data that indicate little more than a gross picture, to volumes of data measuring far more than what is important or useful. The output of a cost data system, like any other, must be that which indicates what is important for user decision making, and it must be in the appropriate form. Data have to be collected and reported in a manner that is a measurement or indicator of what management is trying to understand. A major shortcoming of most cost reporting systems is that the data are too general to be applicable to specific situations. For example, in multiple product plants the production costs of each product, beyond just the cost of the labor and material directly used, is not known with any reasonable accuracy. In fact it has been found that the most common collection systems distort the true costs, leading management to the wrong conclusions about product costs and their profitability. This weakness also makes these systems too limited to be useful in process quality improvement decision making. They do not provide *process* costs.

The basic mechanism in TQM is process improvement teams. They must have access to useful cost data, particularly overhead activities that often are a greater part of a product cost than material or labor. All these costs are quality costs under the process improvement concept. The idea of a cost of quality has existed for many years. It was developed and fostered primarily by quality control specialists. Some or most of its elements can be found in industrial enterprises, in particular those doing business with the DOD. Its content and limitations will be discussed later, but different cost data are needed for process quality analysis and improvement. The appropriate data are not available from the prevailing accounting cost systems or the traditional quality cost data. A cost system well suited to process analysis is called activity-based costing (ABC). This system can provide both product costs for each product (its original design objective), as well as good estimates of the cost of the elements driving each process. These are the kind of costs needed by process improvement teams. This cost system can also fill a growing need to more accurately determine a new product cost in its early stages, that is, introduction and growth. Other cost systems, like standard costs, are unreliable in these early stages. Knowing costs during introduction and growth have become more important with the emphasis on shorter cycle times and shorter product lifetimes. Also, the application of JIT philosophy requires a cost system like ABC because of its emphasis on reducing waste and cycle time. This requires process cost information.

THE TRADITIONAL QUALITY COST APPROACH

Measuring the cost of quality has been essentially an industry activity. It began as a measurement to determine the cost of quality control activities like inspection and to determine the cost of production waste. For example, many companies collect the cost of the direct labor and materials expended in scrap and rework in the factory and try to reduce those costs. As Figure 15.1 illustrates, however, those costs represent only the tip of the iceberg. Many other costs are incurred but not reported. They are not recognized as a cost of product defects. Some companies, in estimating the *total* cost of poor quality, were shocked to find that they approached 30 percent of sales. These hidden costs were major detractors from profit.

As the quality function evolved primarily from inspection (quality control) to more preventive activities (quality assurance), quality cost collection was expanded into the cost of activities for prevention, appraisal, and internal and external failure. These are defined in Table 15.1. This has been the standard categorization used by quality organizations in industry since the 1950s. Few organizations, however, had a cost collection system that could begin to separate all of these costs, so that categorization remained an ideal. In most cases the costs reported were mostly those of the quality organization in those categories.

The Quality Costs Committee of ASQC has published several volumes on the subject of quality costs and results based on those categories. It has also established something of a standard regarding the cost elements within each category (Table 15.2). It illustrates how extensive a collection system would have to be to report all the quality costs. It also demonstrates the pervasiveness of quality costs throughout all organization functions. But even when many of the listed quality costs have been

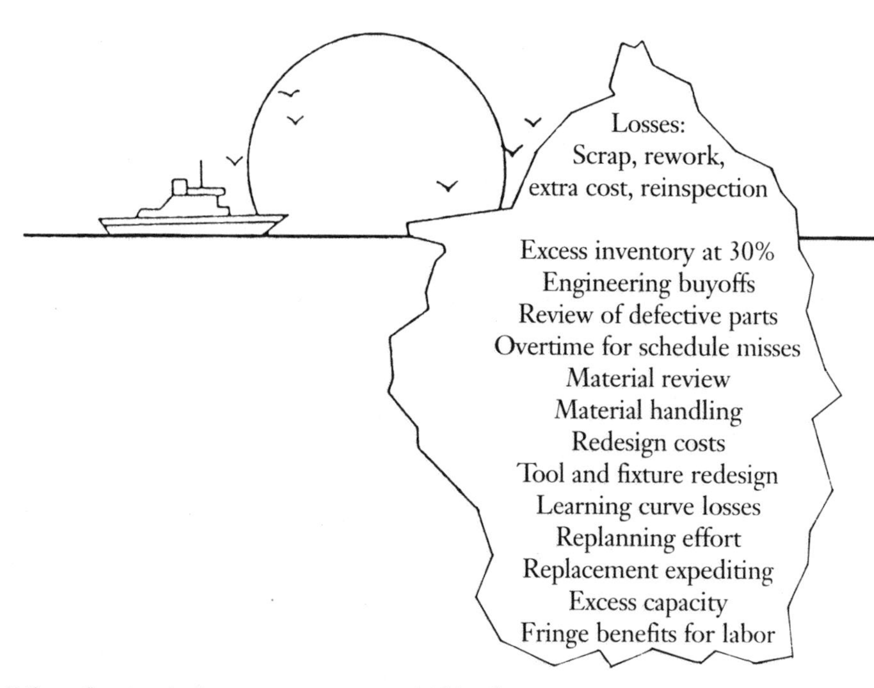

Like a floating iceberg, most costs are hidden but extensive.

Figure 15.1 The Unrecognized Costs of Poor Quality in Industry

Table 15.1 Standard ASQC Quality Cost Definitions

Prevention:	Costs associated with personnel engaged in designing, implementing, and maintaining the quality system, including auditing the system.
Appraisal:	Costs associated with measuring, evaluating, or auditing products, components, and purchased materials to ensure conformance with quality standards and performance requirements.
Internal failure:	Costs associated with defective products, components, and materials that fail to meet quality requirements and cause manufacturing losses.
External failure:	Costs generated by defective products being shipped to customers.

Table 15.2 The Traditional Quality Cost Categories and Their Elements as Established by ASQC

Detailed Quality Cost Description Summary

1.0 PREVENTION COSTS	2.0 APPRAISAL COSTS
1.1 Marketing/customer/user	2.1 Purchasing appraisal costs
1.1.1 Marketing research	2.1.1 Receiving or incoming inspections and tests
1.1.2 Customer/user perception surveys/ clinics	2.1.2 Measurement equipment
1.1.3 Contract/document review	2.1.3 Qualification of supplier product
1.2 Product/service/design development	2.1.4 Source inspection and control programs
1.2.1 Design quality progress reviews	2.2 Operations (manufacturing or service) appraisal costs
1.2.2 Design support activities	2.2.1 Planned operations inspections, tests, audits
1.2.3 Product design qualification test	2.2.1.1 Checking labor
1.2.4 Service design qualification	2.2.1.2 Product or service quality audits
1.2.5 Field trials	2.2.1.3 Inspection and test materials
1.3 Purchasing	2.2.2 Set-up inspections and tests
1.3.1 Supplier reviews	2.2.3 Special tests (manufacturing)
1.3.2 Supplier rating	2.2.4 Process control measurements
1.3.3 Purchase order tech data reviews	2.2.5 Laboratory support
1.3.4 Supplier quality planning	2.2.6 Measurement equipment
1.4 Operations (manufacturing or service)	2.2.6.1 Depreciation allowances
1.4.1 Operations process validation	2.2.6.2 Measurement equipment expenses
1.4.2 Operations quality planning	2.2.6.3 Maintenance and calibration labor
1.4.2.1 Design and development of quality measurement and control equipment	2.2.7 Outside endorsements and certifications
1.4.3 Operations support quality planning	2.3 External appraisal costs
1.4.4 Operator quality education	2.3.1 Field performance evaluation
1.4.5 Operator SPC/process control	2.3.2 Special product evaluations
1.5 Quality administration	2.3.3 Evaluation of field stock and spare parts
1.5.1 Administrative salaries	2.4 Review of test and inspection data
1.5.2 Administrative expenses	2.5 Miscellaneous quality evaluations
1.5.3 Quality program planning	
1.5.4 Quality performance reporting	
1.5.5 Quality education	
1.5.6 Quality improvement	
1.5.7 Quality audits	
1.6 Other prevention costs	

(continued on next page)

3.0	INTERNAL FAILURE COSTS	4.0	EXTERNAL FAILURE COSTS
3.1	Product/service design failure costs (internal)	4.1	Complaint investigations/customer or user service
3.1.1	Design corrective action	4.2	Returned goods
3.1.2	Rework due to design changes	4.3	Retrofit costs
3.1.3	Scrap due to design changes	4.3.1	Recall costs
3.1.4	Production liaison costs	4.4	Warranty claims
3.2	Purchasing failure costs	4.5	Liability costs
3.2.1	Purchased material reject disposition costs	4.6	Penalties
		4.7	Customer/user goodwill
3.2.2	Purchased material replacement costs	4.8	Lost sales
3.2.3	Supplier corrective action	4.9	Other external failure costs
3.2.4	Rework of supplier rejects		
3.2.5	Uncontrolled material losses		
3.3	Operations (product or service) failure costs		
3.3.1	Material review and corrective action costs		
3.3.1.1	Disposition costs		
3.3.1.2	Troubleshooting or failure analysis costs (operations)		
3.3.1.3	Investigation support costs		
3.3.1.4	Operations corrective action		
3.3.2	Operations rework and repair costs		
3.3.2.1	Rework		
3.3.2.2	Repair		
3.3.3	Reinspection/retest costs		
3.3.4	Extra operations		
3.3.5	Scrap costs (operations)		
3.3.6	Downgraded end product or service		
3.3.7	Internal failure labor losses		
3.4	Other internal failure costs		

collected, success in using the data or reducing those costs has had limited success for the following reasons:[21]

1. Business management has not been comfortable with the concept of quality costs. The categorization of prevention, appraisal, and failure was too parochial; it did not correlate with accounting practices.
2. Management's attitude has been that the reduction of quality costs was the responsibility of the quality organization even though these costs were primarily driven by engineering, manufacturing, and supplier performance.

3. The concept of prevention costs was intangible and even ambiguous. The working relationship between prevention expenditures and resultant lower costs was difficult to demonstrate. Appraisal costs (inspection and test) were considered a normal part of the process.
4. Quality costs were not used as a factor in the measurement of management performance. This reduced management's interest.
5. The prevailing definition of quality as "meeting requirements" was fundamental to management's limited interest in quality costs. Meeting requirements means producing anywhere within the engineering tolerance. Dependence was placed on the appraisal of process output to ensure that only "within tolerance" products proceeded to the customers. It was accepted that some production output did not meet requirements. These nonconformances were reworked or scrapped. This resulted in a management focus on the quality costs of inspection, test, scrap, and rework. In practice, production and quality control management constantly wrestled with the question as to what level of these costs was acceptable. The answer often depended on what budget level the quality function could negotiate, not what was needed to ensure that requirements were met.

QUALITY COSTS AND TQM

The difference between the traditional quality assurance and TQM has been explained in previous chapters. To repeat briefly, in TQM higher quality is related to reduced process variation, both in and between all organization activities and functions, for example, contracts to engineering, to production, and so on. Therefore, the kind of cost data needed in process improvement is different from the traditional quality costs. However, appraisal and failure costs may be indicators of where process improvement is needed.

A major difference between the old and new cost needs is that when the focus was on just meeting requirements, improvement efforts would stop when they were satisfied. The TQM objective, in comparison, is to eliminate all variation, that is, to improve capability and reduce cycle time. Here improvement efforts continue even if zero defects is achieved in a process and when scrap, rework, and internal failure costs would be zero. This is when process costs are needed to achieve TQM objectives. A different cost system is needed to do so.

The type of cost data necessary is also influenced by the practice of using employee teams to improve processes. This is reflected in a study by Winchell and Hohner, sponsored by ASQC and the National Association of Accountants.[22] Some conclusions they reached include the following:

1. Traditional quality costs were not a method for exercising control over costs in companies visited that supported continuous improvement. These costs facilitate problem resolution and organizational improvements by improvement teams. Therefore, flexibility is needed, not periodic reporting as has been the common quality function practice.
2. The traditional quality cost systems were not used to support continuous improvement. They are excellent for implementing a structured information system that makes preplanned periodic reports. Such a system would be useful if control is desired. Historically, however, quality cost reporting has not survived when used for this purpose.
3. Stand-alone quality cost systems, a common practice, were not effective and were short lived. They were perceived as nonvalue-added activities and not tied to improvement efforts.
4. The traditional quality cost categories did not fit the terminology of service organizations. As a result, quality cost was unfamiliar to them.
5. Quality improvement efforts drive the need for cost information in TQM. It is the other way around in traditional quality cost systems, where cost information precipitates improvement.

Item 5 reflects the important change in the nature of the quality cost information needed. Many industrial quality organizations have published quality cost reports and, from these, items causing high failure costs were identified and corrective actions taken to reduce them. The costs drove the action. The corrective actions were often ineffective because they were not based on improving the process. Instead, actions are taken to change a single event without considering what that change did to the process variation. An emphasis on process improvement will drive the need for cost information that will aid in selecting improvement targets.

QUALITY AND TOTAL COST MANAGEMENT

Quality costs for a TQM organization ideally should be one part of a total cost management system—a system that allows a focus on the internal management needs of the business and not just on the financial accounting requirements for external reporting. Management should ask itself why it collects costs. What costs are needed in relation to the way the business is conducted? If it is a business adopting or using a continuous improvement philosophy, it needs process activity costs. ABC provides such a cost management system. In this method the important costs of product development/production activities are identified, with reasonable accuracy, to be used to understand what each product and process actually costs.

Traditional cost accounting systems are based on the concept that products consume resources. ABC is based on the concept that products consume activities and that activities consume resources. Ideally in such a system it would be possible to measure, for example, the cost of all direct and indirect activities consumed by each product or its parts (or the cost of activities in a nonindustrial process in a white-collar operation). This is very difficult to define in most collection systems that allocate those factors proportionately to each product *equally* on a common basis, such as direct labor used. In the allocation method, a piece of expensive equipment may be used on some of the products but all the products are charged with its cost. As a result, low-cost products are made noncompetitive by having to carry the cost of other, under-costed products. This difference is significant because the use of support labor, facilities, and equipment can vary widely among different product items. ABC provides a costing method that more accurately reflects their differences.

Process improvement teams need the same kind of accurate product and process costs if they are to make intelligent decisions. Otherwise poor data can lead to counterproductive changes and even an erroneous conclusion that process improvement methodology does not work.

The two main elements of a simple ABC system, process value and cost driver analysis, are basic to the approach.

PROCESS VALUE ANALYSIS

Process value analysis (PVA) is a method for identifying those activities that add value to the process output and those that add cost and little or no value. Value-added is the labor and material directly used in and to make a product. PVA is shown in Figure 15.2. Analyzing value, cost, and cycle time provides economic targets for improvement as well as the true cost for making improvement. The four activities involve:

- Describing the process.
- Analyzing the activity.
- Analyzing the cost driver.
- Identifying the improvement.

Process description involves identifying and describing the important business systems and functional processes in an organization. This is also one of the early steps in implementing TQM. Figure 15.3 shows the common TQM process model with the prime PVA activities noted.

Activity analysis seeks to understand the process. It asks what each step is and why it exists. It requires the measurement of the cycle times and costs for the steps and the separation of value-added from nonvalue-added activities. Analytical tools such as flow charts, process analysis, cause-and-effect charts, and Pareto charts are typical of those used in this analysis. Some elements of this analysis are shown in Table 15.3.

Cost driver analysis associates the value and nonvalue-added activities with their costs. Obtaining these costs is the core of the ABC method. This is difficult when the

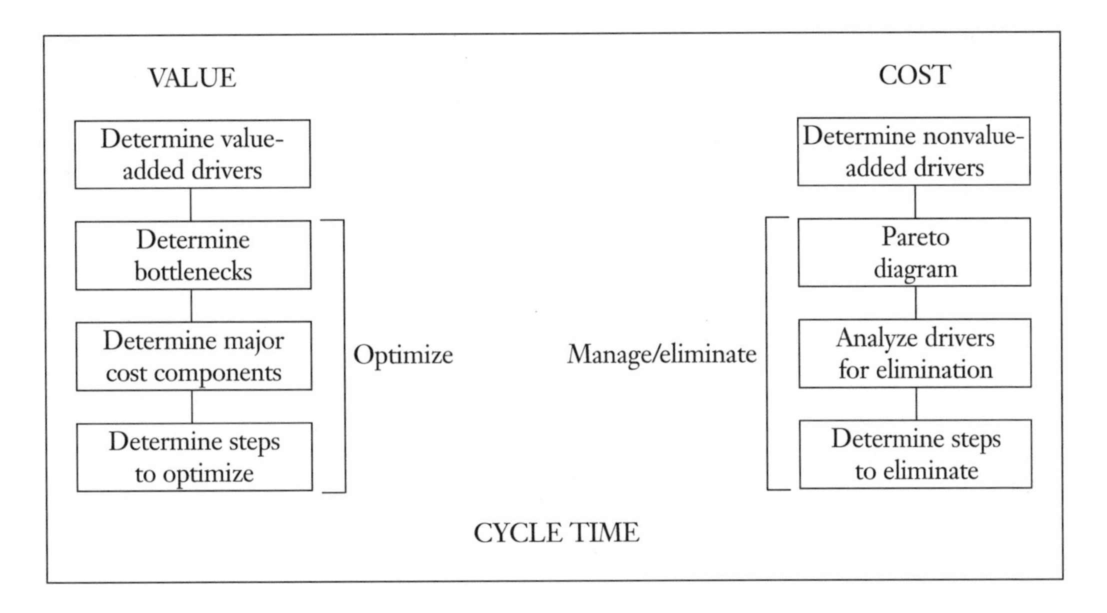

Figure 15.2 Process Value Analysis

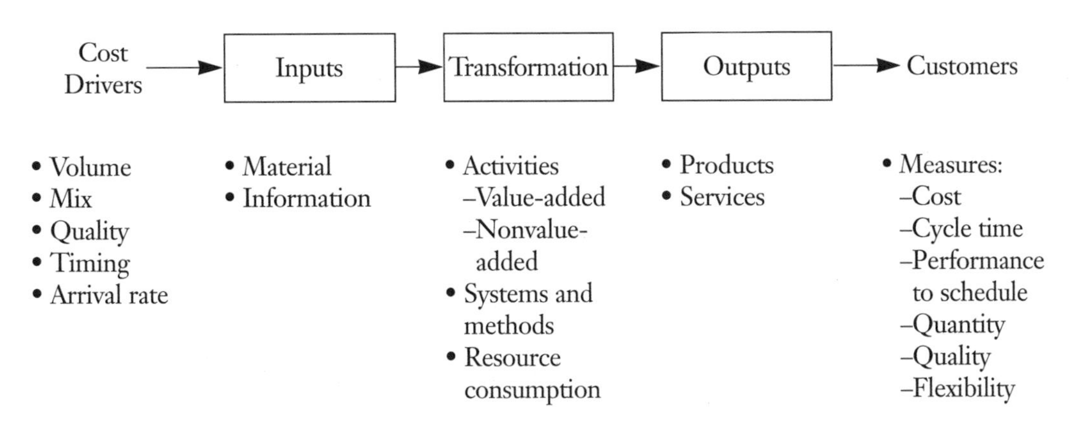

Figure 15.3 Process Description

Table 15.3 Activities and Cost Drivers

Activity	*Cost Driver*
Automatic machine	Machine cycles
Plastic molding	Machine hours
Purchasing	Purchased line items
Assembly	Direct labor hours
Process engineering	Hours
Product complexity	Material handling

This list reflects several different processes. There would be several activities and drivers within each.

accounting system has not been designed to collect them in an appropriate, meaningful manner. These are the costs needed by a process improvement team. Cost drivers in an industrial process may fall into one of the two categories noted in Table 15.4: primary (highly qualitative) and volume based. Typically both are needed because of their different sources. The cost of volume-driven activities is usually available from the cost accounting system. The important primary are not. Each organization will have to devise some informal method to obtain them. The improvement teams can usually play a major role.

Improvement identification is conducted by the teams to increase the process customer satisfaction, optimize value-added activities, reduce or eliminate nonvalue-added activities, and reduce lead time, cycle time, and waste.

BENEFITS OF AN ABC APPROACH

- Provides process improvement teams with cost details related to the process activities affecting variation and cycle time. The result is responsibility and accountability at the lowest levels.
- Monitors results of improvement projects and actions.
- Integrates financial and quality performance. This gives recognition to their interdependence.
- Identifies the true sources of unacceptable variation (quality).
- Allows the allocation of resources for improvement.

Table 15.4 Examples of Process Cost Drivers (Qualitative and Quantitative)

Primary	*Volume*
1. Coordination	1. Number of vendors/suppliers
2. Communication	2. Number of customers of process
3. Capability of staff	3. Number of supplier surveys
4. Quality of material	4. Frequency
5. Quality/age of equipment	5. Number of issues
6. Configuration	6. Number of stocks
7. Availability of tools	7. Number of cars
8. Availability of material	8. Number of moves
9. Availability of machines	9. Number of tool orders
10. Availability of data	10. Lost tool requests
11. Availability of people	11. Production rate
12. Inspection requirements	12. Number of inspections
13. Efficiency	13. Dollar volume
14. Required documentation	14. Number of line items
15. Complexity	15. Number of orders
16. Redundancies	16. Quantity per line item
17. Accuracy of data	17. Number of shipments
18. Change to requirements	18. Number of requests for commitments
19. Outside manufacturing requirements	19. Number of new materials/parts
20. Request for information/data	20. Number of shortages
21. Material characteristics	21. Number of shortage line items
22. Customer requirements	22. Number of outside manufacturing requests
23. Schedule/timing	23. Number of rejects/defects
24. Priority	24. Number of lost parts
25. Safety/environmental requirements	25. Number of approvals
26. Location of resources	26. Number of requests for information/data
27. Timeliness	27. Number of setups
	28. Number of part numbers
	29. Number of log transactions
	30. Number of purchase requisitions
	31. Number of changes to requirements
	32. Number of delinquents
	33. Number of overshipments
	34. Number of minimum buys
	35. Number of receipts

- Provides visibility to management and the process members as to the process performance in business terms. They get more accurate product and process costs and can thereby more fully understand their competitive position and how to change it.

TOTAL COST MANAGEMENT AND JIT

The interdependent relationship of TQM and JIT is discussed in Chapter 14. There is a similar relationship between JIT and total cost management, including ABC.

Briefly, before an enterprise can approach and rely on JIT, it must get its systems and processes under control so that the variation in their outputs is known, predictable, and reduced to its economically achievable minimum. The systems and processes must also reach the same state of knowledge regarding the capability and output of their suppliers' processes. Until this control level is reached, sole dependence on JIT would be high risk if not disastrous. An adequate cost system is basic to provide the foundation for high-return JIT improvements.

SUMMARY

TQM is the continuous improvement of all important process activities in an organization. The definition and scope of quality cost has to include the cost of the activities driving those processes. Some of the traditional quality costs are useful indicators of malfunctioning processes but are of limited use in the continuous process improvement team activities wherein improvements are made beyond the minimum capability and zero defects. What is needed is a cost collection system such as ABC. The data from this system will drive improvements and affect the management of multifunctional processes, resulting in functional improvement as well.

NOTES

1. The GM Manufacturing Divisions and Outside Suppliers of Production Materials and Service Products, Targets for Excellence, 1987.
2. J. D. Powers and Associates. *Wall Street Journal*, July 1990.
3. Specification MIL-Q-9858, *The Quality Program.* Now superseded by ISO 9000.
4. Transferring inspection/testing to production employees is now more than shifting an activity. Application of the continuous process improvement principles results in a reduction of those activities, regardless of who does them.
5. McEachron, N. B., and A. Weinerskirch. *The Future Role of the Quality Assurance Function.* Palo Alto, CA: SRI International, Report D88-1204, 1988.
6. Ford Motor Company Operating Philosophy.

7. Greenwood, R. G. "Management by Objectives." As developed by Peter Drucker, assisted by Harold Smiddy. *Academy of Management Review* 6, No. 2 (1981): 225.
8. Statistical principles are discussed in Chapter 4.
9. The standard deviation is expressed in the same dimension as the process measurement.
10. Ouchi, W. *Theory Z.* Reading, MA: Addison-Wesley, 1981.
11. Melan, E. H. "Focusing on the Process: Key to Quality Improvement." In *Annual Quality Congress Transactions.* Milwaukee: ASQC, 1988.
12. Another reason for the disappointment in quality circles is that they did not involve middle and upper managers. They were only for workers.
13. Breisch, W. E., and R. E. Breisch. "Employee Involvement." *Quality* (May 1990): 49-53.
14. Mohrman, S., and T. Cummings. "Implementing Quality of Work Life Program." Los Angeles: Graduate School of Business Administration. University of Southern California, 1982.
15. Skinner, B. F., Business Behaviorism and the Bottom Line, Video Recording, McGraw-Hill Films, NY, 1972.
16. Beaer, M. C. "Corporate Change and Quality." *Quality Progress* (February 1988): 33.
17. The probable range of a process variation can be easily calculated from samples.
18. Rosenblatt, A., and G. Watson. "Concurrent Engineering." *IEEE Spectrum* (July 1991): 22.
19. The specified full tolerance would be $\pm 3\sigma$ in this example.
20. Maass, R. A. "Supplier Certification—A Positive Response to Just-In-Time." *Quality Progress* (September 1988): 22.
21. Baker, W. M. "Why Traditional Standard Cost Systems Are Not Effective in Today's Manufacturing Environment." *Industrial Management* (July/August 1989).
22. Winchell, W. O., and G. Hohner. "Implementing Quality Cost Systems." In *Annual Quality Congress Transactions.* Milwaukee: ASQC, 1990.

SECTION II

Chapter 16

Benchmarking

Benchmarking is the first technique described in this section because it is the most valuable in achieving improvement. Companies like Xerox, AT&T, ALCOA, Motorola, and the Malcolm Baldrige National Quality Award winners found that it provided the greatest improvements and was the most effective change agent of all their TQM activities.

It isn't, however, a panacea. It won't solve all company problems. Edward Tracy, AT&T vice president, stated, "If AT&T had not been into quality, I'm not sure we could have pulled off benchmarking because of the culture that is needed. You need to understand that benchmarking is a vital piece of the quality process. You need to understand quality principles and you must have the necessary quality skills, structure, and environment in place." He also said that "AT&T's benchmarking process has been not just mildly successful, but enormously successful."[1]

BENCHMARKING

U.S. business has always measured success by profit, growth, and return on investment. At the same time, management always believed that improvement was possible. It annually prepared plans to improve. The basis of its plans was mostly an extrapolation of its latest (one year) performance data. To improve the odds, management often put its most aggressive people in charge of the plan elements. "Make it happen" was the battle cry. Sometimes management was successful, sometimes not. Typically, no one was sure why the outcome was as it was. If successful, those leaders were rewarded. If not, replacements were found or they tried again. Various fads were adopted, like MBO, but they fell out of use because they didn't prove consistently beneficial.

The Japanese have not used extrapolation planning as their fundamental policy. They spent many years analyzing in detail how the rest of the world's businesses worked. They identified how the successful companies worked, then adopted the best there was, often improving on it. They also exchanged this information with each other. This process has now been somewhat systematized and identified in the United States as benchmarking.

American companies did occasionally use benchmarking but on an incremental basis. The most common use was in making detailed comparisons of competitive products. Some companies made occasional use of it in determining competitive manufacturing costs and salaries. However, the practice was not widespread or systematic. Comparisons were not made for all the important activities in all functions as they are in benchmarking today. Noncompetitive processes were rarely benchmarked even if they were similar. American business management has not been process management oriented. Typically, it has believed that only another business in the same market was worth evaluating.

Benchmarking is a comparison process. It is continuously identifying the best business practices anywhere and adopting or adapting them to your organization. It's a renewal process; it's not based on an evolutionary or extrapolation change rate, but on rapidly mutating into a higher order of effectiveness and efficiency. It's leapfrogging into the highest competitive position, process by process.

BENEFITS

As has been demonstrated now by several U.S. companies, such as Xerox, IBM, and Motorola, benchmarking has several valuable benefits.

- It is highly motivating for an organization to know that it is performing as well or better than the best. It frequently stimulates creativity for even greater improvement.
- A business with all its functions performing equal to, or better than, the competitors is in an advantageous market position.
- An organization that has experienced the benefits of benchmarking tends to want to continue the activity and remain the best.
- The benchmarking process fosters a new in-depth understanding by managers and employees of how organizations truly function. This makes the members more interested and motivated.
- Focusing on outside competition avoids nonconstructive internal competition. Need for improvement is more acceptable if it's recognized that someone outside is measurably better.

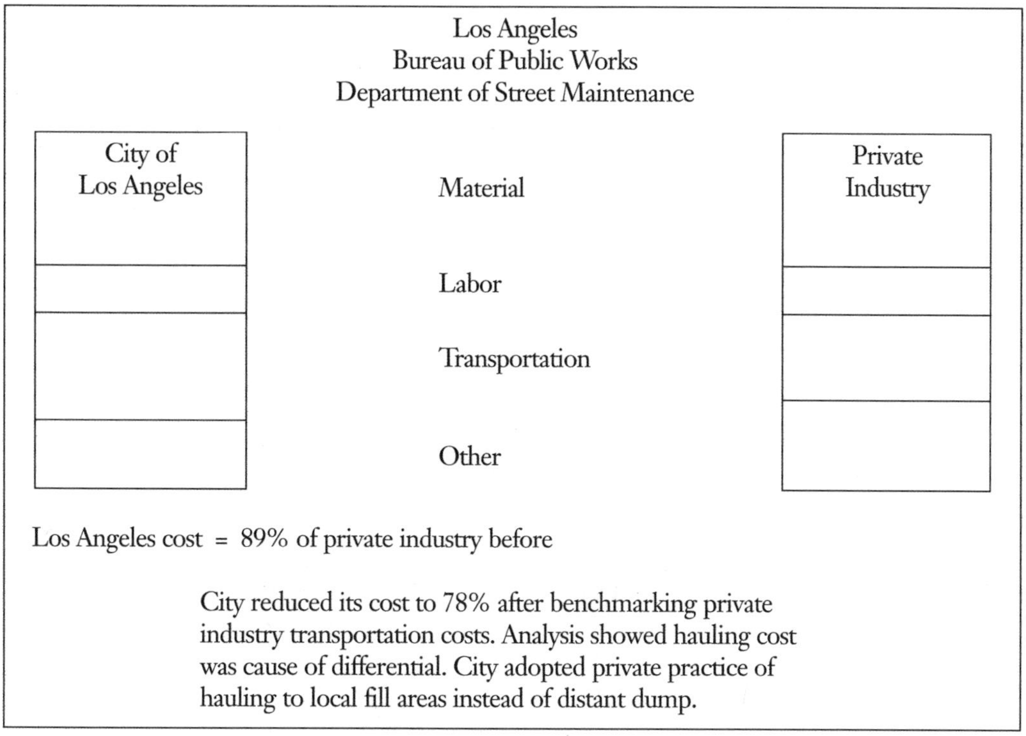

Los Angeles
Bureau of Public Works
Department of Street Maintenance

City of Los Angeles

Material

Labor

Transportation

Other

Private Industry

Los Angeles cost = 89% of private industry before

City reduced its cost to 78% after benchmarking private industry transportation costs. Analysis showed hauling cost was cause of differential. City adopted private practice of hauling to local fill areas instead of distant dump.

Figure 16.1 An example of benchmarking a competitor: The Street Maintenance Department of Los Angeles found one process in which private industry was more competitive, adopted it, and became the most competitive.

- It results in the most valuable productivity improvement, that is what the minimum output cost should and can be with resources properly applied.

Benchmarking can be illustrated by a simple example shown in Figure 16.1. The Street Maintenance Department of Los Angeles made a breakdown of its operating costs and compared them to those of private industry. It found that its costs were only 89 percent of private industry's costs. However, in its analysis it found that its transportation costs for hauling debris was higher. In investigating, it discovered that private industry used local sites where such fill material was needed, while the city used outlying designated dump sites. When the city also adopted this practice, its costs dropped to 78 percent of private industry, thus increasing its competitive advantage.

BENCHMARKING AND TQM

Benchmarking is a very valuable tool for accomplishing the TQM objective of customer satisfaction and continuous improvement. By copying what someone else has proven effective, companies can save time and money that would otherwise be spent on internally determined evaluation and process improvement.

Benchmarking has some additional advantages that make it even more important than relying just on self-improvement and innovation.

- It identifies goals and objectives related to what the marketplace (competition) is now achieving (which may determine what customers expect).
- It satisfies a basic TQM objective—reduced cycle times. Small tasks or big tasks get done faster. This has a positive effect on all business performance measurements.
- It identifies a new standard that must be achieved and exceeded to remain competitive.

SCOPE

The technique is applicable to all kinds of organizations within government and business, profit and nonprofit. It requires only the desire and understanding of management to make benchmarking a part of the way it manages and to provide the resources to make the analysis and do the research.

PRINCIPLES

Benchmarking, like the other TQM techniques, involves measurement. Measurement, however, is not the objective. The objective is adopting the best practices, although measurement is necessary to know what is better or best.

The measurement can be qualitative or quantitative. It can be a description of the better practice or it can describe differences in quantitative terms like dollars, hours, or elapsed time. The best results are obtained by using both measures.

Since benchmarking can be applied to any organization, it is an appropriate technique for improving any activity, function, or process. Many functions within an organization are common to many other outside organizations even in different kinds of business. For example, most companies make purchases, pay bills, and train employees. Which company or organization is the best at performing the same activities that you do? Which has the best process and best satisfies its customers?

Benchmarking may also include comparisons between intercompany activities as well as those of competitors. There is no limit in the search for the best practices anywhere.

MANAGING

As with all other TQM activities, benchmarking represents a tool, methodology, and policy for managing. Therefore, it requires involvement and support by upper management. In addition, since implementing benchmarking findings requires acceptance and change by the people in the organization affected, those people must be convinced that management actively supports it. Lip service or delegation to a staff function won't result in acceptance. The benchmarking activity requires resources: the time of people to investigate, evaluate, and implement competitive processes. Providing the funding and resources is management's most visible and tangible evidence of its support.

THE STEPS IN BENCHMARKING

From a broad perspective, benchmarking can be depicted as a continuous process represented by the plan, do, check, act sequence of the Deming wheel, shown in Figure 16.2.

In more detail it can be described as a sequence or a process as represented by the flowchart in Figure 16.3. Depicted is an 11-step process used by the Northrop Corporation, based on implementation of benchmarking as described by Robert Camp.[2]

A common concern when initiating benchmarking is where and how the information about outside organization processes is obtained. There are several good sources:

1. Libraries. Access to a good business library with the capability to use the voluminous data available is a major asset and the place to begin. Business organizations in particular publish a great deal of useful information.
2. Direct contact. The orientation in benchmarking is processes performance measurement and methodology. Companies in competition are traditionally fearful of providing data but the issue can be made of interest to both parties if it is presented on a process information sharing basis. That is the reason why it is necessary to define and measure the key processes first. Only then do you have something of interest to exchange. Exchanges with noncompetitors who have a similar process are usually much easier.
3. Data centers. These are voluntary groups of like businesses formed to share benchmark information. There are independent centers at some universities and there are consultant businesses developing process information to sell.
4. Trade and professional associations. Members can find books on benchmark contacts.

TRAINING

Benchmarking training programs and seminars are available. The best strategy is to plan to train a specialist or two who can then train other employees.

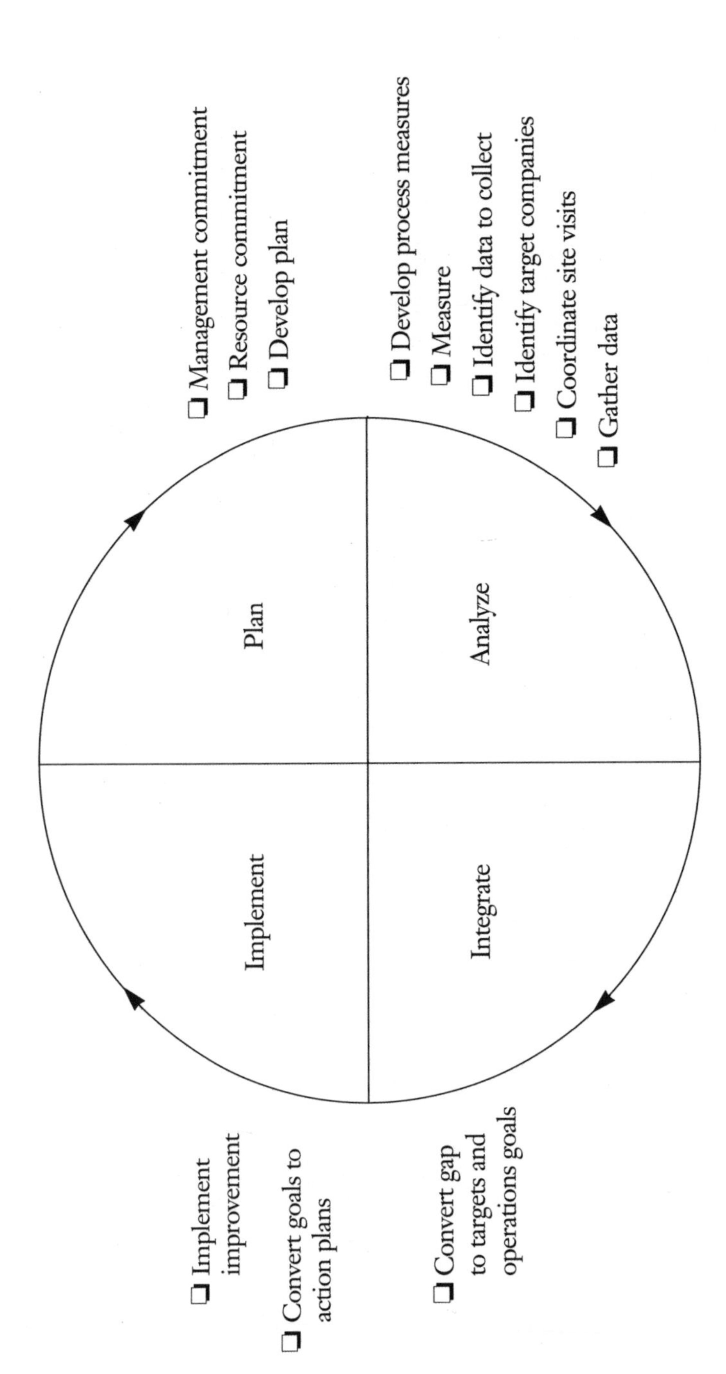

Figure 16.2 The Deming Wheel Applied to the Benchmarking Process

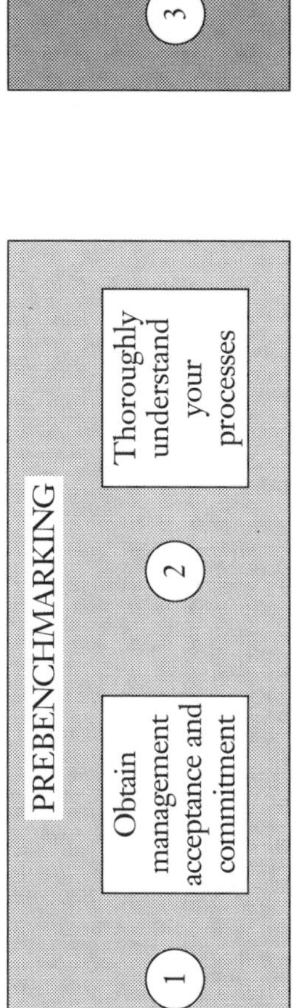

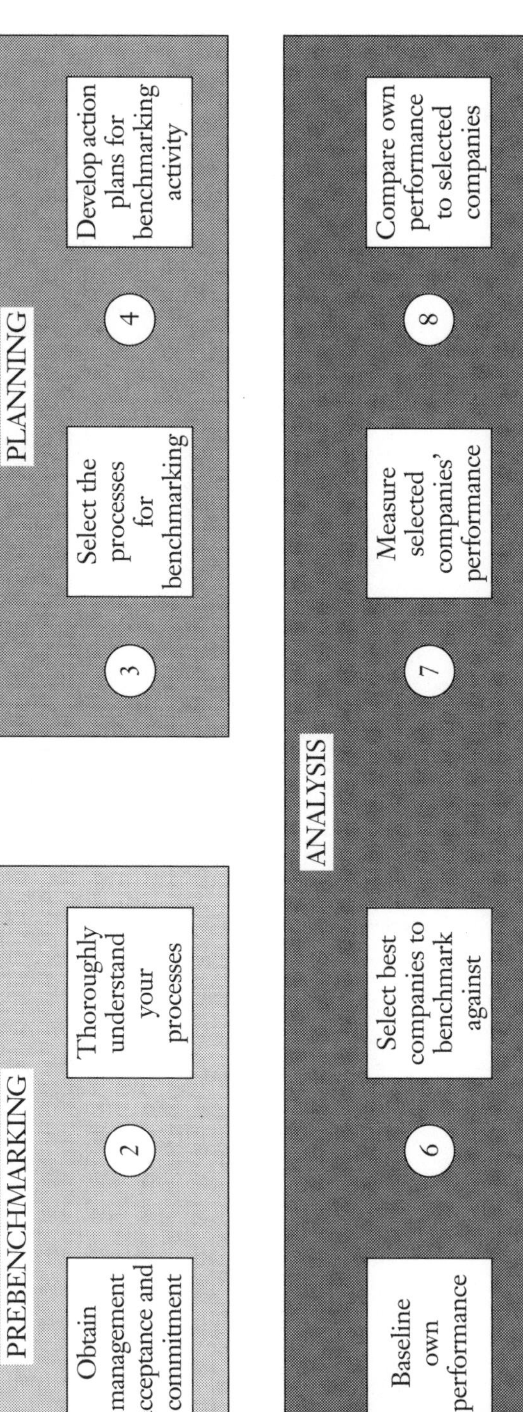

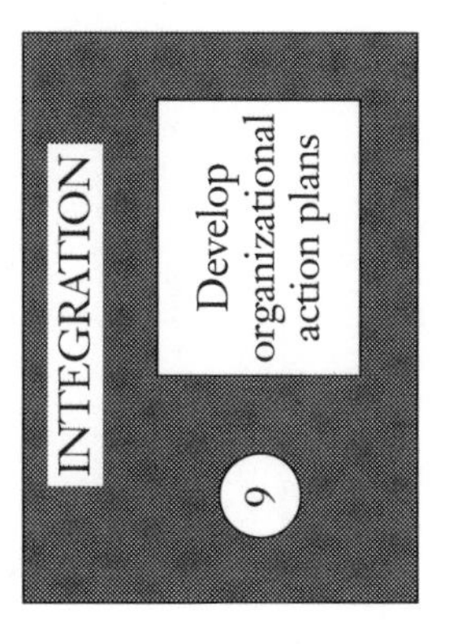

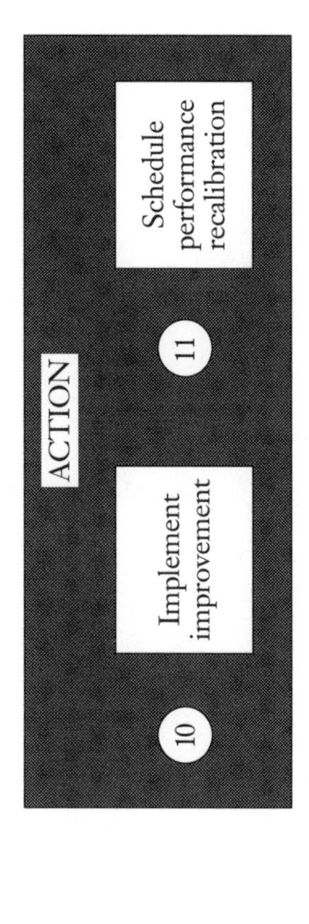

Figure 16.3 Eleven-Step Benchmarking Process

(continued on next page)

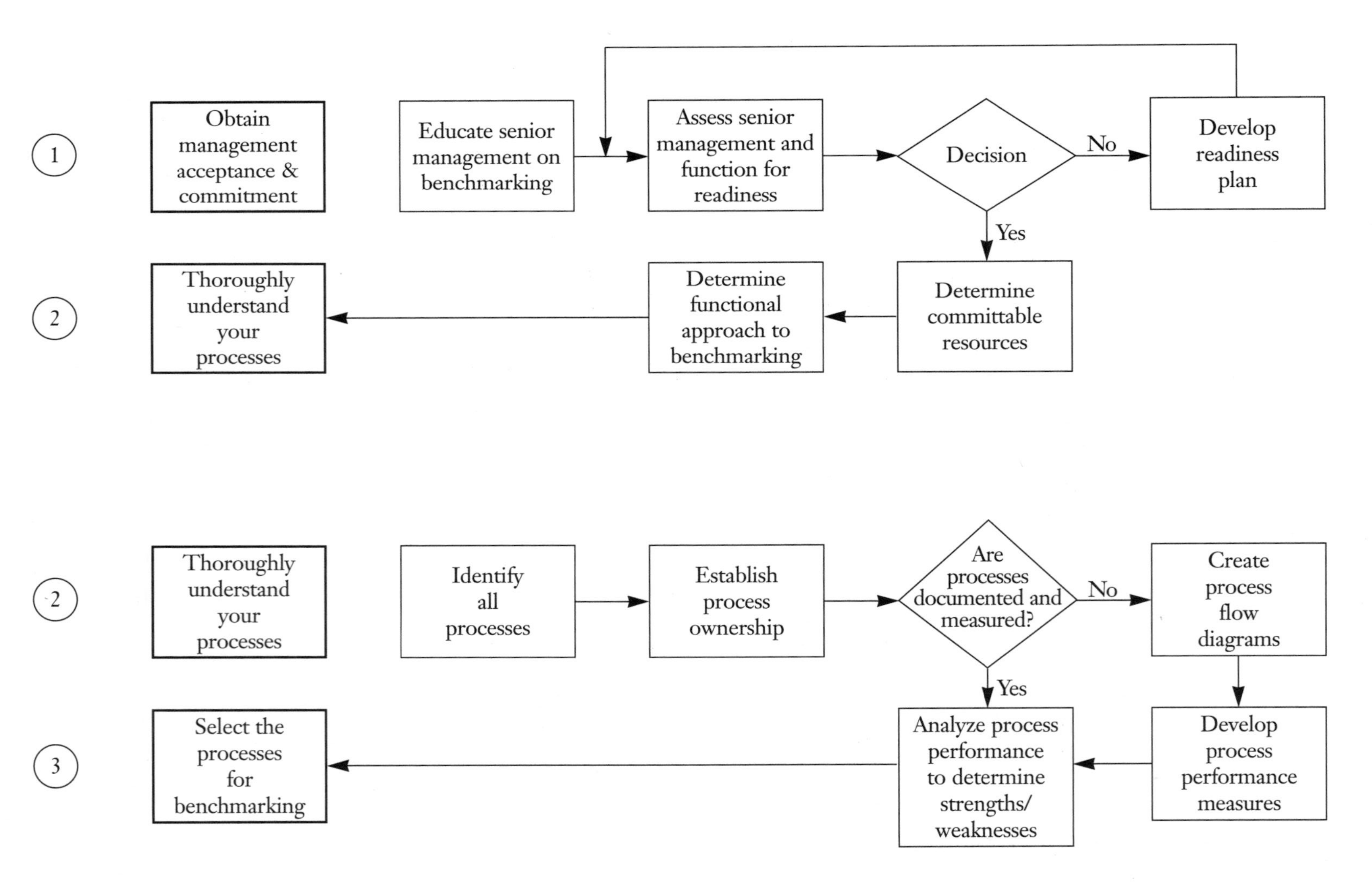

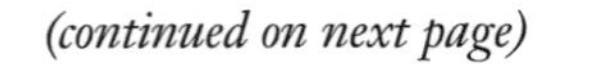
(continued on next page)

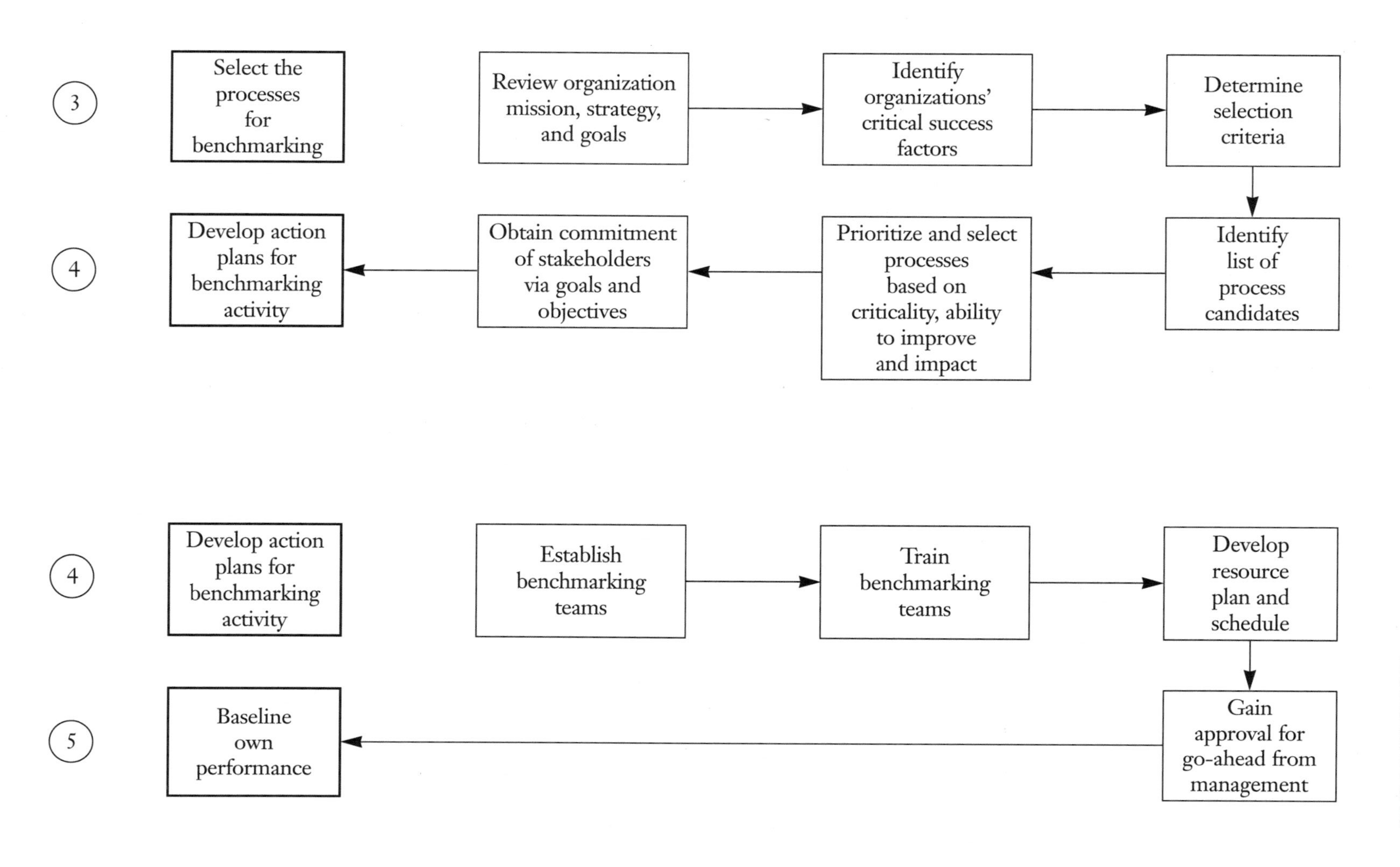

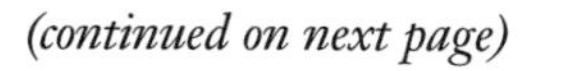
(continued on next page)

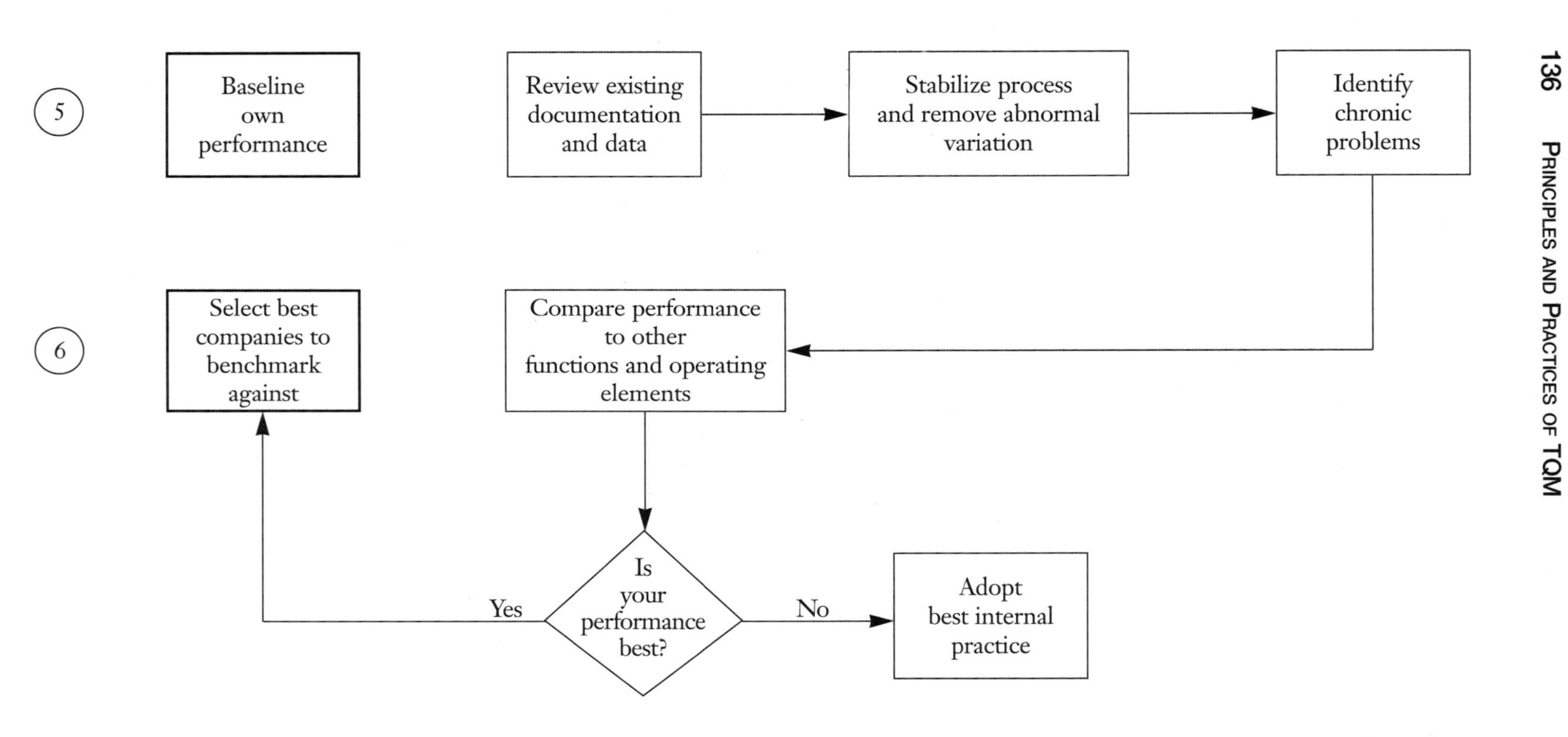

(continued on next page)

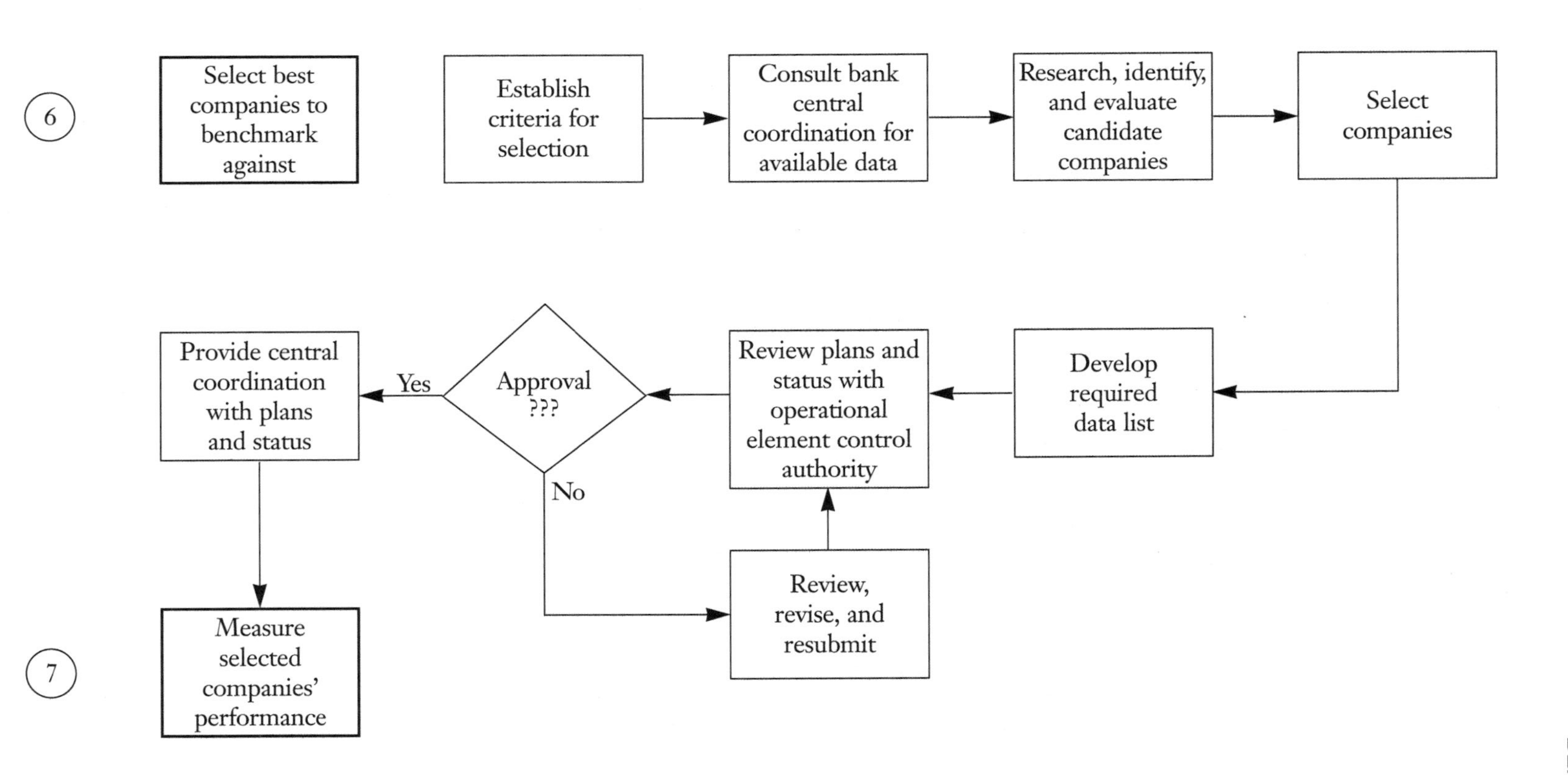

(continued on next page)

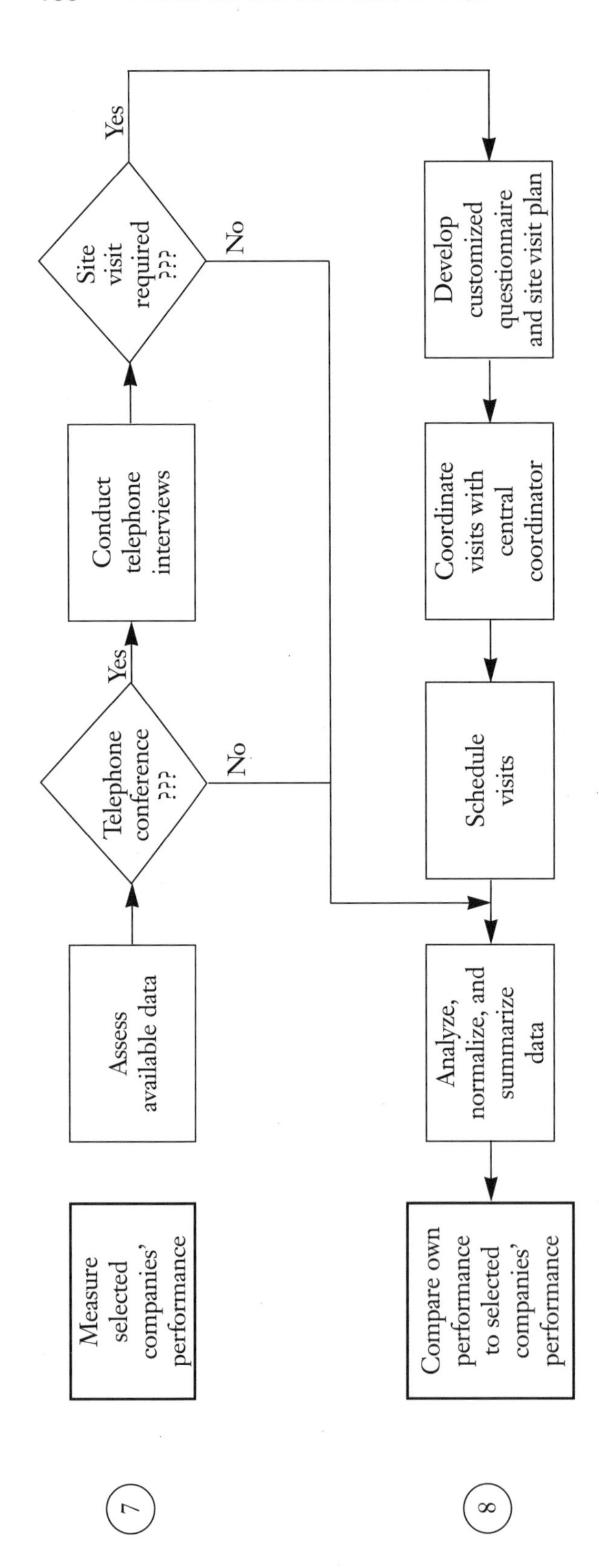

(continued on next page)

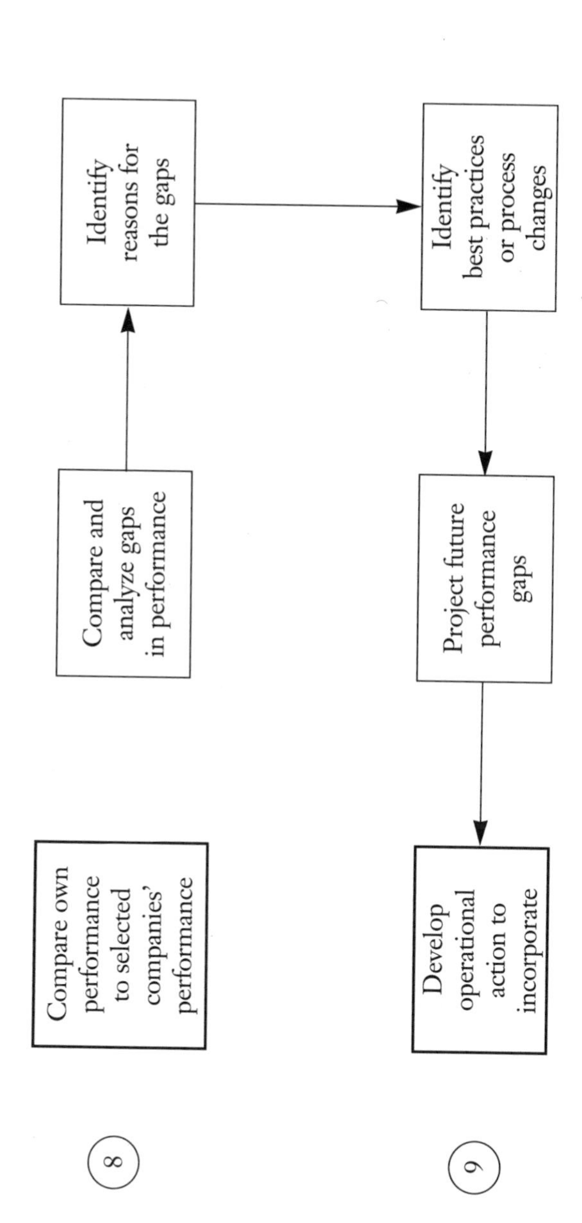

(continued on next page)

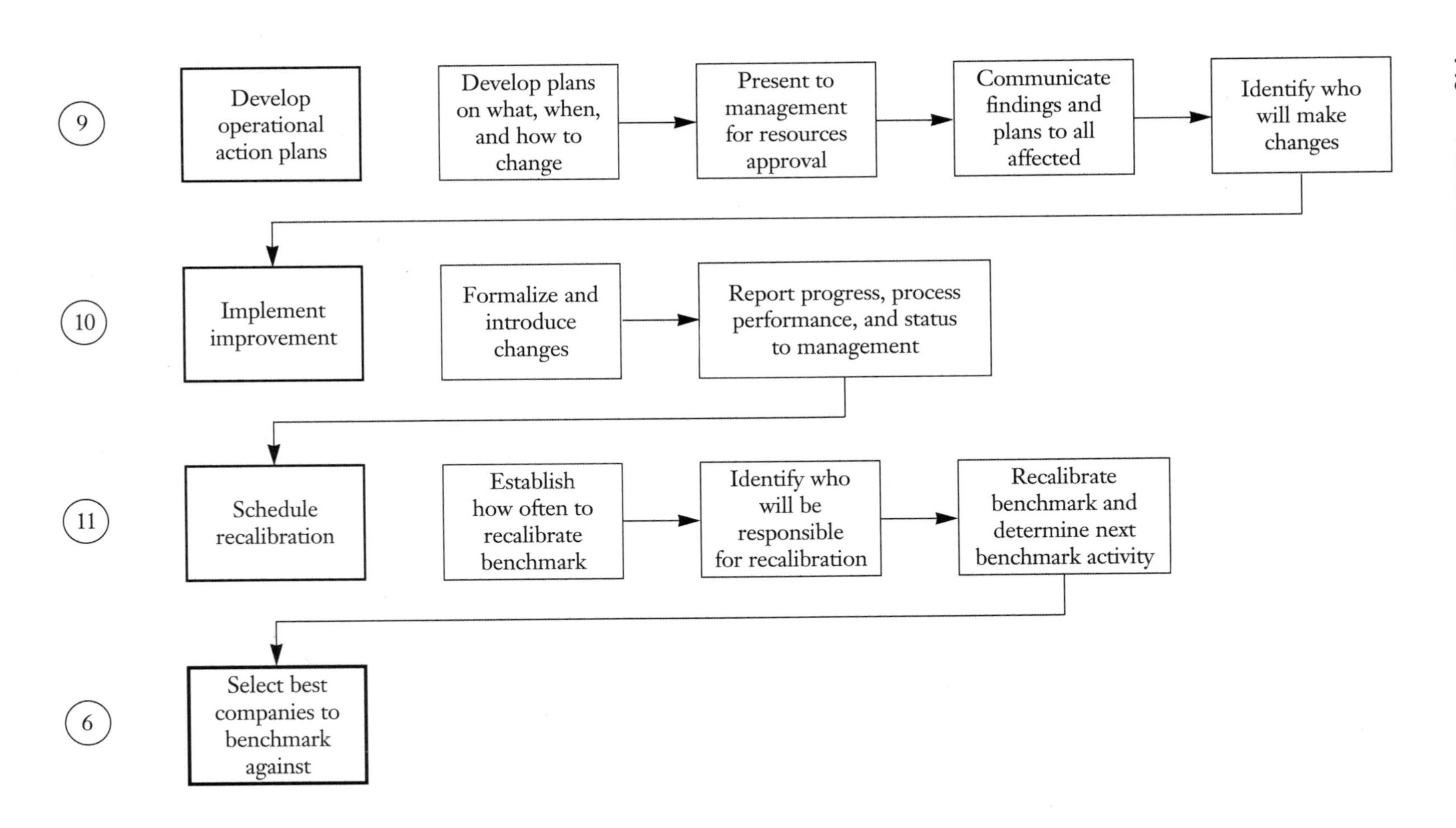
9
Develop operational action plans
Develop plans on what, when, and how to change
Present to management for resources approval
Communicate findings and plans to all affected
Identify who will make changes
10
Implement improvement
Formalize and introduce changes
Report progress, process performance, and status to management
11
Schedule recalibration
Establish how often to recalibrate benchmark
Identify who will be responsible for recalibration
Recalibrate benchmark and determine next benchmark activity
6
Select best companies to benchmark against

COMMUNICATING RESULTS

One of the benefits of using benchmarking is its ability to motivate people to look outside for ideas. One way to foster this reaction is to communicate benchmark findings to employees. Let them know how their activities compared to the best. It stimulates a constructive competitive attitude.

One way to do this is to use a so-called spider (arachnoid) chart as shown in Figure 16.4. Key process measures and comparisons can be seen at a glance. Figure 16.5 is an example related to a materials organization processes.

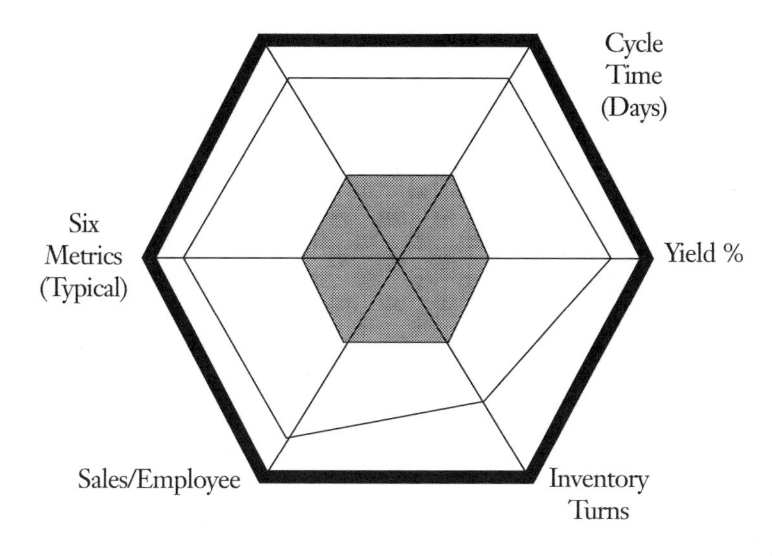

Figure 16.4 Arachnoid Chart Example—Communicate Findings

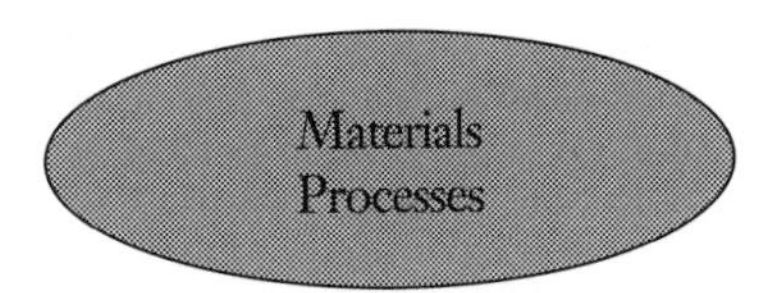

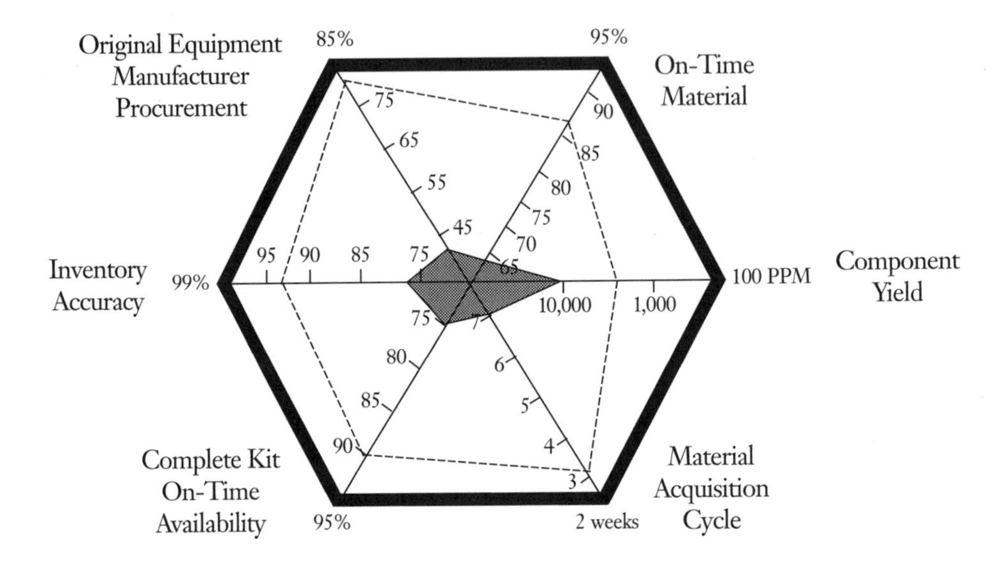

Figure 16.5 Arachnoid Chart Example—Benchmark Analysis

Chapter 17

Quality Function Deployment (QFD)

The purpose of QFD is to ensure that quality is produced in every stage of product and process development. The objective, in every step, is to ensure that customer requirements are accurately identified and then maintained in every decision and activity involved in product delivery. Thus, quality is methodically deployed to ensure that the customer receives the product or service exactly as initially identified. QFD recognizes that quality is produced by a sequence of planned and controlled events, that is the quality system. QFD also recognizes that a product consists of a system of assembled parts. Achieving quality requires the control of the decisions in the system and of the processes that are a part of it. This is the quality function that is deployed to achieve customer satisfaction. It is useful in any business or nonbusiness process.

The basis and emphasis of QFD is on planning. Knowledgeable team members should have a clear understanding and definition of organization practices and processes. It is designed for the team approach. The inputs to the plan must be multifunctional. QFD can vary in its application from a one-step product definition (one matrix) to a complex detailed plan of all the steps in the production and control process through delivery. The determinate of its complexity is the extent of the resources management commits to this planning and definition activity and the complexity of the process. It is also an iterative methodology. It isn't likely that the first plan will satisfactorily yield all of the final answers. But that is one of its strengths. Comprehensively applied it forces answers to important design, process, and control issues that have otherwise not been faced until later in time when earlier decisions in the sequence are fixed, based on schedule and monetary factors. Without this planning, issues faced at the initial stages have to be settled with shortsighted compromises. Those often result in a product with less than the original objectives—less than the customer expected.

The time spent using QFD, beginning at the period of concept, has proven to reduce time to market by forcing all functions to make detailed decisions that result in product and process integration. This avoids most later design changes with their attendant costly delays and product compromises. Using QFD can surface the lack of information normally available to make good design decisions, that is, function, tolerances, materials, and manufacturing capabilities. Making this known early supports the need for such activities as building evaluation models and experimentation. Without this early disclosure it is easier to postpone or avoid these valuable steps.

QFD is a major TQM tool because it is system and process oriented. Organization functions are secondary to planning the integration of their activities in technical detail. In this respect QFD can even be classified as an organization development tool. Not only do functions have to become process oriented but QFD demands useful information from the cost and information systems—the support functions. QFD also benefits from the application of the problem-solving tools used in continuous process improvement. The initial steps, defining a concept in terms of customer requirements and design characteristics, can be very abstract. This is an ideal application of the seven management tools, the affinity diagram in particular (see Chapter 18).

The QFD technique is to convert customer requirements into design characteristics, through to the part level, and then into manufacturing processes and controls. The mechanism to achieve and display the results is the common matrix diagram that presents one set of ideas or data type against those of another, thereby providing a means to evaluate their relationships.

Figure 17.1[3] is an example of such a matrix, used as a building block in QFD. Each intersection of rows and columns represents a question we must ask about the two sets of information in the figure. All the matrix information relates to the total cost of ownership, an important factor in customer satisfaction and, in TQM/QFD terminology, a true quality requirement. The column features are substitute quality requirements. Its sub-elements are shown to the right of it and compared to product features (of a computer) that will affect them in the columns. The figure shows that there is a strong relationship of design to cheap repairs, but none of the features will help meet the customer's need for an inexpensive warranty.

Other product features would have to be identified to satisfy that need. Therefore, a lack of a relationship between needs and features is highlighted and must be addressed. Strong relationships must be maintained in the subsequent matrices that evaluate design elements and manufacturing processes.

A completed quality plan to satisfy the customer and to present a description of all the design features and manufacturing processes would be a series of interlinked matrices (decisions on one matrix drive the next as depicted in Figure 17.2).

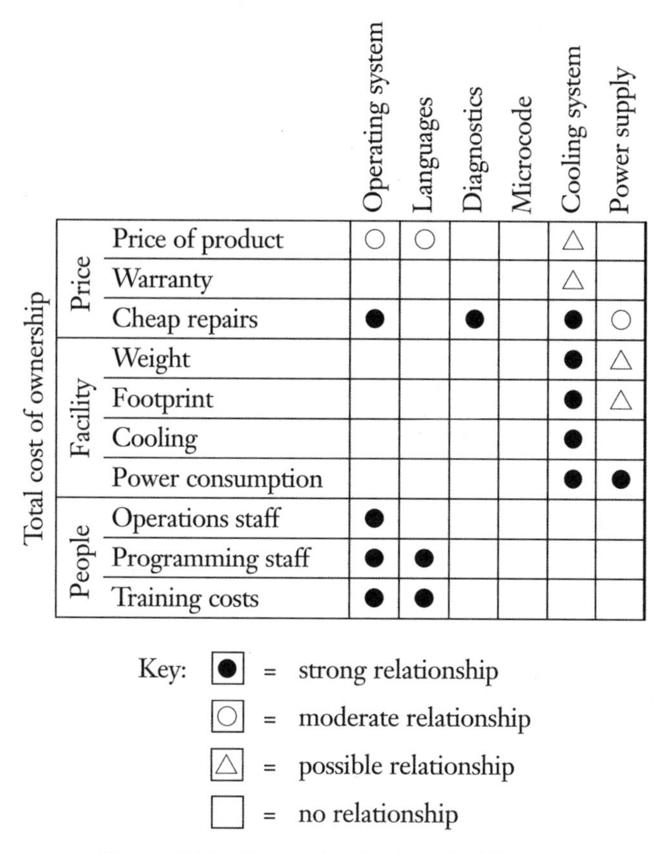

Total cost of ownership		Operating system	Languages	Diagnostics	Microcode	Cooling system	Power supply
Price	Price of product	○	○			△	
	Warranty					△	
	Cheap repairs	●		●		●	○
Facility	Weight					●	△
	Footprint					●	△
	Cooling					●	
	Power consumption					●	●
People	Operations staff	●					
	Programming staff	●	●				
	Training costs	●	●				

Figure 17.1 Example of a Matrix Diagram

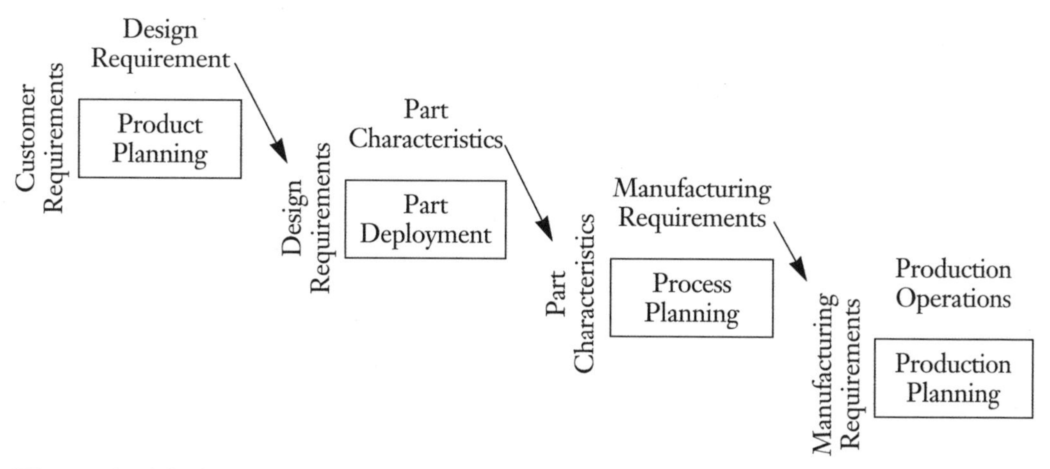

The result of deploying the customer requirements (quality) is a series of interlinked matrices defining all the important design decisions, production process descriptions, and controls. Sub-matrices for any of the four can provide detail to the degree desired. All entries on a matrix are tied to the original customer requirements.

Figure 17.2 Depiction of Matrix Relationships

In QFD the simple matrix format is expanded to extract more information as shown in Figures 17.3 and 17.4. Figure 17.5 shows a completed house of quality for the initial step in a car door design. This matrix would likely be completed by a team composed of marketing and engineering specialists. The matrix depth of detail is determined by the team. The matrix features are, briefly:

1. Design characteristics. These are related to and affect several customer requirements. Those characteristics are measurable and affect customer perceptions. Their integrity must be maintained throughout the production process to ensure customer acceptance.
2. Customer perception. This is an evaluation collected from customer comments comparing the company's car to others' cars. This provides a basis for deciding priorities for design changes.
3. Relationships. The strengths between attributes and characteristics (no symbols or too many weak relationships) are an indication that some customer requirements are inadequately addressed. Conflicting requirements are also identified and resolved.
4. Objective measures. These are a comparison of in-house evaluations of design characteristics against the customer's competitive perceptions. A lack of correlation would suggest that a different characteristic is needed to satisfy the requirement.

Targets are the design characteristics to be attained on the final product. They are established based on customer importance, difficulty, and cost.

The roof matrix is for correlation between characteristics. The objective is to determine the effect of one feature on the others. High correlation indicates product features that must be given consistent attention.

Figure 17.6 is an example of a completed matrix for the good operation and use requirement for a car door. To carry this first customer design evaluation in the direction of production of an actual door all the customer design characteristics would have to be evaluated. Then the design characteristics would have to be developed into a specific door part definition and then into the manufacturing processes for each part as well as the finished doors, using the interrelated matrices depicted in Figure 17.2.

Figure 17.7 is an example of another matrix series that shows a component traced from a customer requirement for a smooth ride through several sub-matrices. The component "spring" is selected to display further quality deployment.

One characteristic, shown in Figure 17.8, is spring length. The process plan, shown in Figure 17.9, indicates that the spring wire is to be drawn and cut to length. It also notes the process controls to be used. Figure 17.10 shows the quality control plan for the process.

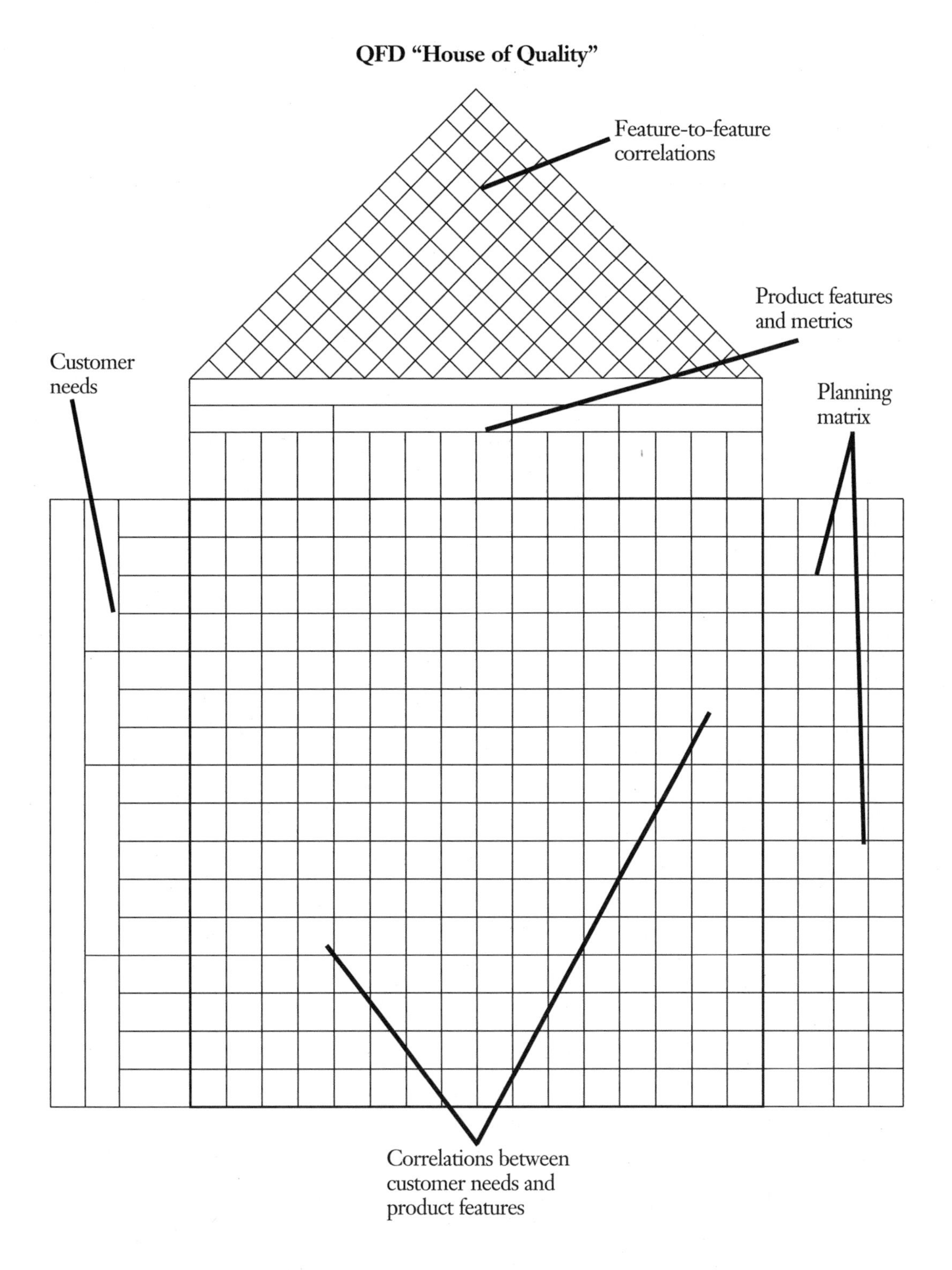

Figure 17.3 The QFD Matrix Expanded to Evaluate/Compare Other Relationships

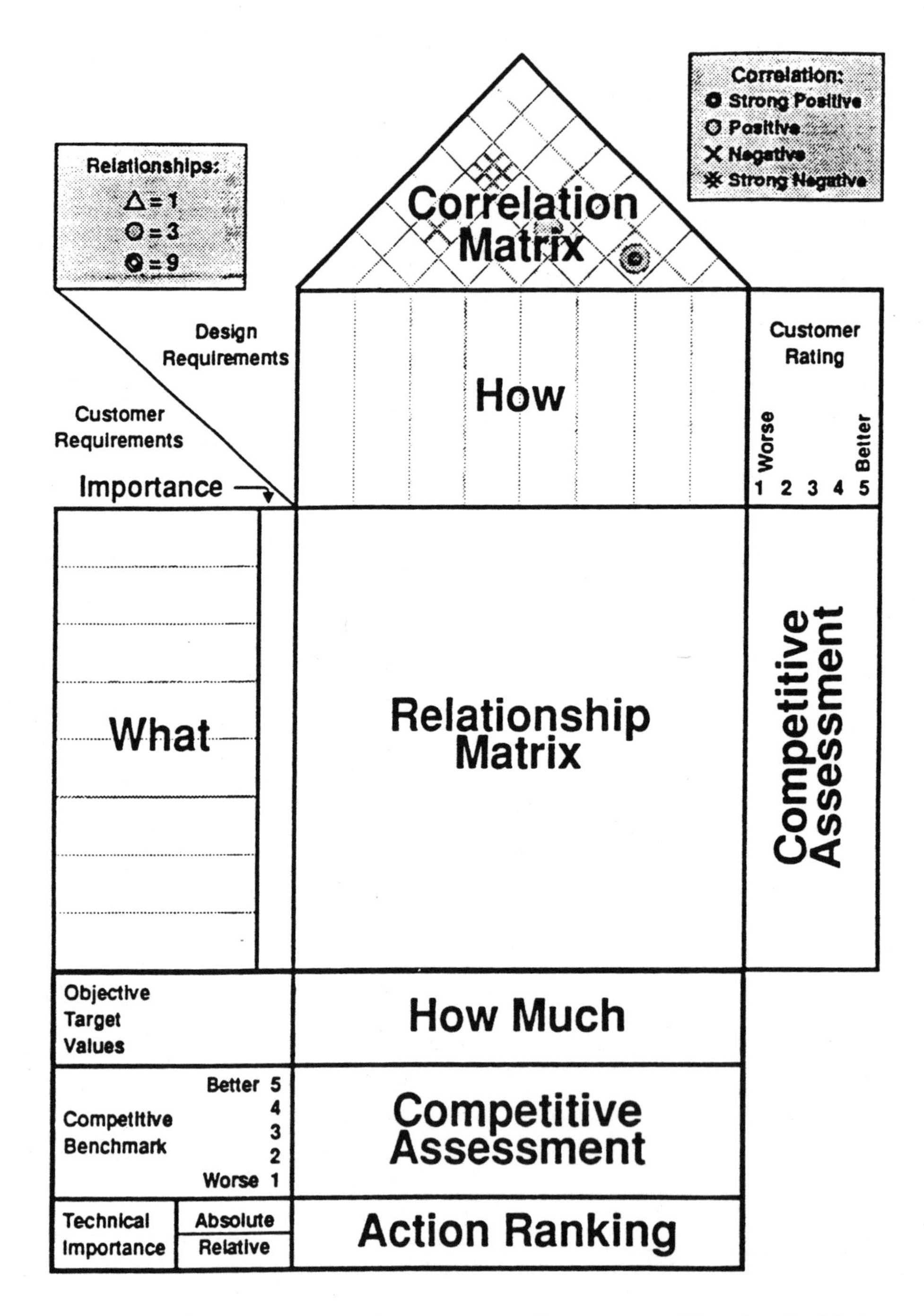

Figure 17.4 The Identification of All the Types of Evaluations That Can Be Made by QFD Teams, From the Initial What and How Elements

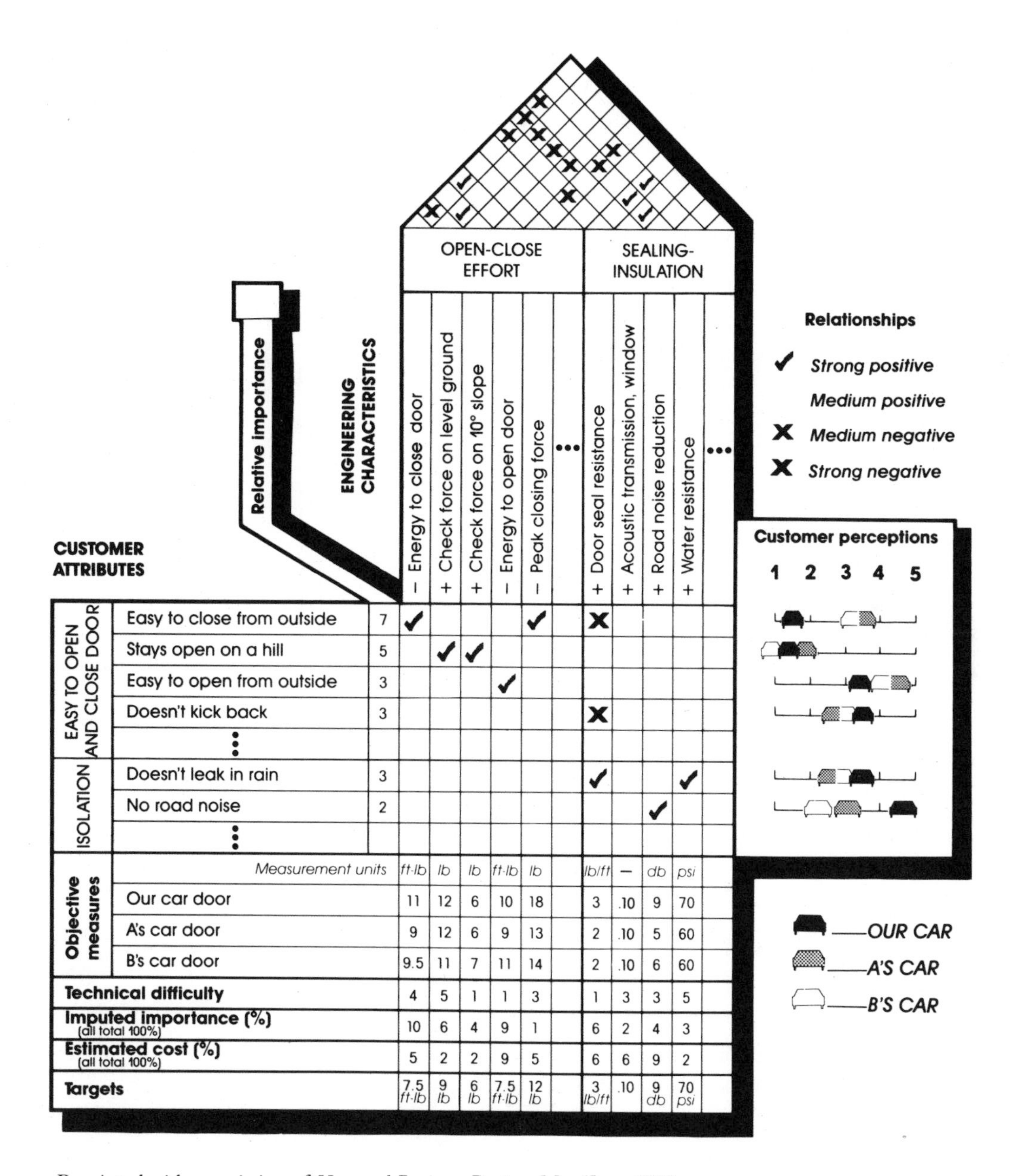

Reprinted with permission of *Harvard Business Review*, May/June 1988.

Figure 17.5 Completed QFD Matrix for Car Door Design

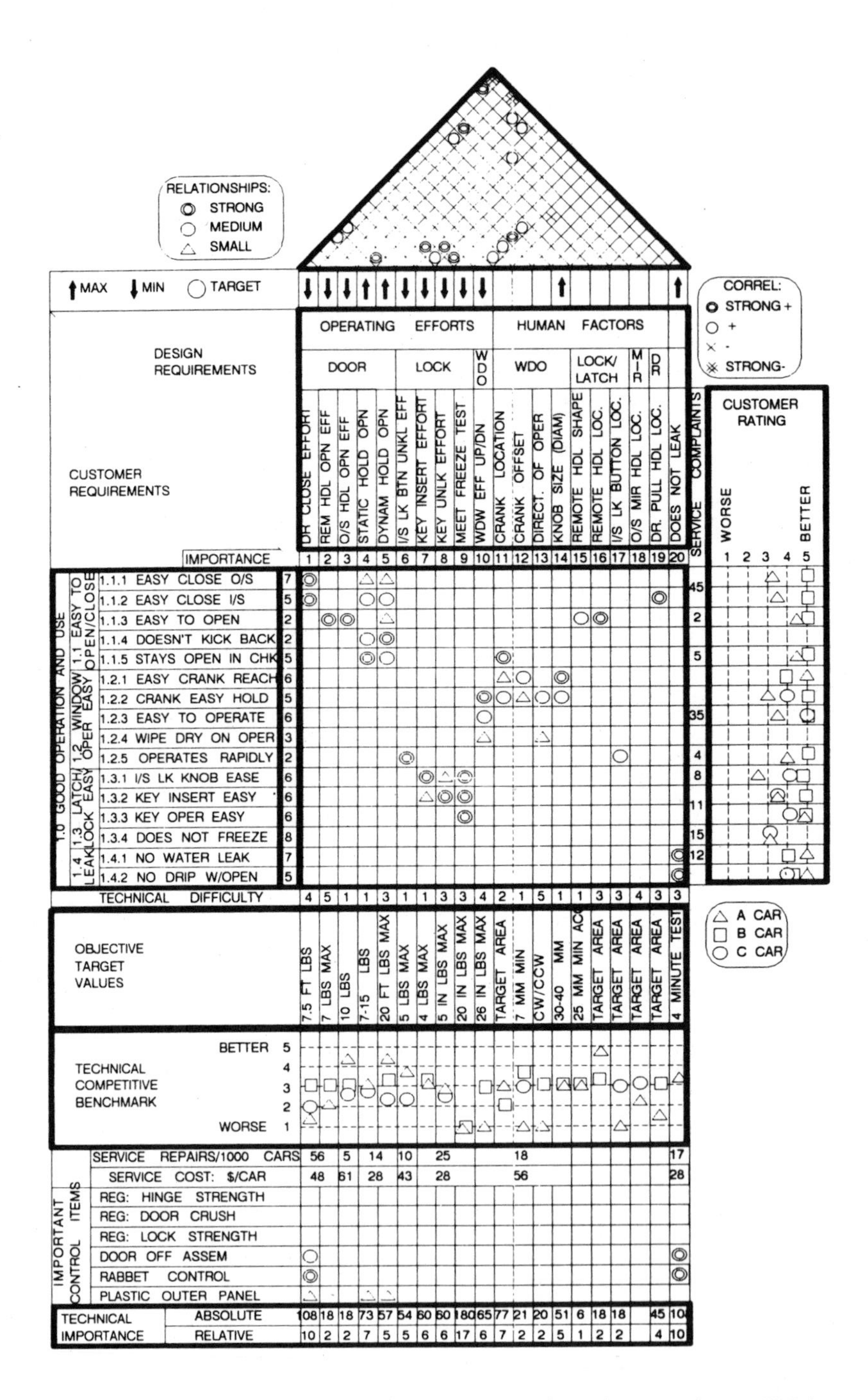

Reprinted with permission of American Supplier Institute, Inc. of Dearborn, Michigan (U.S.A.).

Figure 17.6 Completed Matrix Picturing the Completed Decision Process for the Good Operation and Use Requirement for a Car Door

Finished component characteristic deployment matrix
From Planning Matrix
(Overall Ride Target—115% of Vehicle Z)

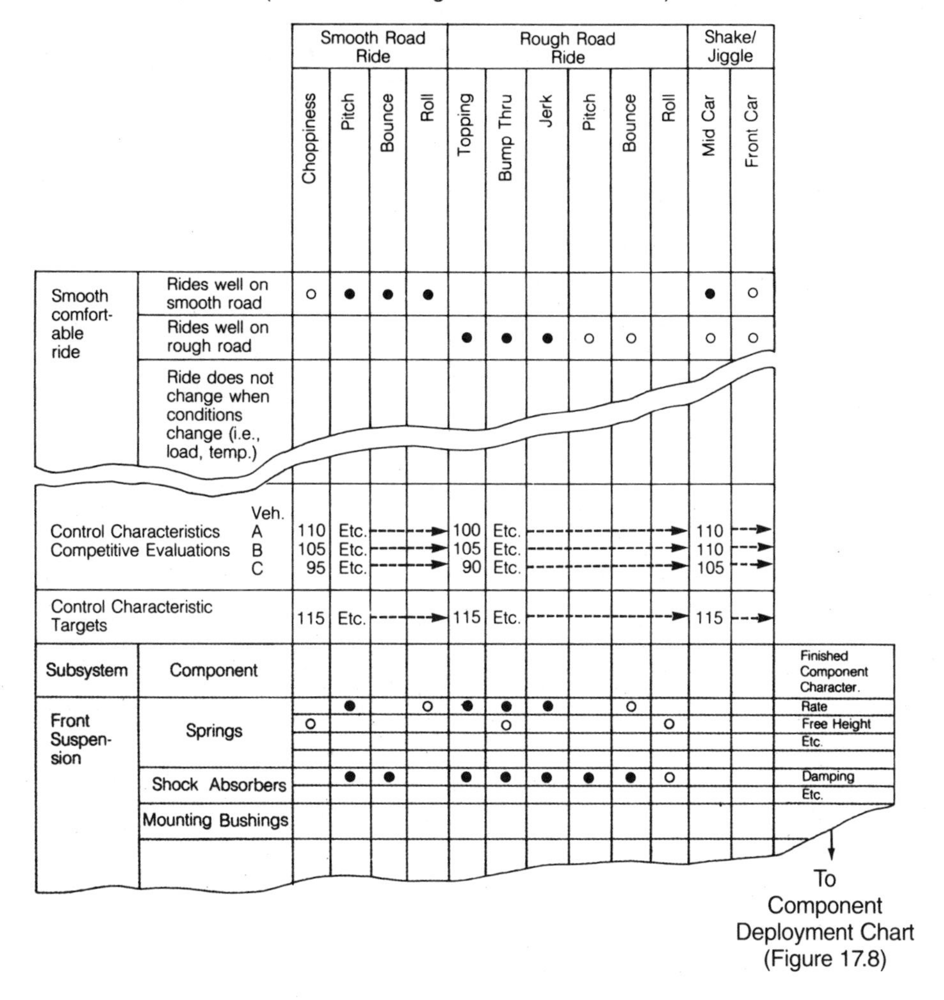

Reprinted with permission from *Quality Progress*, June 1986.

Figure 17.7 Deployment Matrix of One Characteristic—Smooth Ride

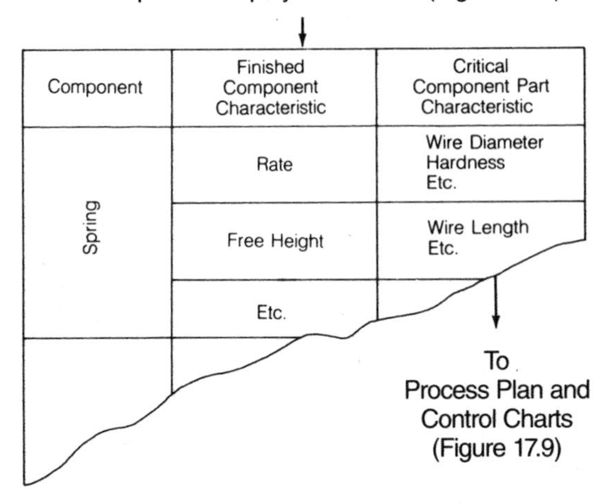

Reprinted with permission from *Quality Progress*, June 1986.

Figure 17.8 Deployment Matrix of One Characteristic—Spring Lengths

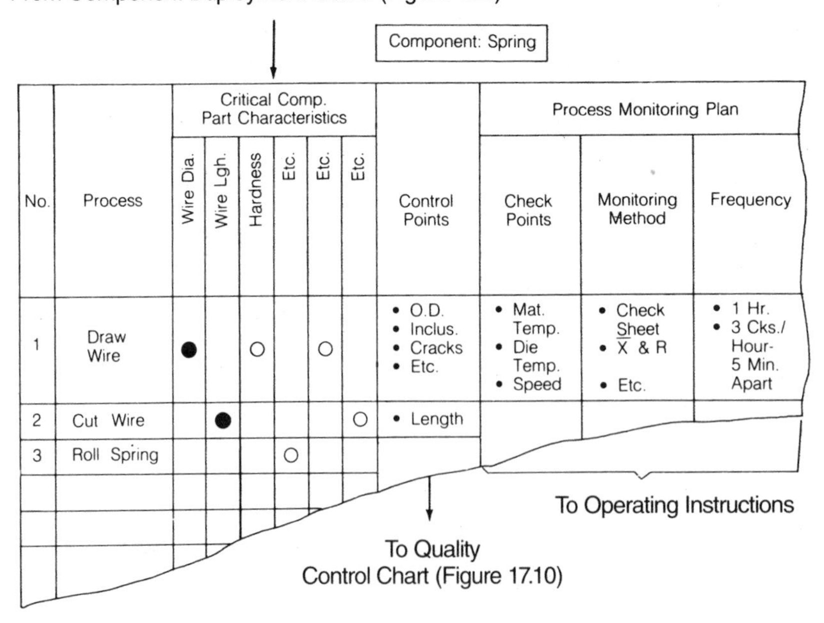

Reprinted with permission from *Quality Progress*, June 1986.

Figure 17.9 Process Plan and Control Chart

Quality Control Plan Chart

From Process Plan Chart

Component: Spring

Process Flow		Control Point	Control Method	Sample Size Frequency	Check method
Raw Material	Process				
▽		• Chemistry	See Supplier Plan		
		• Hardenability			
		• Etc.			
	Draw	• O.D.	$\overline{X}$ & R	5 Pcs./Hr.	Electronic Gage
		• Inclusions • Cracks	N/A	100%	Eddy Current Tester
		• Etc.	Etc.	Etc.	Etc.
	Cut	• Length	$\overline{X}$ & R	3 Pcs./Hr.	Checking Fixture
		• Etc.	Etc.	Etc.	Etc.

To Operating Instructions

Reprinted with permission from *Quality Progress*, June 1986.

Figure 17.10 Quality Control Plan for the Process

This overview of QFD illustrates its comprehensive and unique capabilities, beginning with an accurate definition of customer requirements and describing the connection maintained even down to manufacturing work instructions. This structured planning process is bi-directional. Questions that may require a change in design decisions are resolved before production. When a product completes production, it is the product the customer wants.

HINTS FOR SUCCESS

1. Recognize that the use of QFD requires a significant effort in planning new product design, development, and production processes before release to manufacturing than usual.

   The size of the effort and the affect of the production start are related to the participants' experience with QFD methodology among the other factors.
2. Begin with a simple pilot program.
3. The initial direction should not be charts for every activity. The GOAL/QPC's approach identifies 30 charts that will adequately plan a complex product.[4]
4. Adapt QFD to fit the organization, product, and process. It is a general framework for planning

Chapter 18

TQM Tools

A few quality tools specific to total quality have been developed over the years beginning with the pioneer work of Shewhart at Bell Laboratories in the 1920s. His major contribution was the concept of variation, special and common causes, and statistical control charts.

The next major practical contribution to the QC tool kit was by Kaoru Ishikawa in combining Shewhart's work with his own and identifying seven QC tools.[5] These represent the first practical scientific tools, useable by anyone, in analyzing and improving process performance. Their first significant use in the West was in quality circles, and they are integral to the functioning of process improvement teams. The seven QC tools are primarily a graphic means for process problem analysis through the analysis of data.

At about the same time, the Union of Japanese Scientists and Engineers (JUSE) was fostering the development of the seven management tools for QC.[6] These are tools to qualitatively analyze problems of a complex nature that are not well defined. Both sets of tools are listed in Table 18.1.

The seven management tools are linguistic, for exploring problems, organizing ideas, and converting concepts into action plans, design criteria, and so forth and have application in planning, research and development, designing, and selling products. Both categories of tools are appropriate for problem-solving (process-improvement) teams. These tools bring order to their functioning and an effective synthesis of team knowledge.

Table 18.1 The Seven QC and Seven QC Management Tools

Seven QC Tools	*Seven QC Management Tools*
Pareto diagram	Affinity diagram (K–J)
Cause-and-effect diagram	Relationship diagram
Flowchart	Tree diagram
Check sheet	Matrix chart
Histogram	Matrix data analysis chart
Scatter diagram	Arrow diagram
Graphs and control charts	Process decision program chart
Each set of tools has many applications for problem analysis and solution.	

THE SEVEN MANAGEMENT TOOLS

There are many situations in which there are little or no data to make decisions. New product planning is one such business situation. A customer need or market exists that may be broadly recognized but lacks a clear path to defining it, much less identifying design criteria. Since we think linguistically rather than mathematically, there are often many ideas but no obvious way to distill them into actionable information. The seven management tools for QC (Table 18.2) were developed for this kind of problem solving. They are now beginning to be understood and used in the West. There isn't a simple recipe to use these tools. The application situations are typically nebulous and abstract at the start. They require time to learn and apply, but they produce valuable results.

Affinity Diagram. The affinity diagram facilitates the definition of problems by organizing ideas according to a recognized relationship or affinity for each other. The genesis of this methodology is like that of the Russian chemist, Dmitry Mendeleyev, who described the periodic table of elements in the nineteenth century. He wrote the characteristics of each element on a card. In arranging them, he recognized that they could be organized into families. These family members had a structural affinity for each other and could be so grouped. This reflects the idea of the affinity diagram except that the elements in TQM application are ideas.

For example, a team trying to learn customer requirements with the intention of translating them into design requirements might begin by each member writing an idea on a file card. Then laying the cards on a table without conversation to influence them, the team members would arrange them into whatever logical groups they perceived. That is, they would identify which ideas had an affinity for each other.

Table 18.2 The Seven Management Tools

The Seven Management Tools
Documentation and planning • Affinity diagram (K–J) • Relationship diagram
Intermediate planning • Tree diagram • Matrix chart • Matrix data analysis chart
Detailed planning • Arrow diagram • Process decision program chart

Invariably they would reach a consensus. What had been several seemingly unconnected ideas actually had an inherent organization and pattern. The groups can be prioritized and the same process repeated to connect the groups to the next level of information such as goals and objectives or even design criteria.

It should be recognized that the technique is a form of brainstorming for organizing creative thinking. As an alternate method, Post-its® (adhesive-backed paper) can be used in place of cards. They can then be stuck onto a wall and grouped by the team.

It is often helpful to use another tool, the relationship diagram, in conjunction with the affinity diagram.[7]

Relationship Diagram. This diagram aids the problem-solving process by showing the relationship between problems and ideas in complex situations. It identifies meaningful categories from a mass of ideas. It is useful when relationships are difficult to determine.

In using this tool, the team writes each idea in a circle and clusters the circles in proximity to each other. It then identifies which idea strongly influences another and uses arrows to indicate the direction of influence. The results are evaluated by identifying ideas that have the most arrows entering or exiting. Basic or key ideas are indicated by circles that have only exiting arrows.

Figure 18.1 is pictorial of the tool; Figure 18.2 presents the results of a team brainstorming session that identified 15 major issues involved in developing a company TQM plan.

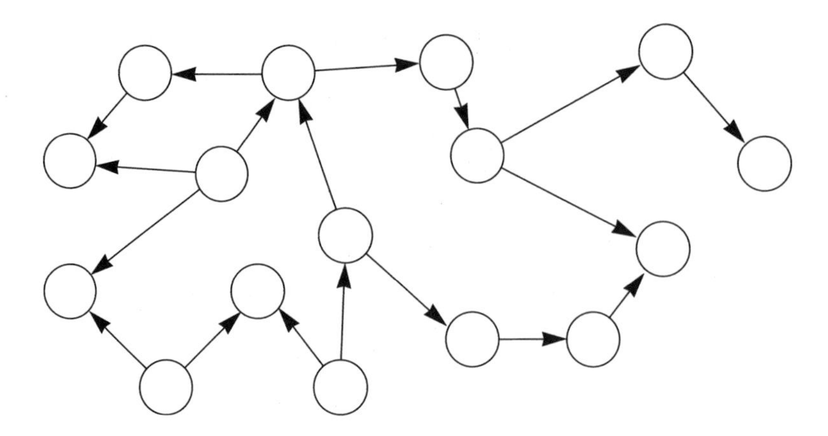

Logically Categorize Ideas
A pictorial of the result of assigning arrows to show cause and effect. Each circle represents a team's selection of the important problems. Assigning cause-and-effect arrows further clarifies relationships.

Figure 18.1 Relationship Diagram

Tree Diagram. A tree diagram identifies the tasks and methods needed to solve a problem and reach a goal. It systematically traces the means and clarifies the problem to be solved by exposing its complete structure. From this analysis, the problem-solving method can be identified.

The tree diagram can supplement the affinity and relationship diagram and identify items that were missed. It's a simple structure, as shown in Figure 18.3. Figure 18.4 is an example of its application.

Matrix Chart. This type of chart yields information about the relationships and importance of task and method elements of the subjects concerned. It typically uses the information developed by the previously mentioned tools.

Figure 18.5 shows the relationships among the issues identified in the relationship diagram (Figure 18.2) including a ranking technique to prioritize their importance.

Matrix Data Analysis. This tool shows all the key data clearly. It can be a rough, two-axis correlation picture. It is not always applicable, but it can provide a picture of such things as different product and market characteristics.

Figure 18.6 gives an idea of what it can be used to display.

Arrow Diagram. An arrow diagram shows the time required to solve the problem and which items can be done in parallel. It is a simplified critical path method of planning and scheduling designed to show the optimum schedule for fulfilling a plan and tracking its progress. Figure 18.7 shows the type of diagram that results from this kind of planning.

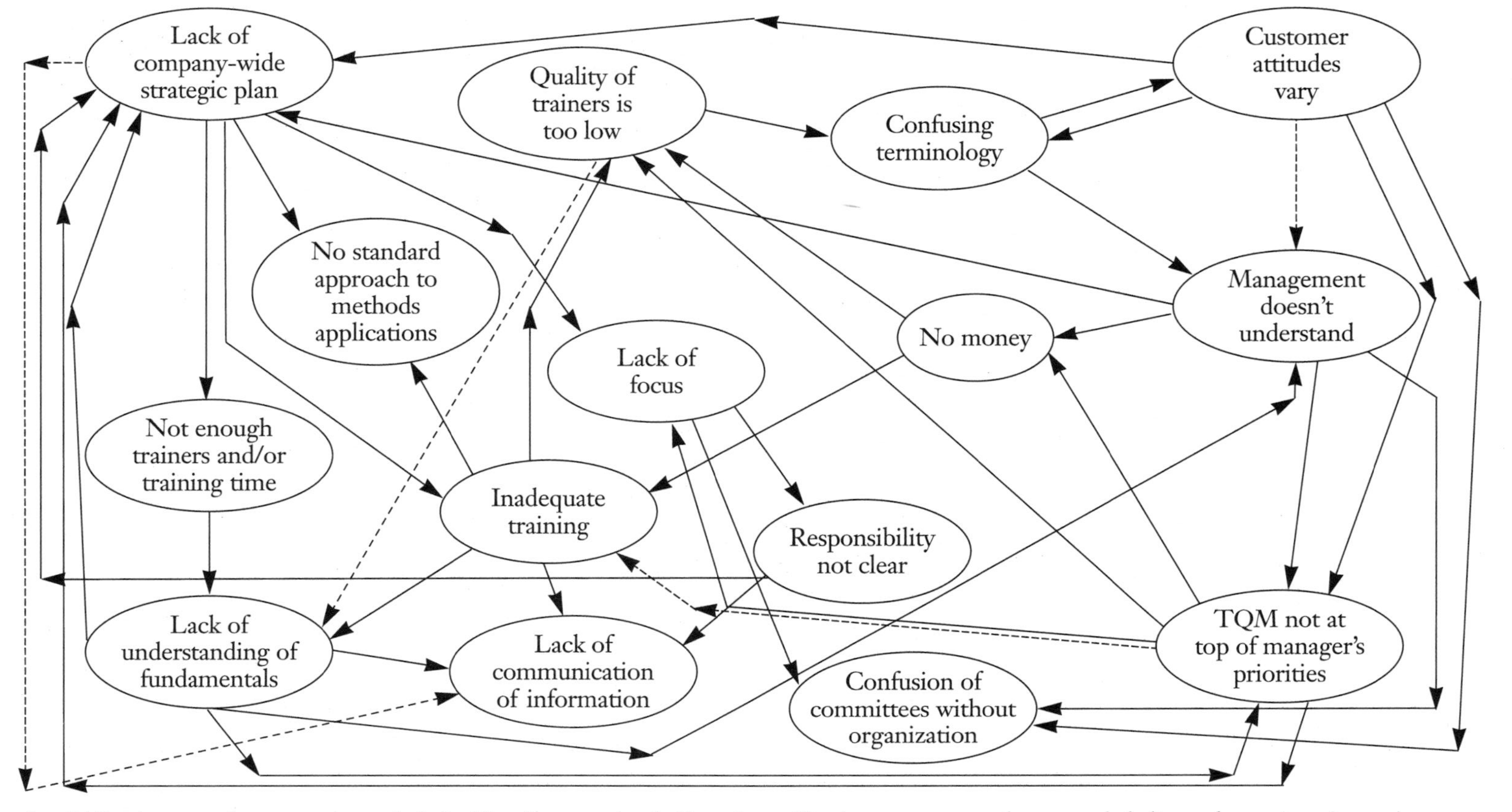

A solid line is counted as one point A dashed line is counted as half a point If only one team member strongly believes that an item is a major cause of another item, then an arrow is not shown on this chart but a quarter point is added to the total

The objective is to determine major cause (most arrows going out) issue that is most interrelated to other issues (most arrows in and out) and the issue that is both a major cause and has most interrelationships to other issues (most arrows going in and out). Results are tabulated in Figure 18.7.

Source: "Using the 7-M Tools for Strategic Planning," Don Murphy, Hughes Aircraft Co.

Figure 18.2 Relationship Diagram—TQM Problems and Concerns

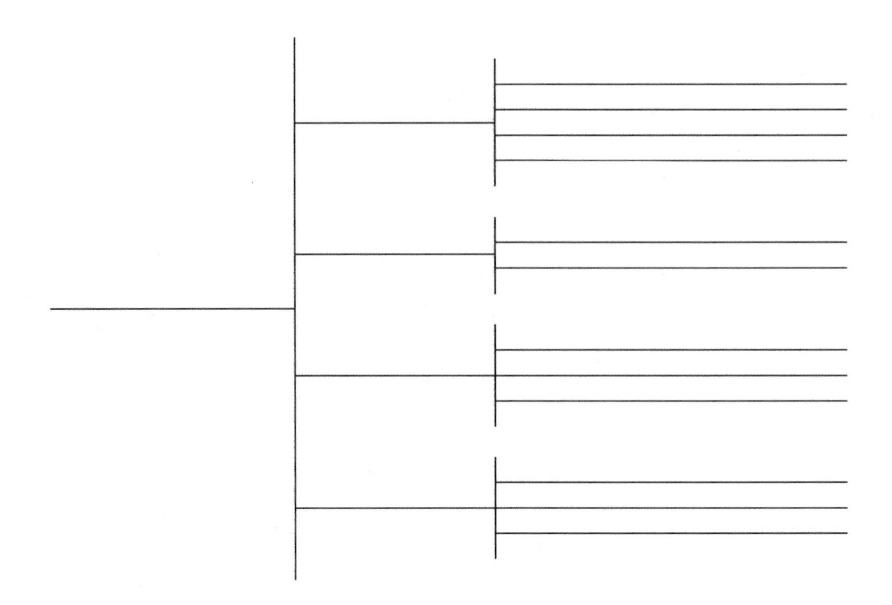

Identify ideas in greater and greater detail

Figure 18.3 Tree Diagram

Process Decision Program Chart. This chart focuses on possible sequences to help lead to a desirable result. This is a chart for contingency planning. It was developed to plan for the future while still in the development stage of problem solution planning. Figure 18.8 depicts a simple application.

THE SEVEN QUALITY CONTROL TOOLS

Hitoshi Kamikubo of JUSE, which has been instrumental in guiding the Japanese industrial success since their first discussions with Deming in 1950, has recently stated that he "believes that the main reason behind the astonishing growth and advance of the Japanese economy, based on industrial exports, is the effective and enthusiastic promotion of QC within companies. The largest contributing factor to this progress has been the many tools for quality control—the seven QC tools."[8]

These tools provide techniques for a structured approach to business problem analysis and solution that is a prerequisite for improvement. They are valuable to anyone who desires to be effective in an organization. Maximum benefit is achieved when they are applied by a team or circle. This elicits the maximum amount of useful data that the tools are designed to manage.

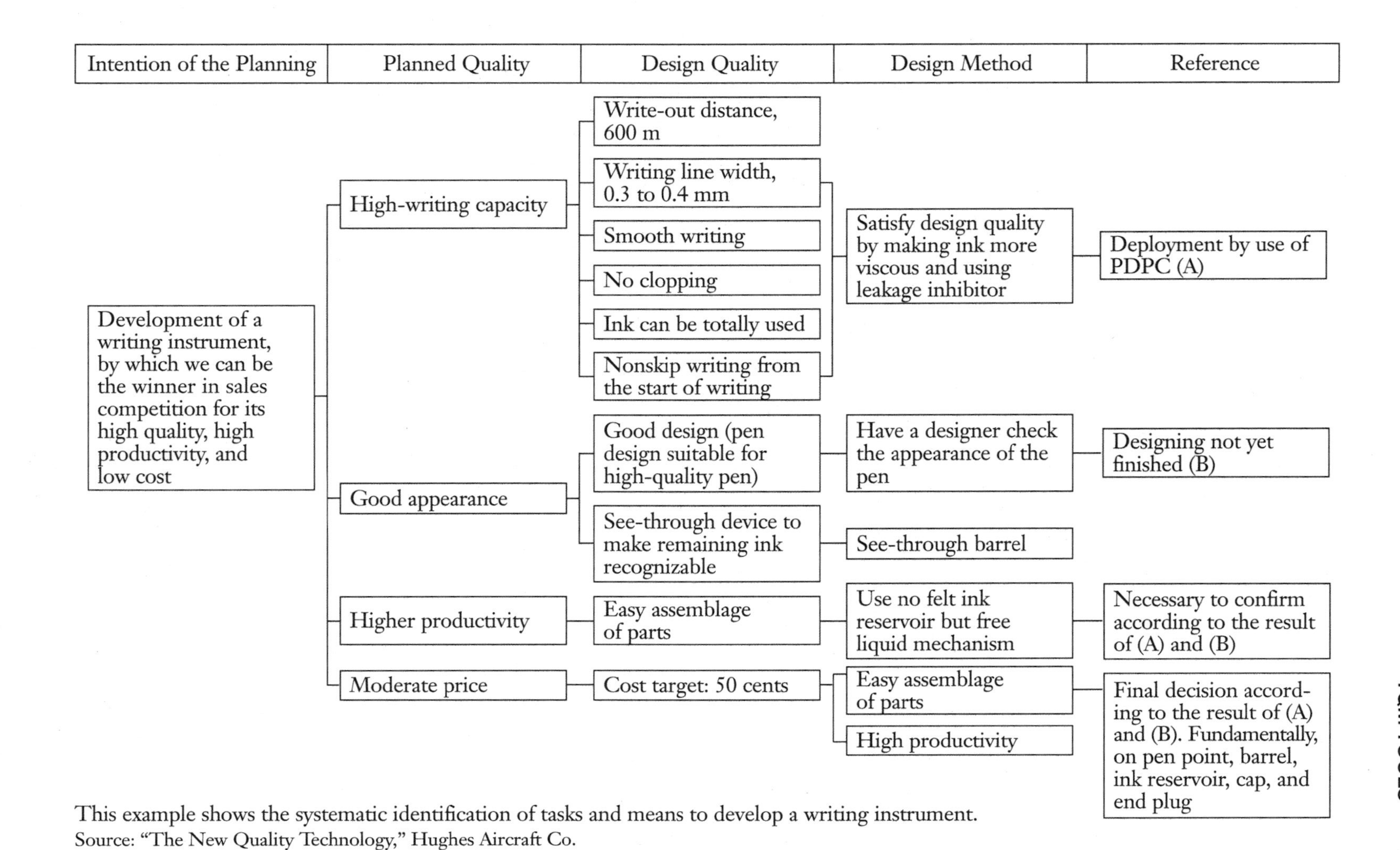

This example shows the systematic identification of tasks and means to develop a writing instrument.
Source: "The New Quality Technology," Hughes Aircraft Co.

Figure 18.4 Tree Diagram for Design Quality

This matrix is used to document the results of the relationship diagram (see Figure 18.2)

		1 Lack of company-wide strategic plan	2 Not enough trainers and/or training time	3 Lack of understanding of fundamentals	4 No standard approach to methods applications	5 Inadequate training	6 Lack of communication of information	7 Quality of trainers is too low	8 Lack of focus	9 Responsibility is unclear	10 Confusing terminology	11 No money	12 Profusion of committees without organization	13 Customer attitudes vary	14 Management doesn't understand	15 TQM not at top of manager's priority list	TOTAL CAUSES (Total arrows going out)	TOTAL INTERRELATIONSHIPS (Total arrows going in and out)	RANK BY CAUSE	RANK BY COLUMN AND ROW TOTAL
1	Lack of company-wide strategic plan	N/A	↑		↑	↑	↑D		↑	↑		↑				↑	7.5	12.5	4	4
2	Not enough trainers and/or training time		N/A	↑		↑↑		●			↑D						2.75	7.75	13	12
3	Lack of understanding of fundamentals	↑		N/A			↑		↑			↑↑			↑	↑↑	6	8.5	6	9
4	No standard approach to methods applications				N/A				↑	↑							2	8.5	14	10
5	Inadequate training			↑↑	↑	N/A	↑	↑	↑		↑				↑	↑	8	14.5	3	1
6	Lack of communication of information						N/A		↑	↑					↑	↑	4	8	8	11
7	Quality of trainers is too low		↑	↑D		↑		N/A			↑						3.5	5.75	11	14
8	Lack of focus				↑	↑			N/A	↑		↑	↑			↑	6	14	5	2
9	Responsibility is unclear	↑			↑	↑D	↑			N/A							3.5	11.5	9	6
10	Confusing terminology				↑D		↑D				N/A		↑D	↑	↑		3.5	7	10	13
11	No money		↑			↑		↑				N/A					3	9	12	8
12	Profusion of committees without organization									↑			N/A				1	4.5	15	13
13	Customer attitudes vary	↑			↑				↑	↑	↑	↑	↑	N/A	↑D	↑	8.5	9.5	2	7
14	Management doesn't understand	↑	↑		↑	↑D			↑	↑		↑	↑		N/A	↑	9.5	13	1	3
15	TQM not at top of manager's priority list	↑	↑			↑D			↑	↑		↑				N/A	5.5	12.5	7	8
	TOTAL EFFECTS (total arrows going in)	5	5	2.5	6.5	6.5	4	2.25	8	8	3.5	6	3.5	1	4.5	7				

LEGEND

An arrow placed in row 1 and column 2 indicates that item 1 is a major cause of item 2 ("Major" and "Cause" are the key words used when developing this matrix)

↑↑	A double arrow was used to indicate a very strong (almost unanimous agreement) within the team and/or a very strong significant relationship but was still only counted as one point
↑	A single arrow was used to indicate a majority agreement within the team and was counted as one point
↑ D	A dashed line was used to indicate a major disagreement within the group (i.e., half felt that there was a major cause and half did not). A dashed line is counted as half a point
●	A dot was used when one team member had a strong belief that a major cause existed. This condition was counted as a quarter point
N/A	This symbol represents that this column and row relationship is not applicable

Source: "Using the 7-M Tools for Strategic Planning," Hughes Aircraft Co.

Figure 18.5 The Relationship Matrix of Problems, Issues, and Concerns From Team Findings Shown in Figure 18.2

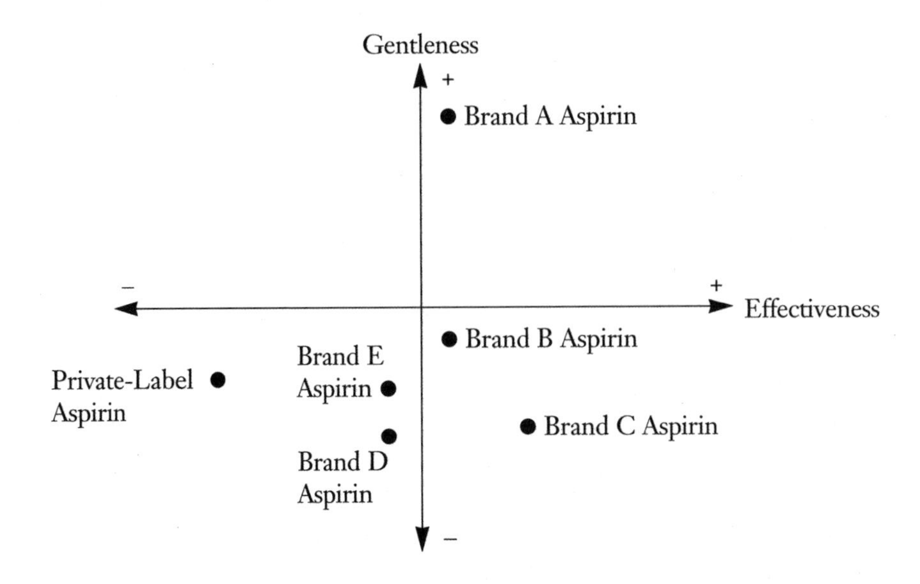

Figure 18.6 Matrix Data Analysis Comparing the Relationship of Different Products to Two Main Characteristics

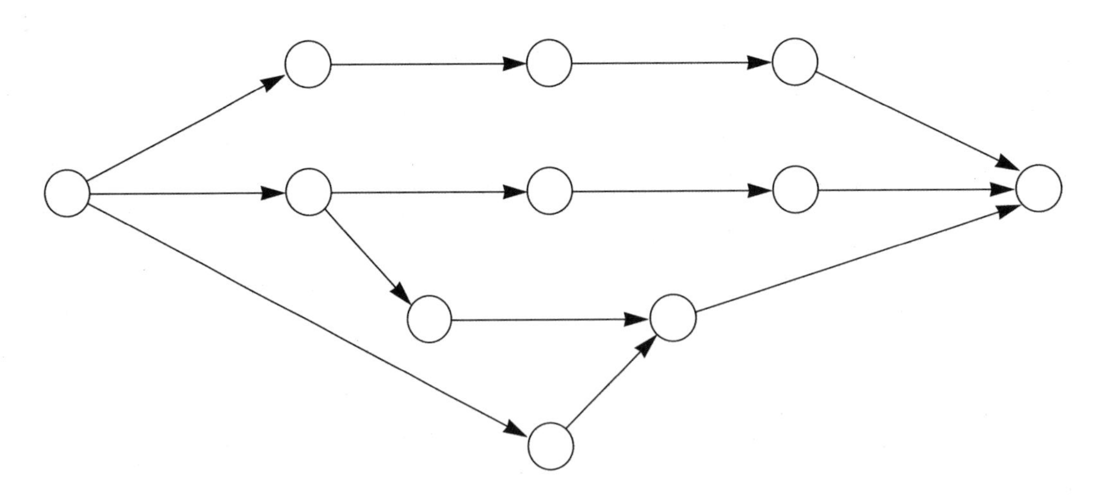

Equivalent to CPM (critical path method)/PERT (program evaluation and review technique), but kept simple. The completion of an event is shown by a circle with the arrows depicting the time for completion.

Figure 18.7 Arrow Diagram

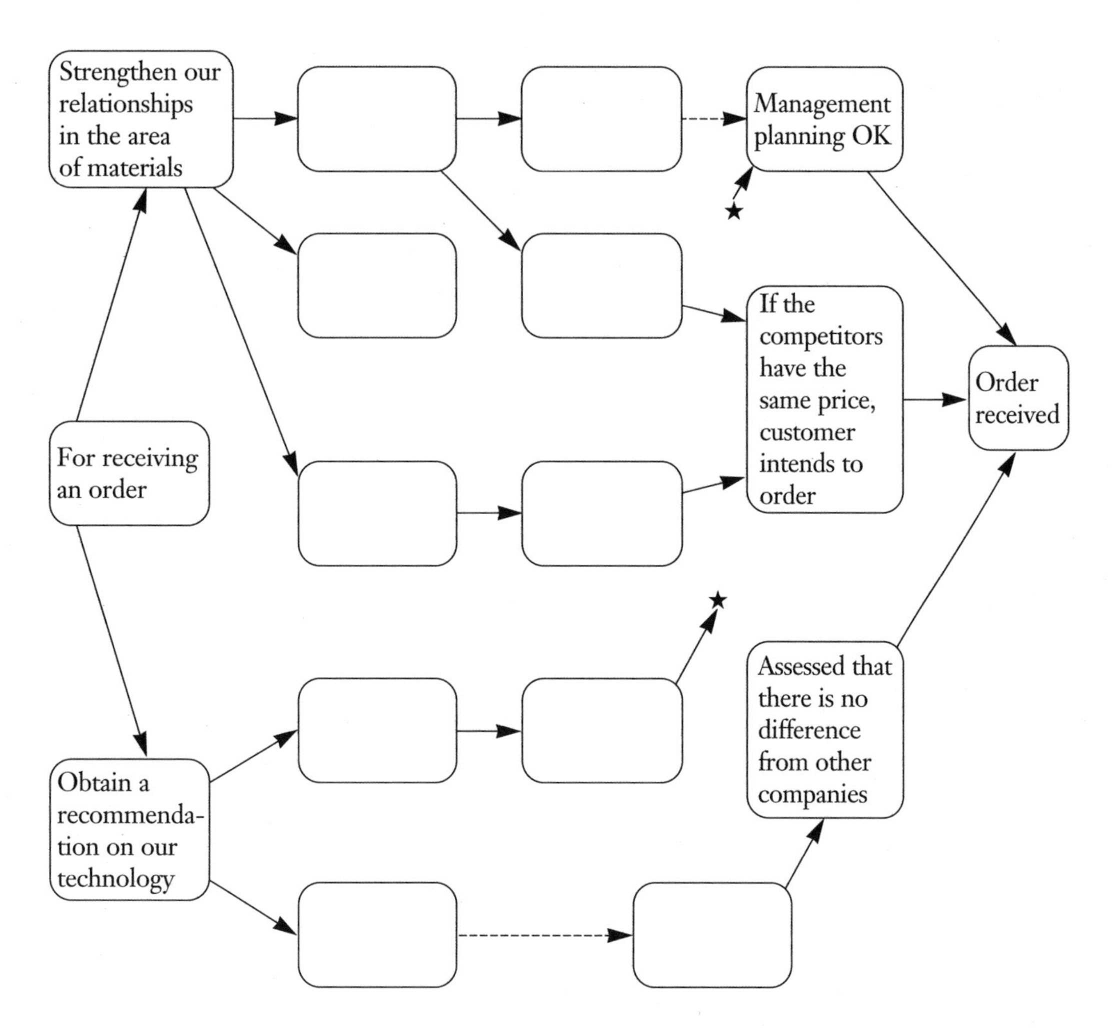

Note: Revise whenever situation changes.

The process decision program chart method was designed to help predict the future of an event while it is still in a developing stage and, thereby, help lead it to a desired result.

The process decision program chart method has two types of applications:

- Sequential extension: To design a plan to achieve a desirable objective, to deal with problems found while implementing the plan, and to make a correct decision and enhance the plan, thereby achieving the objective.
- Forced connection: To conceive countermeasures to avoid an undesirable situation by simulating a process of events leading to an undesirable result.

Source: "The New Quality Technology," Hughes Aircraft Co.

Figure 18.8 Process Decision Program Chart

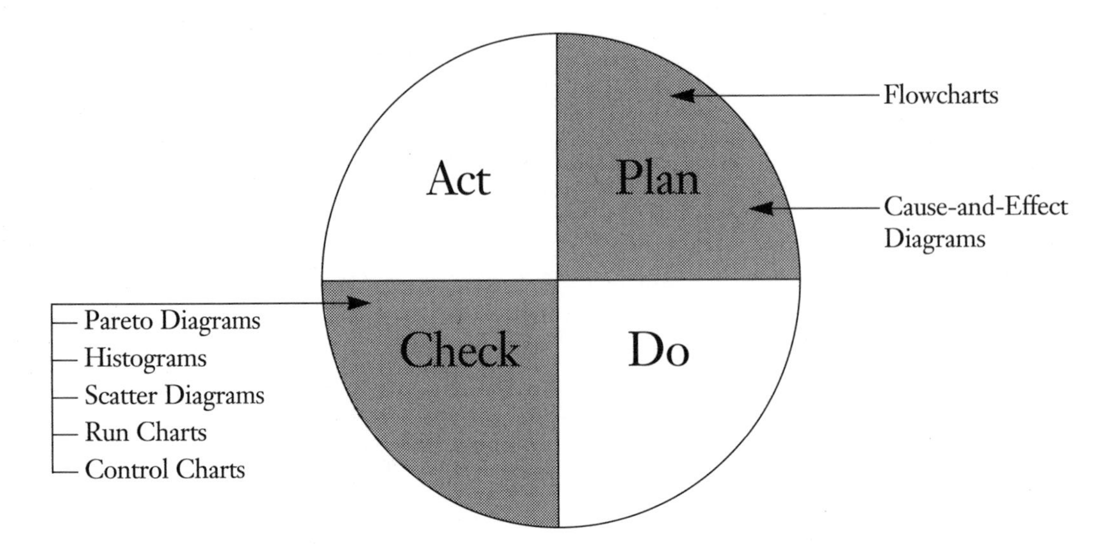

Figure 18.9 Basic Graphic Methods

Figure 18.9 illustrates the most common application when following the Deming Wheel for continuous improvement. The tools can be divided into two broad types, quantitative and nonquantitative. All use diagrams of some kind.

- Nonquantitative
  - –Flowcharts
  - –Cause-and-effect diagrams
- Quantitative:
  - –Scatter diagrams
  - –Pareto diagrams
  - –Run charts
  - –Histograms
  - –Control charts

The nonquantitative tools are used primarily for problem analysis although solutions or partial solutions are sometimes reached through their use. The quantitative tools require data—some measurement of characteristics or events.

The two categories are most frequently used in various combinations depending on the nature of the problem and the objective. For example, in working to improve a business process, it is fundamental to first describe it in adequate detail. The flowchart showing its elements is a simple and powerful first tool. Then after the process has been accurately defined, the various problems in its operation are prioritized using the Pareto diagram. The cause-and-effect diagram would be the next logical tool to analyze causes methodically from which the most likely are selected (by the process team). Means for correction are determined and tried. After the corrections are made, the data are collected. The Pareto chart tool is then used to prioritize the problems that exist, and the effectiveness of the corrective action is determined.

A run chart may then be used to collect performance data over time to determine the trend and to get an idea of the extent of variation with respect to required limits or goals. Used repeatedly on some activity, particularly in nontechnical or mechanized processes, these five tools alone invariably yield significant improvements.

As can be seen in the tool descriptions that follow, ideas from the team's experience are captured and used. There may be some simple data taking, but no knowledge of statistical theory is required. These tools require only organized thinking and simple arithmetic.

The remaining tools—histograms and control charts—can add a great deal more power to the analytical phase and are very important in improving process yield and customer satisfaction. These techniques can be understood and used by the average organizational member without understanding the theory. However, a knowledgeable person, such as an ASQC certified quality engineer, should provide the training and assist in implementing the tools. In time, more sophisticated statistical techniques will be beneficial and require the assistance of an industrial statistician. Figure 18.10 depicts another way to identify the use of the tools applied to the process improvement activity.

FLOWCHARTS[9]

Making and using flowcharts are among the most important actions in bringing process control to both administrative and manufacturing processes. While it is obvious that to control a process one must first understand that process, many companies are still trying to solve problems and improve processes without first describing how they are actually operating.

The easiest and best way to understand a process is to draw a picture of it—that's basically what flowcharting is. There are many styles that can be used. Some people use pictures, some use engineering symbols, and others just use squares or rectangles for the whole diagram. There really is no right or wrong way to display the information. The true test of a flowchart is how well those who create and use it can understand it and work with it.

Constructing Flow Diagrams

Every process is supplied with services and products from some supplier(s). Likewise, every process provides products or services to some other process—its customer(s). Figure 18.11 shows a generic process. Using this figure as a guide, making a flowchart

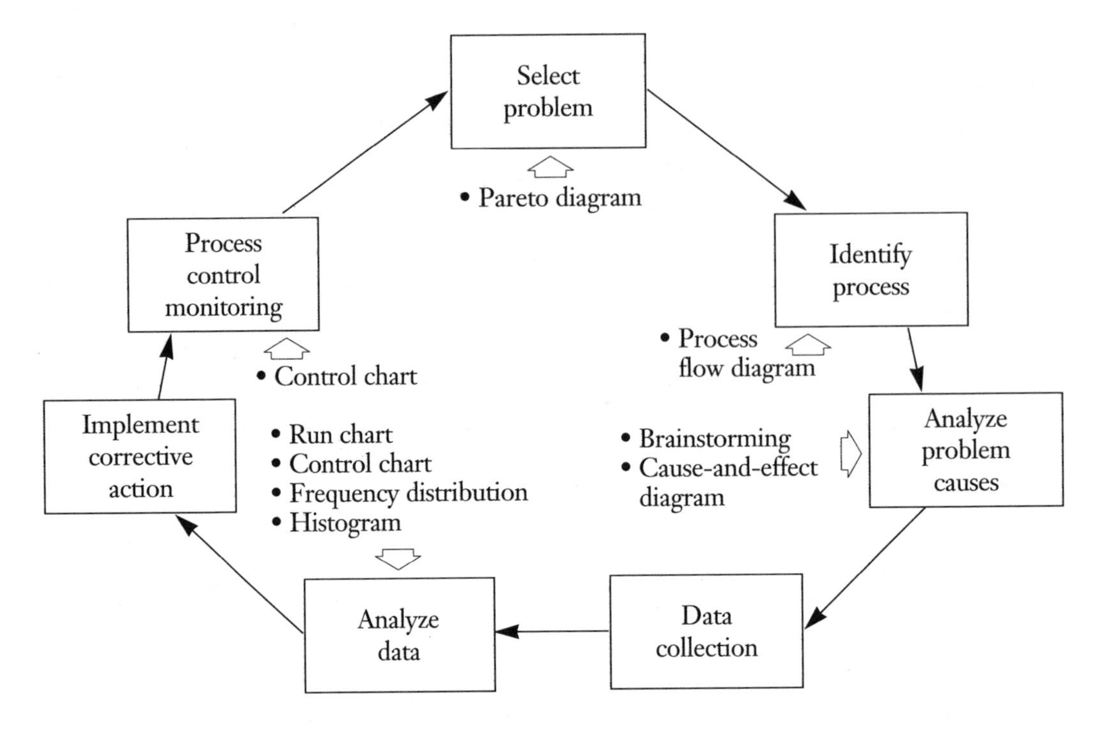

Figure 18.10 The Improvement Process

is simple as long as the designer(s) follows these rules:

Rule 1. The most important rule is that the right people must be involved in making the chart. This includes those who actually do the work of the process, suppliers to the process, customers of the process, the supervisor of the area with which the process functions, and an independent facilitator.

Rule 2. Key members of the group should participate. Ideally it would be all members, but in large processes that isn't always practical. If all are not part of the team then all must be kept current on progress.

Rule 3. During team sessions all data must be visible to all the people all the time. Using large sheets of paper and masking tape is imperative for a good flow-charting session. As one sheet is completed, it should be taped on the wall in sequence with previous work. Rarely should a session be completed without at least some rework of previous parts of the flowchart as the group members reflect on the information in front of them.

Rule 4. Enough time must be allotted. Experience shows that much more time is required to make a flowchart than is usually expected. More than one session might be required. Group members may need more time to obtain more information on the functioning of the process.

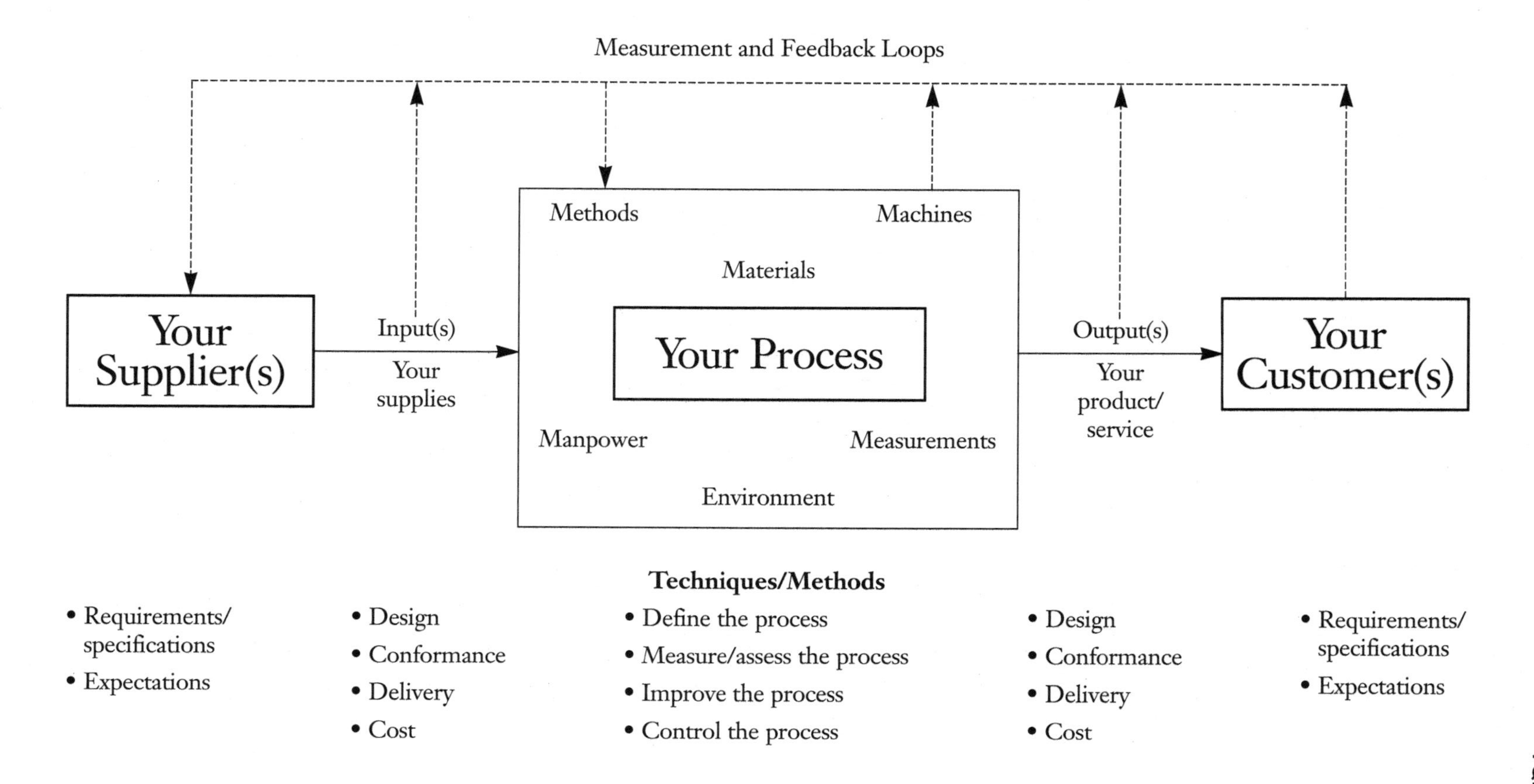

Figure 18.11 Flow Diagram

Rule 5. The more questions everyone asks the better. Questions are the key to the flowcharting process. There are many questions that can be asked by both the facilitator and the group members. What is the first thing that happens? What is the next thing that happens? Questioning should continue throughout the process. Questions that will be helpful at certain times during the process include:

- Where does the service or material come from?
- How does the service or material get to the process?
- Who makes the decision if a service or material is needed?
- What happens if the decision is "yes"?
- What happens if the decision is "no"?
- Is there anything else that must be done at this point?
- Where does the product or service of this operation go?
- What tests are performed on the product at each part of the process?
- What tests are performed on the process?
- What happens if the test is out of tolerance?

Even more questions will arise during the session(s). Also, teams should not get bogged down on any one question. Keep moving. Answers can be researched and reported on later.

Rule 6. Finally, be sure that the final chart is verified against what is actually taking place. It is not uncommon for one person to think he or she knows what is happening only to find out later that he or she was only partially correct.

Applications

There are many ways to use flowcharts, and employees should get used to working with them. The charts can be even more helpful if employees ask the questions listed in Rule 5, particularly the questions about what could be measured.

While flowcharts are important in manufacturing, substantial improvements can be made by using them in staff or administrative functions at any level.

The Benefits of Flowcharts

Companies that use process flowcharting reap many benefits:

- The people who work in the process understand the process. They begin to control it instead of being victims of it.

- Once the process can be seen objectively in the flowchart, improvements can be easily identified.
- Employees realize how they fit into the overall process, and they visualize their suppliers and customers as a part of that overall process. This leads directly to improved communication between departments and work areas (system thinking).
- The people who participate in flowcharting sessions become enthusiastic supporters of the entire quality effort. They will continue to provide suggestions for even further improvement.
- Process flowcharts are valuable tools in training programs for new employees.
- Work procedures written around current process flowcharts will be the most effective and are more likely to be followed.

In short, perhaps the most important benefit of using process flowcharts is that the people in the process will all understand it in the same terms. That understanding leads to employees who can better control their destinies, more economical processes, less waste in administrative functions, and better customer-supplier relationships between departments.

CAUSE-AND-EFFECT DIAGRAMS

One unique and valuable tool for obtaining the maximum information is the cause-and-effect diagram. This tool was first developed in 1943 by Ishikawa at the University of Tokyo; he used it to explain to a group of engineers from the Kawasaki Steel Works how various factors could be sorted and related.

The cause-and-effect diagram is a method for analyzing process dispersion. The diagram's purpose is to relate causes and effects. This tool is not only invaluable for virtually any issue requiring attention, but can easily be learned by people at all levels of the organization and applied immediately.

There are three basic types of cause-and-effect diagrams: dispersion analysis, process classification, and cause enumeration. Figure 18.12 depicts the basic format for the cause-and-effect diagram. Note the hierarchical relationship of the effect to the main causes and their subsequent relationship to the sub-causes. For example, main cause A has a direct relationship to the effect. Each of the sub-causes is related in terms of its level of influence on the main cause.

While a cause-and-effect diagram can be developed by an individual, it is best when used by a team. This tool is well suited for team applications. One of the most valuable attributes of this tool is that it provides an excellent means to facilitate a brainstorming session. It will enable the participants to focus on the issue at hand and immediately allow them to sort ideas into useful categories, especially when dispersion analysis or process classification methods are used.

Dispersion Analysis

Let's assume there are difficulties with customer complaints. Let us further assume that a team of about seven individuals from various functions throughout the organization is formed. Each of these individuals has sound knowledge of the overall business as well as an area of specific expertise. This team will provide a good example of the way to construct a cause-and-effect diagram using the dispersion analysis methods. There are three steps:

Step 1. It is quite simple to construct the diagram. First determine the quality characteristic you wish to improve—perhaps customer satisfaction. There must be consensus when the problem statement is written. For example, "Customers are dissatisfied."

In a manufacturing process, you might use a specific characteristic of a product as the effect, such as a problem with paste thickness in a surface mount line, poor paint coverage, or welding errors. In an administrative or service area, use customer complaints, decreased sales volume, or increased accounts receivables past due.

Step 2. Now the team must generate ideas as to what is causing the effect and contributing to customer dissatisfaction. The causes are written as branches flowing to the main branch. Figure 18.13 shows the main cause headings resulting from an actual session in a service/distribution business. In this case, the team determined five areas—product quality, service, order processing system, distribution system, and order fulfillment—as the potential main causes of dissatisfied customers. If there is difficulty in determining the main branches or causes, use generic headings—such as methods, machines, people, materials, environment, or training—to help start the team.

Step 3. The next step is to brainstorm all the possible causes of problems in each of the major cause categories. These ideas are captured and applied to the chart as sub-causes. It is important to continually define and relate causes to each other. It is acceptable to repeat sub-causes in several places if the team feels there is a direct, multiple relationship. This effort will ensure a complete diagram and a more enlightened team.

Returning to Figure 18.13, it can be seen that the team identified five main causes of customer dissatisfaction. Now the team members must ask themselves, "What could contribute to each of these five main causes?" Once several sub-causes have been identified, the team continues asking the same question until the lowest level causes are discovered.

Figure 18.14 shows the completed portion of the diagram for one of the main causes: service. The team identified reliability issues, carrier issues (for example, a trucking company), poor communications, and lack of, or poor, training.

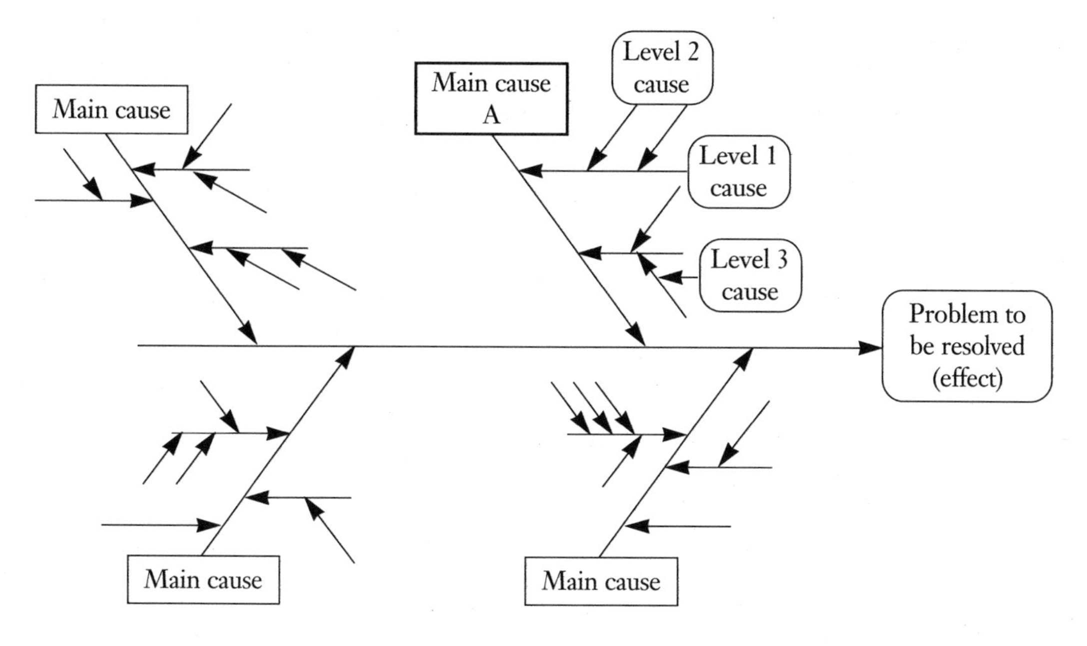

Reprinted with permission from *Quality Progress*, July 1990.

Figure 18.12 Basic Cause-and-Effect Diagram

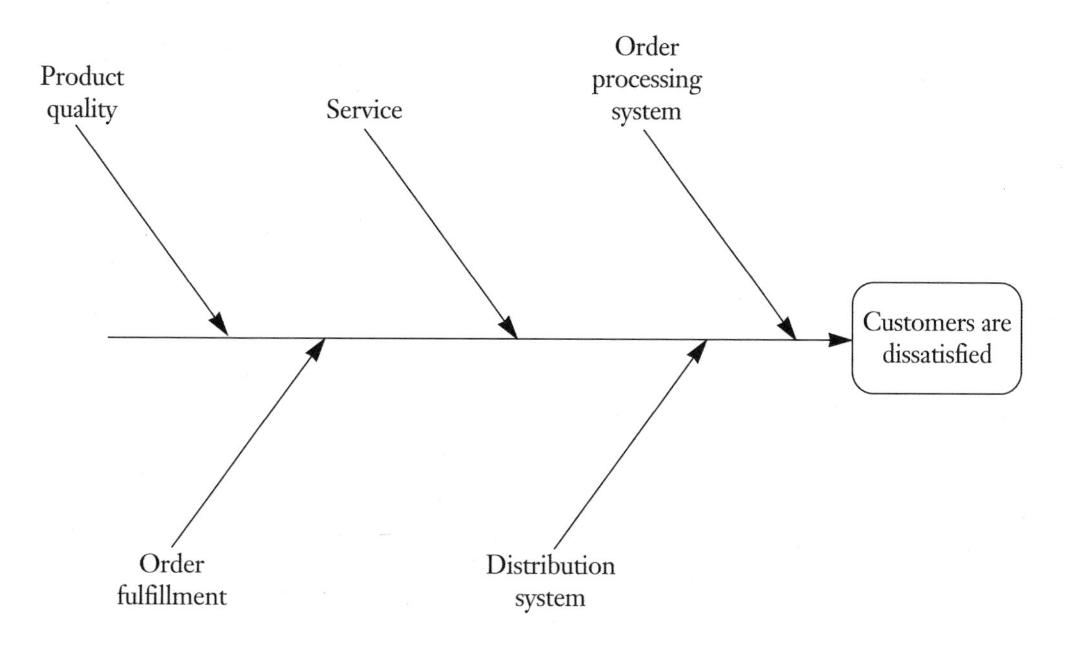

Reprinted with permission from *Quality Progress*, July 1990.

Figure 18.13 Main Cause Headings

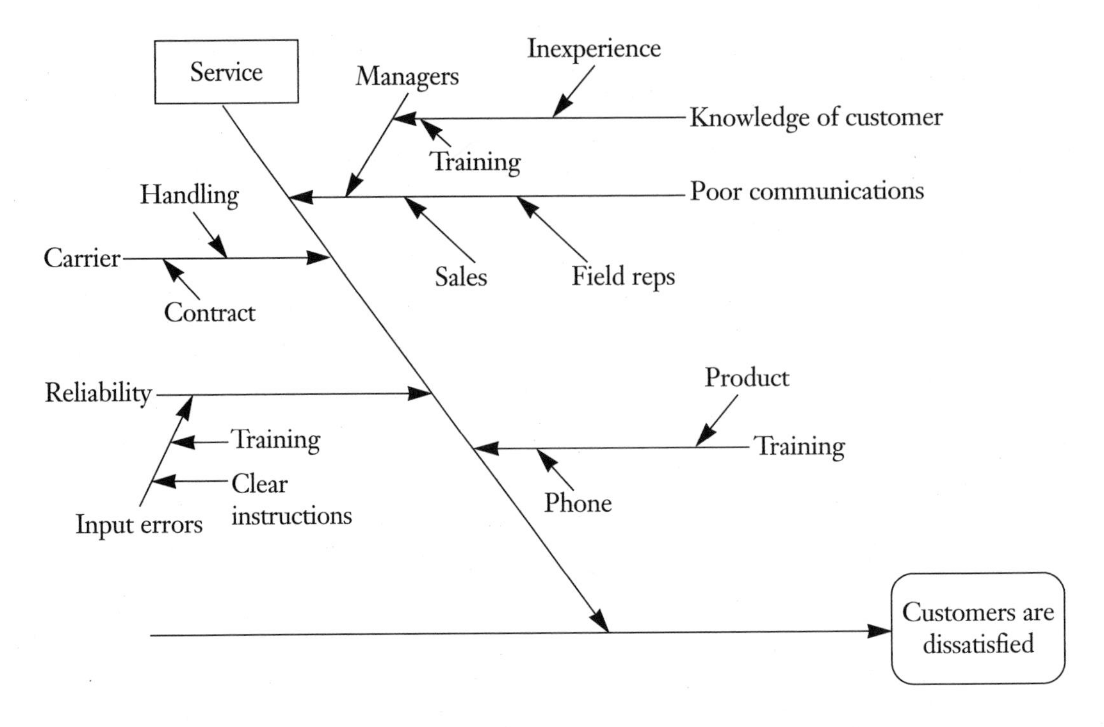

Reprinted with permission from *Quality Progress*, July 1990.

Figure 18.14 A Detailed Look at One Main Cause

The next level of causes is identified by asking the question, "What could cause a problem in these areas?" In the case of the poor communications, the team focused on functions and jobs—sales people, field representatives, and managers—as potential causes. It can be seen that a lack of knowledge of the customer can cause managers to communicate poorly. Subsequently, you can see that inexperience and training can be two key contributors to a manager's lack of customer knowledge. Thus, there are six levels of causes in this example.

Process Classification

Another type of diagram is known as the process classification diagram. This tool is as valuable in service-based businesses as it is in manufacturing companies since every product or service is the result of a process. Although the basic process for constructing this type of diagram is similar to the one used for dispersion analysis, there are some differences. These differences are driven by the application. For the process classification method, identify the flow of the process to be improved and then list key quality-influencing characteristics at each of the steps.

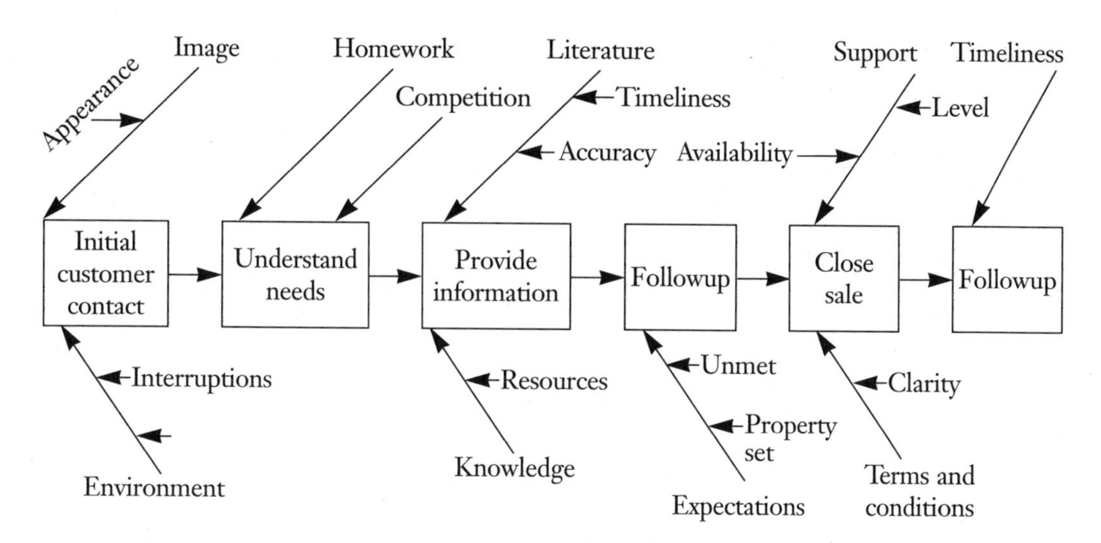

Reprinted with permission from *Quality Progress*, July 1990.

Figure 18.15 Completed Process Classification Diagram

Step 1. Identify the process and develop a flow diagram of the primary sequential steps. For example, in a generic selling process, the following steps might be identified: make initial customer contact, develop an understanding of customer needs, provide information to the customer, follow up, close the sale, and follow up on the sale.

Step 2. Now add all the things that might influence the quality of each step. Use the method described in the previous section. Brainstorming with a team of knowledgeable people will make the finished diagram more like the actual process.

Figure 18.15 shows an example of a completed process classification diagram. The intent is to take the cause and effect to the lowest level to understand all the contributing factors to improve the process. It is also advisable to consider the connecting steps from process step to process step. Everywhere there is a handoff from one step to the next, there are likely to be possible causes of dispersion. Many opportunities for improvement can be found in these areas.

Cause Enumeration

The cause enumeration method involves simply brainstorming all possible causes and listing them in the order they are offered. Once the brainstorm has exhausted itself, the team begins the process of grouping the causes as it did for the dispersion analysis diagram. The end result looks exactly the same.

This process can be enhanced dramatically using the affinity diagram process. It is a valuable method for gaining insight and organizing ideas.

Convert to Action

Understanding processes, using teams, and identifying areas of opportunity are excellent ways to move toward continuous improvement while solving some of today's tough issues. But they are only the beginning. To obtain the full value from the cause-and-effect diagram, it must be turned into action. It is therefore wise to quantify the problem and as many of the causes as possible. Once this has been done, the business can determine the priority areas to be addressed and can track improvements.

In the example of Figure 18.14, the business was able to quantify the problem of customer dissatisfaction by measuring several key parameters, including the number of calls about problems, the number of requests to return material for specific reasons, and delays in customer payments. In the area where sub-causes were identified, various parts of the organization were surveyed to determine the primary areas of opportunity for addressing the causes identified by the cause-and-effect diagram. For example, one need was for training in simple statistical problem-solving methods. This need was quantified not only by the number of people needing training, but also by the results of the training applications.

As the team and business move to quantify the causes, other tools play key roles. Pareto analysis, histograms, control charts, scatter plots, and multivariate analysis might be particularly valuable.

Understanding Processes

In the past decade, quality has gained recognition as a competitive imperative for all businesses. The root of all quality improvement lies in understanding processes. Many existing tools assist managers, engineers, and others in this work. It isn't necessary to look for the newest tool, software, or management theory to construct a sound foundation on which to build improvements. The cause-and-effect diagram, which can be used for virtually any issue your business might face, fosters teamwork, educates users, identifies lowest level issues on which to work, helps show a true picture of the process, and guides discussion.

HISTOGRAMS

A histogram is a graphic summary of variation (dispersion) in a set of data. The pictorial nature of the histogram lets you see patterns that are difficult to see in a simple table of measures.

A Case Study

The importance of using data and facts is stressed in problem-solving and quality improvement efforts. But sometimes the data can seem overwhelming or of little value as the problem at hand is tackled. Consider the following example.

A manufacturer of electronic telecommunications equipment was receiving complaints from the field about low volume on long-distance circuits. A string of amplifiers manufactured by the company was being used to boost the signal at various points along the way. The boosting ability of the amplifiers (engineers call it the "gain") was naturally the prime suspect in the case.

The design of the amplifiers had called for a gain of 10 decibels (dB). This means that the output from the amplifier should be about 10 times stronger than its input. Amplification is needed to make up for the weakening of the signal over the long-distance connection. Recognizing that it is impossible to make every amplifier with a gain of exactly 10 dB, the design allowed the amplifiers to be considered acceptable if the gain fell between 7.75 dB and 12.2 dB. These permissible minimum and maximum values are sometimes called the specification (or spec) tolerance limits. The expected value of 10 dB is the nominal value. There were literally hundreds of amplifiers boosting the signal on a long connection. The average gain of the amplifiers should have provided adequate overall amplification to the signal over the wires. This was the assumption of the designer.

The quality improvement team investigating the low volume condition arranged to test the gain of 120 amplifiers. The results of the tests are listed in Figure 18.16.

Gain of 120 Tested Amplifiers

8.1	10.4	8.8	9.7	7.8	9.9	11.7	8.0	9.3	9.0
8.2	8.9	10.1	9.4	9.2	7.9	9.5	10.9	7.8	8.3
9.1	8.4	9.6	11.1	7.9	8.5	8.7	7.8	10.5	8.5
11.5	8.0	7.9	8.3	8.7	10.0	9.4	9.0	9.2	10.7
9.3	9.7	8.7	8.2	8.9	8.6	9.5	9.4	8.8	8.3
8.4	9.1	10.1	7.8	8.1	8.8	8.0	9.2	8.4	7.8
7.9	8.5	9.2	8.7	10.2	7.9	9.8	8.3	9.0	9.6
9.9	10.6	8.6	9.4	8.8	8.2	10.5	9.7	9.1	8.0
8.7	9.8	8.5	8.9	9.1	8.4	8.1	9.5	8.7	9.3
8.1	10.1	9.6	8.3	8.0	9.8	9.0	8.9	8.1	9.7
8.5	8.2	9.0	10.2	9.5	8.3	8.9	9.1	10.3	8.4
8.6	9.2	8.5	9.6	9.0	10.7	8.6	10.0	8.8	8.6

This material is contained in the in-house training package, "Quality Improvement Tools.®" Contact: Juran Institute, Inc., 11 River Road, Wilton, CT 06897-0811.

Figure 18.16 Results of Tests of 120 Amplifiers

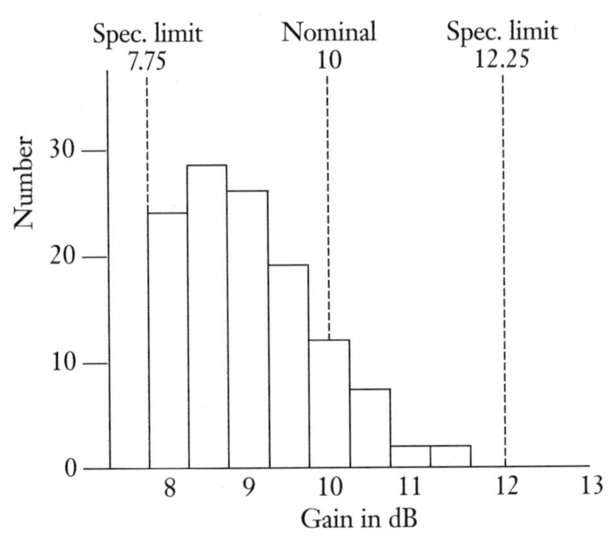

This material is contained in the in-house training package, "Quality Improvement Tools.®"
Contact: Juran Institute, Inc., 11 River Road, Wilton, CT 06897-0811.

Figure 18.17 A histogram clearly shows that most of the amplifiers had a lower-than-nominal value of gain.

This table of data contains 120 measurements to examine. The gain of all the amplifiers fell within the specification limits. This didn't seem to identify the problem. One could jump to the conclusion that a 10 dB gain is not enough. However, the data in the tables do not give a useful "picture" for analysis.

The team members decided to construct a histogram to give them a better "picture" of the 120 data point. They divided the specification range into nine intervals of 0.5 dB each and counted the number of data points that fell in each interval. They found that there were 24 amplifiers whose gain reading was between 7.75 dB and 8.24 dB, 28 amplifiers between 8.25 dB and 8.74 dB, and so on.

The histogram of the data is shown in Figure 18.17. The height of each bar on the histogram represents the number of amplifiers with gain readings that fell within the dB range that the bar covers on the horizontal axis. For example, the histogram indicates that 19 amplifiers had a gain reading between 9.25 dB and 9.74 dB. The histogram of the data gave the team a very different view of the situation. While all the amplifiers fell within the specification limits, the readings were certainly not evenly distributed around the nominal 10 dB value. Most of the amplifiers had a lower-than-nominal value of gain. This pattern was hard to see in the table of data but the histogram clearly revealed it.

If most of the amplifiers in the series on a long-distance connection boost the signal a little bit less than expected (less than the 10 dB expected), the result will be a low volume level.

The histogram gave the team a clearer and more complete picture of the data. The team could now concentrate its investigation in the factory to find out why the manufacturing line was not producing more amplifiers that were more evenly distributed around the nominal value.

Histograms in Problem Solving

As this example illustrates, the histogram is a simple but powerful tool for elementary analysis of data. Key concepts about data and the use of histograms in problem solving can be summarized as follows:

1. Values in a set of data almost always show variation. Although the amplifiers were designed for a nominal value of 10 dB gain, very few of them actually had a measured gain of 10 dB. Furthermore, few amplifiers had exactly the same gain. This variation is due to small differences in literally hundreds of factors surrounding the manufacturing process—the exact values of the component parts, the nature of the handling that each amplifier receives, the accuracy and repeatability of the test equipment, even the humidity in the factory on the day the amplifier was made. Everything varies. It is inevitable in the output of any process: manufacturing, service, or administrative. It is impossible to keep all factors in a constant state all the time.
2. Variation displays a pattern. In the amplifier example, the pattern of variation shown in Figure 18.17 had a number of characteristics. For example:
   - All values fell within the specification limits.
   - Most of the values fell between the nominal and the lower specification limit.
   - The values of gain tended to bunch up near the lower specification limit.
   - More values fell in the range of 8.25 dB to 8.75 dB than in any other 0.5 dB category.

   Different phenomena will have different variation, but there is always some pattern to the variation. For example, we know that the height of most 10-year-old boys will be close to some average value and that it would be relatively unusual to find an extremely tall or extremely short boy. If we gathered the data on the time required to repair an appliance for a customer or the time required to process paperwork or the time required to complete a transaction at a bank, we would expect to see some similar pattern in the numbers. These patterns of variation in data are called "distributions."

   The purpose of this discussion is to point out that there are usually discernible patterns in the variation and that these patterns often tell a great deal about the cause of a problem. Identifying and interpreting these patterns are the most important topics discussed here. There are three important characteristics of a histogram: its center, width, and shape.

3. Patterns of variation are difficult to see in simple tables of numbers. Again, recall the amplifier example and the table of data in Figure 18.16. Looking at the table of numbers, we could see that no values fall outside the specification limits, but we cannot see much else. While there is a pattern in the data, it is difficult for our eyes and minds to see it. Unless it is exposed, the wrong conclusions may be reached and improper actions may be taken.

Typical Patterns of Variation

Figure 18.18 shows common patterns of variation. The following list contains general explanations of each type and provides suggestions for further analysis:

- The bell-shaped distribution is a symmetrical shape with a peak in the middle of the range of data. This is the normal, natural distribution of data from a process. Deviations from this bell shape might indicate the presence of complicating factors or outside influences. While deviations from a bell shape should be investigated, such deviations are not necessarily bad. As we will see, some nonbell-shaped distributions are to be expected in certain cases.
- The double-peaked distribution is a distinct valley in the middle of the range of the data with peaks on either side. This pattern is usually a combination of two bell-shaped distributions and suggests that two distinct processes are at work, and two different sets of data have been tabulated.
- The plateau distribution is a flat top with no distinct peak and slight tails on either side. This pattern is likely to be the result of many different bell-shaped distributions with centers spread evenly throughout the range of data.

  Diagram the flow and observe the operation to identify the many different processes at work. An extreme case occurs in organizations that have no defined processes or training—each person does the job his or her own way. The wide variability in process leads to the wide variability observed in the data. Defining and implementing standard procedures will reduce this variability.
- The comb distribution is high and low values alternating in a regular fashion. This pattern typically indicates measurement error—errors in the way the data were grouped to construct the histogram—or a systematic bias in the way the data were rounded off. A less likely alternative is that this is a type of plateau distribution. Review the data collection procedures and the construction of the histogram before considering possible process characteristics that might cause the pattern.

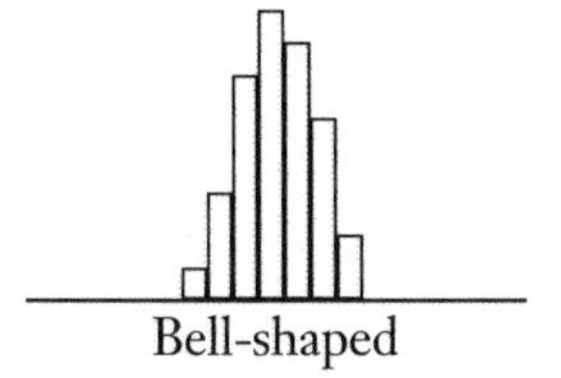
Bell-shaped

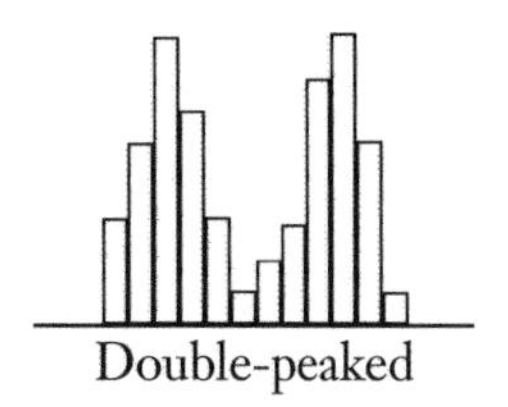
Double-peaked

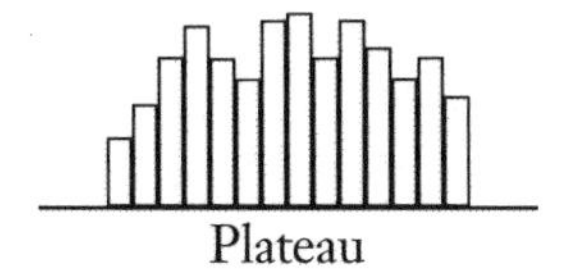
Plateau

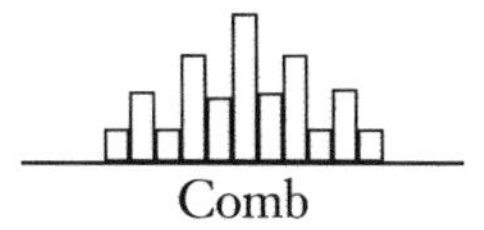
Comb

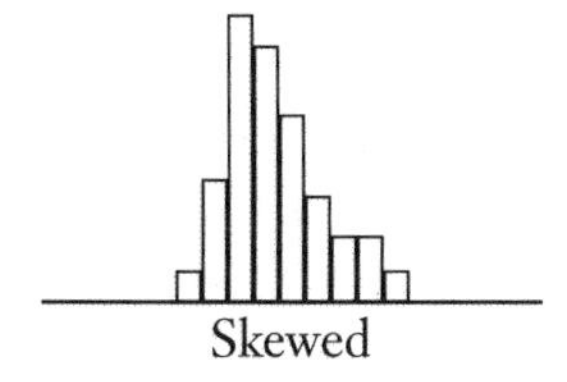
Skewed

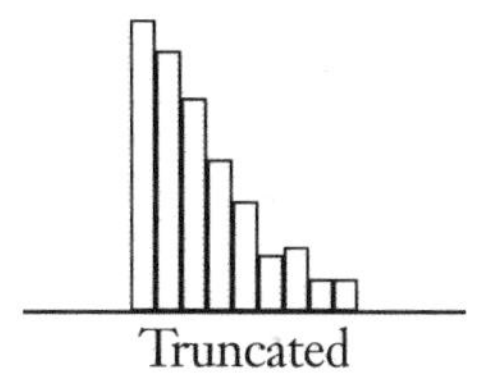
Truncated

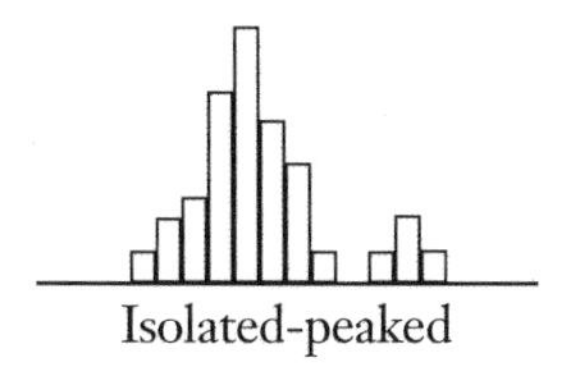
Isolated-peaked

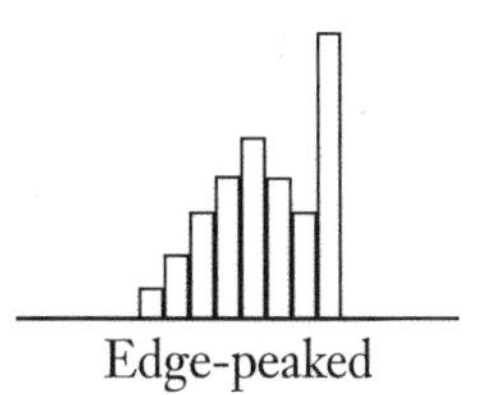
Edge-peaked

This material is contained in the in-house training package, "Quality Improvement Tools.®" Contact: Juran Institute, Inc., 11 River Road, Wilton, CT 06897-0811.

Figure 18.18 Common Histogram Patterns

- The skewed distribution is an asymmetrical shape in which the peak is off-center in the range of data and the distribution trails off sharply on one side and gently on the other. The illustration in Figure 18.18 is called a positively skewed distribution because the long tail extends rightward, toward increasing values. A negatively skewed distribution would have a long tail extending leftward toward decreasing values. The skewed pattern typically occurs when a practical limit or a specification limit exists on one side and is relatively close to the nominal value. In these cases, there simply are not as many values available on one side as there are on the other. Practical limits occur frequently when the data consist of time measurements or counts of things.

  For example, tasks that take a very short time can never be completed in zero or less time. Those occasions when the task takes a little longer than average to complete create a positively skewed tail on this distribution of task time. The number of weaving defects per 100 yards of fabric can never be less than zero. If the process averages about 0.7 defects per 100 yards, then sporadic occurrences of three or four defects per 100 yards will result in a positively skewed distribution.

  One-sided specification limits (a maximum or minimum value only) also frequently give rise to skewed distributions.

  Such skewed distributions are not inherently bad, but a team should question the impact of the values in the long tail. Could they cause customer dissatisfaction (for example, long waiting times)? Could they lead to higher costs (for example, overfilling containers)? Could the extreme values cause problems in downstream operations? If the long tail has a negative impact on quality, the team should investigate and determine the causes for those values.
- The truncated distribution is an asymmetrical shape in which the peak is at or near the edge of the range of the data, and the distribution ends very abruptly on one side and trails off gently on the other. The illustration in Figure 18.18 shows truncation on the left side with a positively skewed tail. Of course, one might also encounter truncation on the right side with a negatively skewed tail. Truncated distributions are often smooth, bell-shaped distributions with a part of the distribution removed, or truncated, by some external force such as screening, 100 percent inspection, or a review process. Note that these truncation efforts are an added cost and are, therefore, good candidates for removal.
- The isolated-peaked distribution is a small, separate group of data in addition to the larger distribution. Like the double-peaked distribution, this pattern is a combination and suggests that two distinct processes are at work. But the small size of the second peak indicates an abnormality, something that doesn't happen often or regularly.

Look closely at the conditions surrounding the data in the small peak to see if you can isolate a particular time, machine, input source, procedure, operator, and so on. Such small isolated peaks in conjunction with a truncated distribution might result from the lack of complete effectiveness in screening out defective items. It is also possible that the small peak represents errors in measurements or in transcribing the data. Recheck measurements and calculations.

- The edge-peaked distribution is a large peak appended to an otherwise smooth distribution. This shape occurs when the extended tail of the smooth distribution has been cut off and lumped into a single category at the edge of the range of the data. This shape very frequently indicates inaccurate recording of the data (for example, values outside the "acceptable" range are reported as being just inside the range).

Potential Pitfalls in Interpretation

There are four important pitfalls that a quality improvement team should be aware of when interpreting histograms:

1. Before stating a conclusion from the analysis of a histogram, make sure that the data are representative of typical and current conditions in the process. If the data are old (such as, the process has changed since the data were collected) or if there is any question about bias or incompleteness in the data, it is best to gather new data to confirm and enhance the conclusions.
2. Don't draw conclusions based on a small sample. As pointed out earlier, the larger the sample, the more confidence exists that the peaks, spread, and shape of the histogram of the sample data are representative of the total process or group of products. As a rule of thumb, if the intent is to construct before-and-after or stratified histograms to examine differences in variability or the location of peaks, use a sample large enough to give you 40 or more observations for each histogram to be constructed. For example, if the plan is to stratify the data into three groups, the minimum sample size should be around 120 (3 x 40). If this is not practical, consult a statistical adviser to design an appropriate sampling and hypothesis testing scheme.
3. It is important to remember that the interpretation of the histogram is often merely a theory that must still be confirmed through additional analysis and direct observation of the process in question. The first conclusion and interpretation might not be correct—even if it sounds perfectly reasonable. Always take time to think of alternative explanations for the pattern seen in the histogram.

4. A histogram from an ongoing activity is a picture of only one instant in time. A series of such "snapshots" at fixed intervals may give additional and valuable information to an improvement team. A series of such histograms is the initial step in establishing the control charts discussed in Chapter 19.

What Do We Do Next?

The key accomplishments of a histogram analysis are as follows:

1. Some aspect of the process has been quantified by facts, not opinions.
2. There is a better understanding of the variability inherent in the process; there is a more realistic view of the ability of the process to produce acceptable results consistently.
3. There are new ideas and theories about how the process operates or about the causes of a problem. The stage is set for additional investigative efforts.

PARETO DIAGRAMS

The Pareto principle is several things. It is a ranking system. It is also a way of managing project by prioritization. Finally, it is a process—an orderly way of thinking about problems that affect us.

The Principle

The Pareto principle was first defined by Juran in 1950. During his early work, Juran found that there was a "maldistribution of quality losses." Not liking such a long name, he named the principle after Vilfredo Pareto, a nineteenth-century Italian economist. Pareto found that a large share of the wealth was owned by relatively few people—a maldistribution of wealth. Juran found this was true in many areas of life, including quality technologies. In 1975, he published a retraction of his use of Pareto's name in an article called "The Non-Pareto Principle; Mea Culpa." Nevertheless, the term "Pareto principle" is here to stay.

In simplest terms, the Pareto principle suggests that most effects come from relatively few causes. In quantitative terms, 80 percent of the problems come from 20 percent of the machines, raw materials, or operators. Also, 80 percent of the wealth is controlled by 20 percent of the people. It is a well-used idea in inventory measurement that 80 percent of the dollars are represented by 20 percent of the items. Finally, 80 percent of scrap or rework quality costs come from 20 percent of the possible causes.

In the quality technologies, Juran calls the 20 percent of causes the "vital few." He originally called the rest of the causes the "trivial many." However, he and other quality professionals came to understand that there are no trivial problems on the manufacturing floor and that all problems deserve management's attention. Juran has

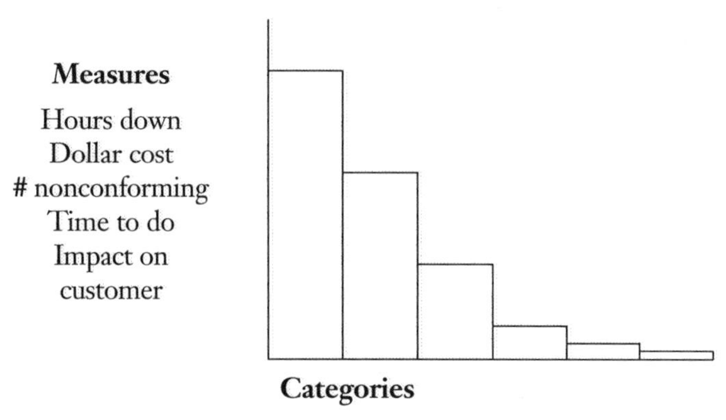

Reprinted with permission from *Quality Progress*, November 1990.

Figure 18.19 Generalized Pareto Diagram Showing Examples of the Kinds of Data That Can Be Plotted

since renamed the trivial many the "useful many." But no matter the labels, the Pareto principle is a powerful tool.

A Management Tool

Data can be collected on the state of scrap, rework, warranty claims, maintenance time, raw material usage, machine downtime, or any other cost associated with manufacturing a product or providing a service. In the case of providing a service, for example, data can be collected on wasted time, number of jobs that have to be redone, customer inquiries, and number of errors. The data should be organized as illustrated in Figure 18.19. The most frequent (highest cost) cause is placed on the left, and the other causes are added in descending order of occurrence.

Figures 18.20 and 18.21 are examples of Pareto diagrams. It is quite obvious which causes or problems have to be reduced or eliminated to have any real impact on the system. A double Pareto diagram, as in Figure 18.22, can be used to contrast two products, areas, or shifts, or it can be used to look at a system before and after improvement.

A Way of Thinking

Figure 18.23 is not a Pareto diagram but a set of data on problems encountered with boxes used to package a number of different products. The most frequent problem is on only one of the box types. Talking to the supplier about the specific problem (warping on box style C) will solve almost half of the difficulties. This would also

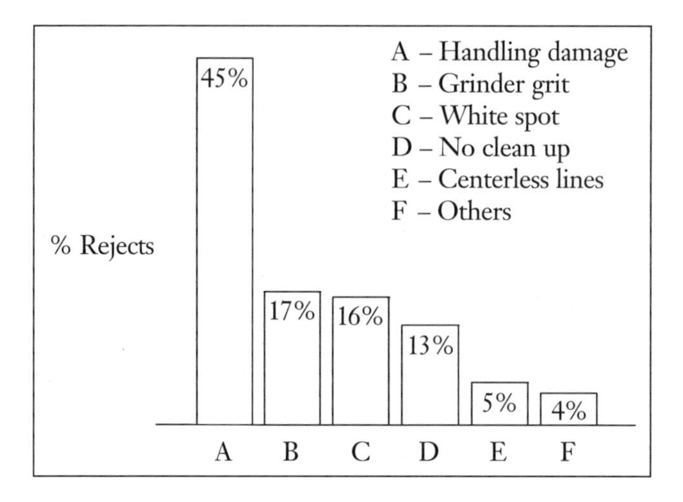

Reprinted with permission from *Quality Progress*, November 1990.

Figure 18.20 Strut Rod Rejects

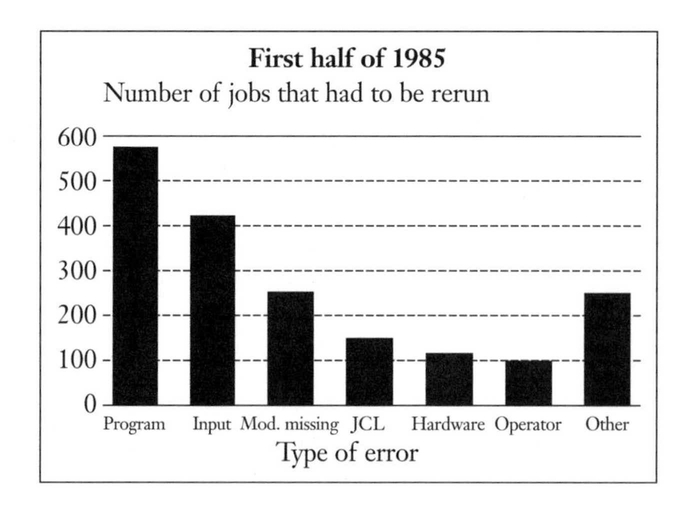

Reprinted with permission from *Quality Progress*, November 1990.

Figure 18.21 Information Systems

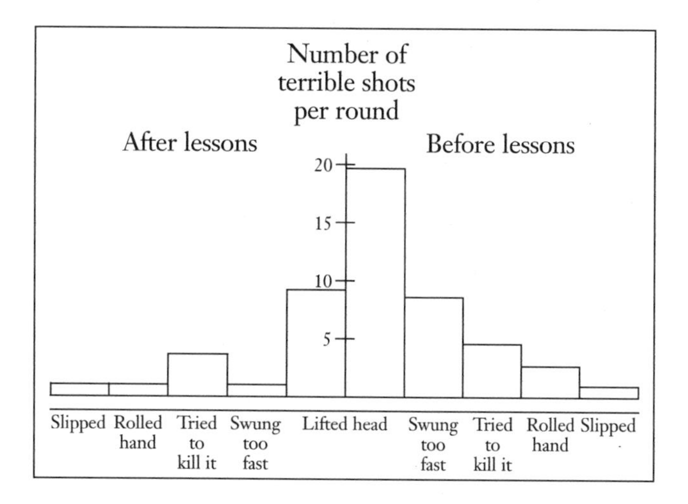

Reprinted with permission from *Quality Progress*, November 1990.

Figure 18.22 Poor Golf Shots

Product	Labels	Liner	Glue	Score	Warp	
			Problem			
A	2		8			10
B	1		4			5
C		1		7	28	36
D		2			4	6
E	3		11			14
F	1				1	2
G	1					1
H				2		2
I	2					2
	10	3	23	9	33	

Reprinted with permission from *Quality Progress*, November 1990.

Figure 18.23 Data Collected on Supplied Boxes

probably lead to less warping of box style D, particularly if the boxes are made on the same line.

The next most frequent problem is glue. The problem occurs over several box types. Are they made on a common line? Is the glue or glue lot the same among these? If so, then a common cause has been identified and should be eliminated. The "mess" of incoming box supply problems will be reduced 80 percent by solving the two problems that have the most impact on quality. Of course, the improvement process is not stopped. The box manufacturing process should be continually analyzed using the Pareto diagram and the other tools of quality.

American industries—manufacturing or service—are some of the greatest collectors of data in the world. The trick is to recognize which data are useful. The Pareto principle describes the way causes occur in nature and human behavior. It can be a very powerful management tool for focusing personnel's effort on the problems and solutions that have the greatest potential payback.

SCATTER DIAGRAMS

The other tools in this study are all methods for handling one type of data at a time. Scatter diagrams show the relationship between *paired* data such as that encountered in analyzing a process using the other QC tools. For example, the cause-and-effect analysis identifies individual factors but does not provide a means to establish whether a measurable relationship exists between them. It doesn't describe which variables relate to each other, which vary at the same time, which is cause, and which is the effect.

With a scatter diagram, several corresponding groups of data are collected and plotted with respect to each other. Figure 18.24 depicts the technique. Figure 18.25 is an example of the relationship between viscosity of oil with respect to temperature. Drawing a trend line through the plots shows how strong a relationship is. The closer the points are to the line, the stronger, and more interdependent the variables are—hence the stronger the cause and effect.

Correlation

The strength of the relationship between two variables can be expressed quantitatively in terms of a coefficient of correlation that varies from zero to one:

- Interpretation. Figure 18.26 shows the basic scatter patterns and how correlation is expressed. The correlation can be calculated mathematically, but in most QC applications a visual analysis is sufficient.
- Application. The scatter diagram can be used for any two variables, but some knowledge has to be used. Variables can be selected and a good correlation indicated when there is actually no relationship. For example, a good correlation

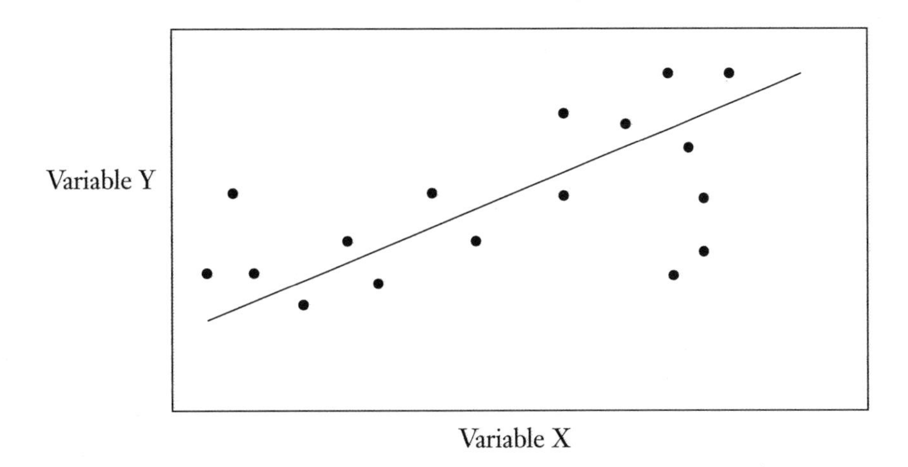

• Diagrams that show the relationship between two variables

The Y axis is usually used for the dependent variable, i.e., the one that changes as a function of variable X.

Figure 18.24 Scatter Diagram

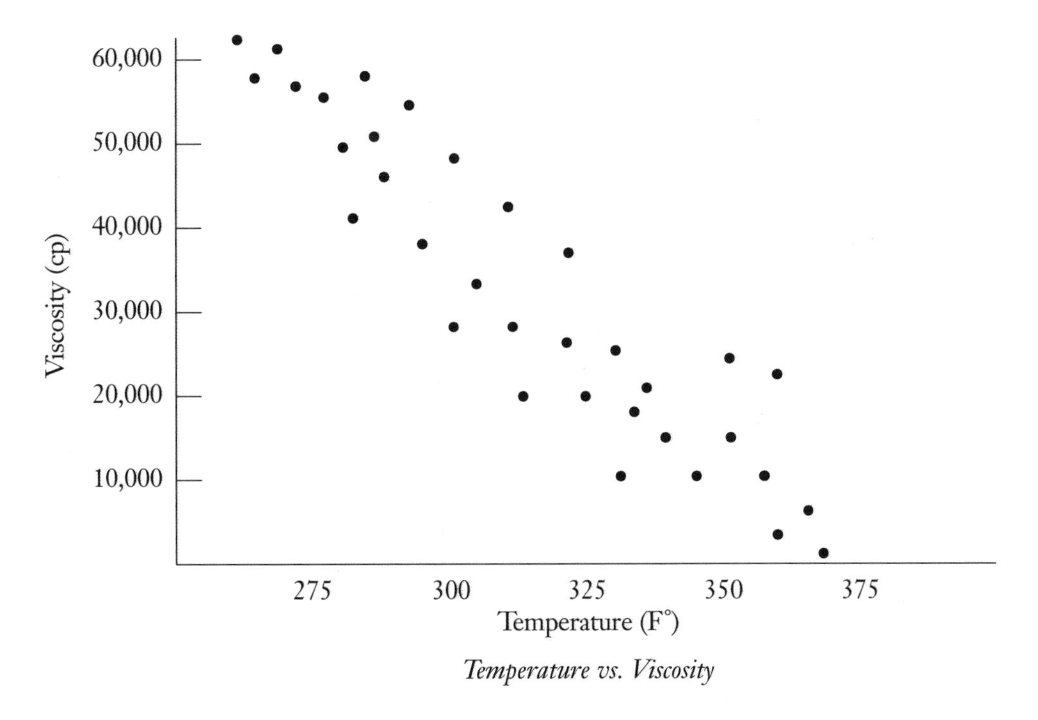

Figure 18.25 Scatter Diagram Showing the Relationship Between Two Variables with a Dependent Relationship and Good (Negative) Correlation

might be seen in a diagram of oil viscosity versus the number of automobiles crossing the Golden Gate Bridge, but the result is meaningless.

CONTROL CHARTS

Various types of control charts and their construction are described in Chapter 19.

Data Collection

An important emphasis of TQM is to make decisions and take action based on facts—data and information. It is also fundamental to success in using any of the QC tools. Quality control has always emphasized measurement and data. It is quite common for quality organizations to have a great deal of data collected and reported over a long period of time. The weakness has been that operating management didn't use them for process management much less process improvement. However, frequently the collected data was only used to report performance (process yield) and wasn't in a form useful for process analysis and improvement. It was symptom-oriented instead of cause-oriented.

Planning

The purpose of process quality data is to use them to take action. Therefore, the data should be in a form and structure to facilitate action. Collecting the most useful data must be planned. Failure to collect the correct data is one of the most common reasons for not taking action or taking the wrong action. The basic axiom is to plan according to how and for what purpose the data will be used.

The first requirement is to understand the process to be studied (flowchart). Identify key performance measures and where in the process they will be measured. In other words, identify what type of data is needed. What collection format will be the most useful in the subsequent analysis? Ishikawa emphasizes the use of what he calls check sheets for this. For example, the proper format could result in developing a histogram in the process of recording the data. Specifically tailored charts for a process operator to record data directly is another example. The result might be a run chart that can easily be converted to a control chart.

Checklists are another format frequently used. They typically provide go/no-go data. An identified event either happened or didn't. However, checklists can be designed with ranges of quantitative measures to be checked. This kind of data is very useful in cause-and-effect analysis. How to collect data can be summarized by following the steps listed in Table 18.3.[10]

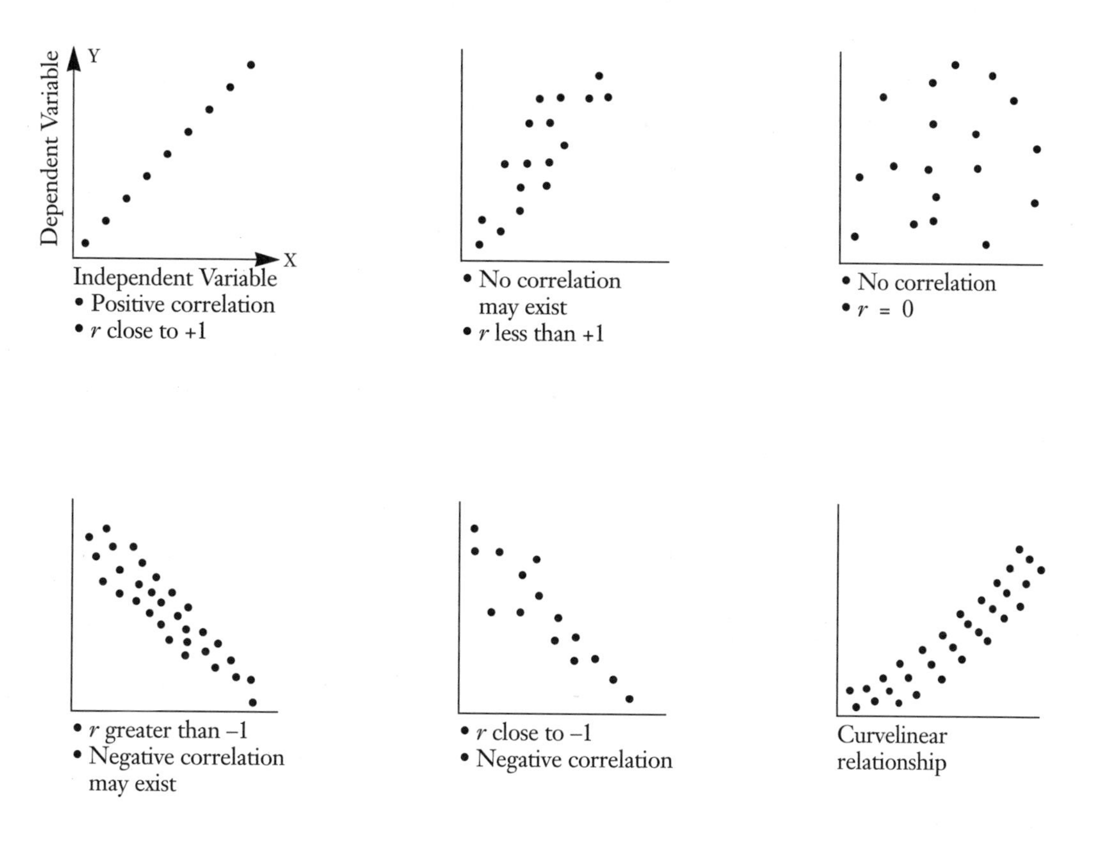

Figure 18.26 The Relationship Between Scatter Diagrams and Correlation

Table 18.3

How to Collect Data

Data collection is a type of production process itself and, like any process, needs to be understood and improved. Generally speaking, 10 points must be addressed when collecting data:

1. Formulate good questions that relate to the specific information needs of the project. It is much easier to get others to help collect data if they believe those in charge know precisely what they are looking for and that they are going to do something with the collected information.
2. Use the appropriate data analysis tools and be certain the necessary data are being collected. Whenever practical, collect continuous variable data. A few minutes of thought before gathering data can often prevent having to recollect data because they are incomplete or answer the wrong question.
3. Define comprehensive data collection points. The ideal is to set the collection point where the job flow suffers minimum interruption. An accurate flowchart of the work process can help immensely.
4. Select an unbiased collector. The collector should have the easiest and most immediate access to the relevant facts.
5. Understand data collectors and their environment. The training and experience of the collectors determine whether they can handle this additional assignment.
6. Design data collection forms that are simple. Reduce opportunities for error and capture data for analysis, reference, and traceability. The forms should also be self-explanatory and look professional. The KISS (keep it simple, stupid) principle applies here.
7. Prepare the instructions for use. In some cases, a special training course might be necessary for data gatherers. In other cases, a simple sheet of instructions will suffice.
8. Test the forms and instructions. Try out the forms on a limited basis to make sure they are filled out properly. If they aren't, the forms or instructions might need revision.
9. Train the data collectors. Training should include the purpose of the study, what the data will be used for, a properly completed form, and a discussion about the importance of complete and unbiased information.
10. Audit the collection process and validate the results. Randomly check completed forms and observe data collection during the process. Look for missing or unusual data, and be wary of variations in the data that might result from biases in the data collection process.

This information is contained in the in-house training package, "Quality Improvement Tools.®" Contact: Juran Institute, Inc., 11 River Road, Wilton, CT 06897-0811.

Chapter 19

SPC, Process Capability, and Continuous Improvement

Some statistical concepts were introduced in Chapter 7 in relation to managing variation and also in the 6σ goal. They are part of the general subject of quality control statistics. SPC and process capability (PC) also fall under that heading.

Another tool is statistical sampling which is actually more widely used. This subject is thoroughly explained in other publications. It is not a significant tool for TQM. Sampling inspection is essentially a cost-saving inspection method. With the emphasis on process control including the supplier's processes and the subsequent elimination of customer receiving inspection, its most common application will disappear. It's likely that remaining application will be in high-volume manufacturing where SPC is not used. Sampling inspection is used in conjunction with AQLs. They are expressed in terms of the percentage of defectives the user is willing to accept before rejecting an entire lot of material. This obviously conflicts with the philosophy of striving for zero defects through process control and improvement.

TQM STATISTICS APPLICATION AND ANALYSIS

Overall, statistics and statistical analysis play a paramount role in TQM. The TQM focus is on reducing process variation. This requires measurement. The only practical way to interpret varying data is by using statistical analysis. The variables at work in any process change with time. Measuring the variation over time is the function of SPC and is what makes it valuable. One measurement, one picture, of all the variables at work in a process, is a histogram; however, it has no predictive power.

It can't show how the process will vary in the future. However, a series of histograms can be analyzed to determine what a process has been doing and whether it's operating properly. Histograms can also determine how a process will probably continue to operate, and whether it will produce acceptable or unacceptable output.

This series of pictures is a control chart: an analytical and decision-making tool for process management. There are several types of control charts so that any process can be measured, pictured, controlled, and improved.

SPC

SPC is sometimes described as one of the seven QC tools (see Chapter 18). Of the seven, statistical concepts and analysis are involved only in histograms, scatter diagrams, and control charts. Those three, plus DOE, are what this book considers SPC.

Figure 19.1a shows the relative power of the common "vary-one-factor-at-a-time" approach compared to the use of statistical techniques that disclose the effect of factor interactions, which, when controlled, can provide significant reduction in variations. This is discussed in the DOE section of Chapter 20.

In Figure 19.1b, H. J. Bajaria and R. P. Copp use the term statistical problem solving (SPS), to include all the quantitative and qualitative techniques used in process problem solving.[11] In the figure, they describe a rational and comprehensive methodology for improving the capability of a process after it is stabilized using control charts. It's an excellent road map that requires a thorough knowledge of modern statistical techniques.

The need for other techniques is shown in Figure 19.2, which shows that applying SPC can result in a process operating at its full capability (or capability index 1.0). If that capability cannot fully satisfy requirements or, if in applying the continuous improvement philosophy, it is necessary to improve the capability further, some other techniques are required. SPC will not improve capability.

Statistical Concepts for Process Control

The statistical tools for process control can be understood and used without mastering the underlying theory. However, setting up an SPC application for the operators of a process requires more understanding. Data collection and initial interpretation of the data for control actions are quite simple. Monitoring the SPC program for anomalies and more sophisticated evaluations requires a greater knowledge of statistical theory.

Basis of SPC. The basis for SPC and the primary tool of interest, control charts, requires recognition of the fact that everything varies and a method is needed to measure the constant changes. Fortunately, most groups or populations of things (such as the tasks in, and products resulting from, process activities) occur in a

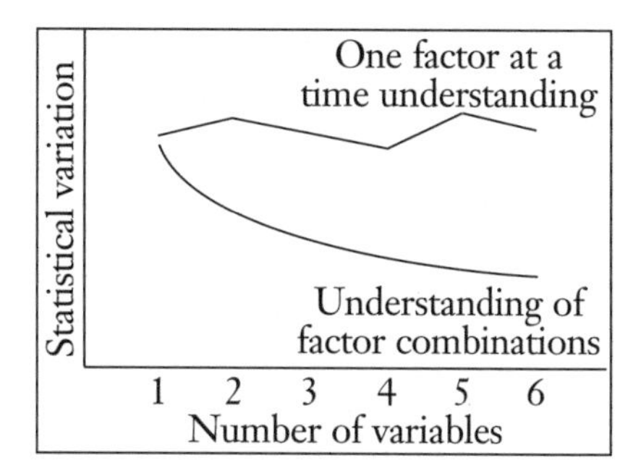

a. Reducing statistical variation through understanding variable combinations.

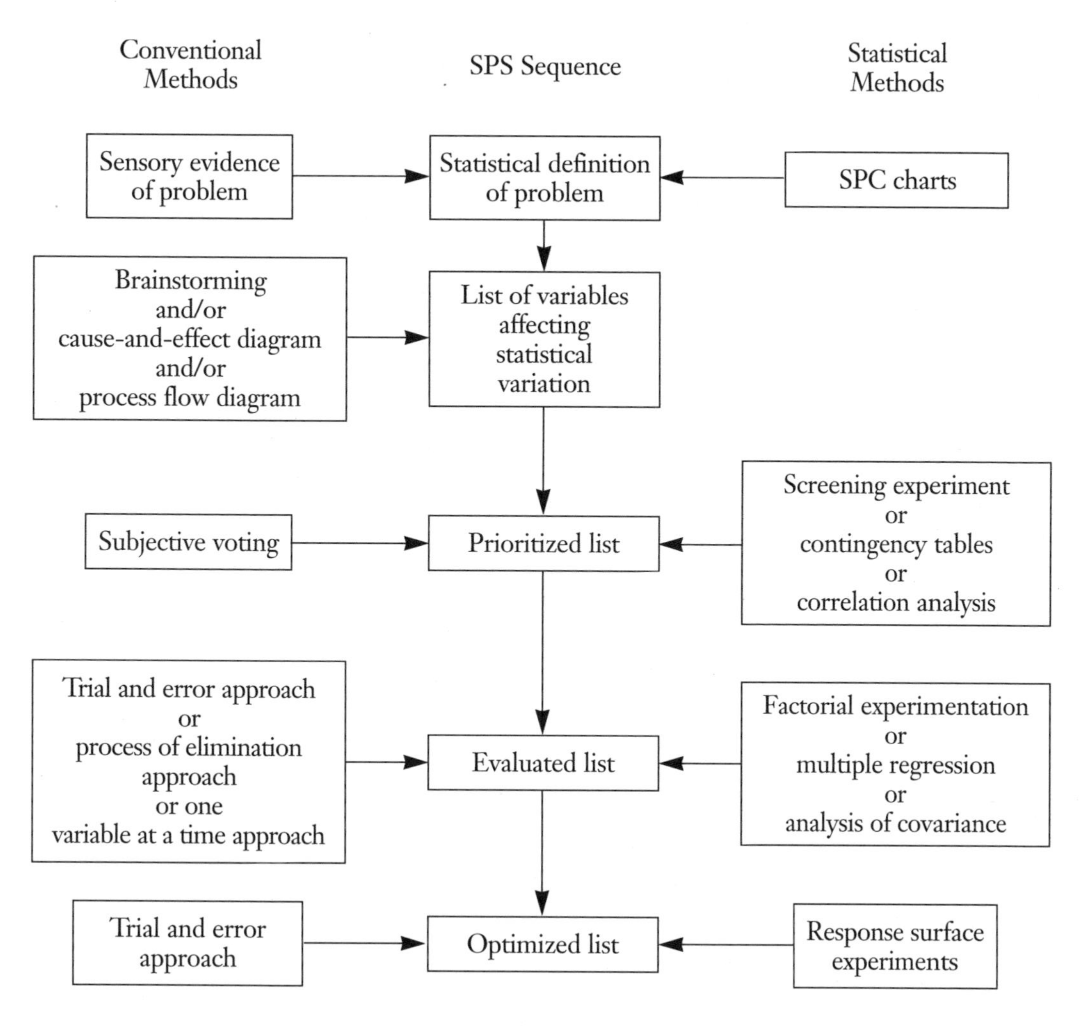

b. SPS sequence showing integration of conventional and statistical methods.

Figure 19.1 Comprehensive Depiction of All the Statistical Methods Available to Reduce Process Variation

common pattern called the normal distribution. For example, intelligence quotients follow this pattern as do the heights of males or females. If a small sequential sample of the process output is measured, it will almost always display this normal distribution pattern also.

Distribution. This term describes the pattern of the measured process output. For example, Figure 19.2a show how pieces from a process may vary. When more samples are taken a pattern appears called a distribution (Figure 19.2b). The most common is a normal distribution represented by the symmetrical curve of the line shown to the extreme right in Figure 19.2b. This distribution has some useful characteristics that will be explained later. The next set of curves shows that distributions can differ and still be normal, as in Figure 19.2c. The fourth set, shown in Figure 19.2d, represents a series of sample pictures, over time, that represent a stable process. It is in statistical control. Pictures taken of an unstable process are shown in Figure 19.2e.

Control Charts. Control charts use the same picture data in a different format. If four or five samples are taken periodically and sequentially, and the average of the measurements is plotted with respect to time, those points represent a normal distribution with the average representing the sample center (mean). The result is a run chart, as in Figure 19.3. A run chart can show trends but doesn't indicate if the process is operating at its best (in statistical control). Therefore, it doesn't predict what future output will be. Control charts provide that additional information.

Figure 19.4 shows the key elements of a control chart. All plotted data are calculated (not directly measured). The plotted data indicate that a process is in statistical control. This means that there is only a 0.27 percent chance that the process will produce outside the control limits.

Construction. The following simplified procedure illustrates the relatively straightforward nature of constructing a common X bar ($\bar{X}$ and R) chart. (Other types are discussed in subsequent paragraphs.)

1. Calculate the average of the sample plotted averages. This is the process operating center ($\bar{\bar{X}}$).
2. Calculate the process control limits using at least 25 consecutive plotted points and draw them. These are also referred to as the plus or minus three sigma ($\pm 3\sigma$) limits. The formulas for calculating control limits for all the common control charts are shown in Figure 19.5.
3. Test the chart for statistical control by using the tests described in Figure 19.6. These tests reflect the fact that just because all points are within control limits does not mean the process is in control. If not in control, the special causes must be removed. The seven QC tools, described in Chapter 18, should be used for this purpose.

a. Pieces vary from each other.

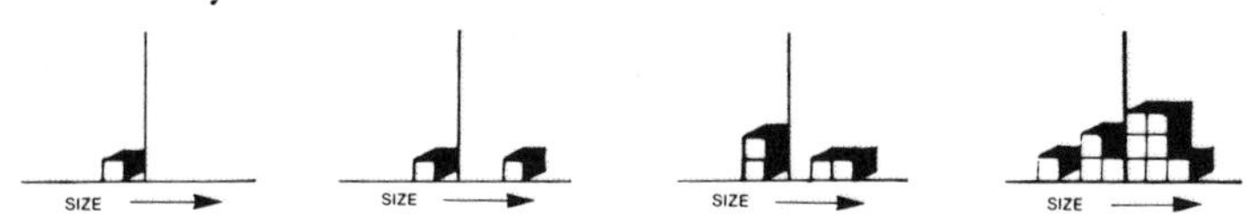

b. But they form a pattern that, if stable, is called a distribution.

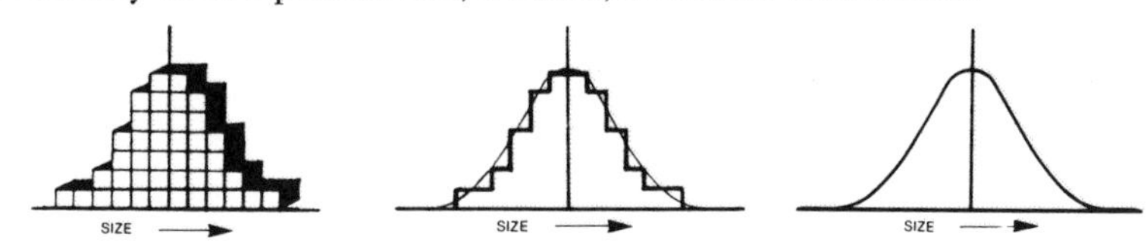

c. Distributions can differ in location, spread, or shape, or any combination of these.

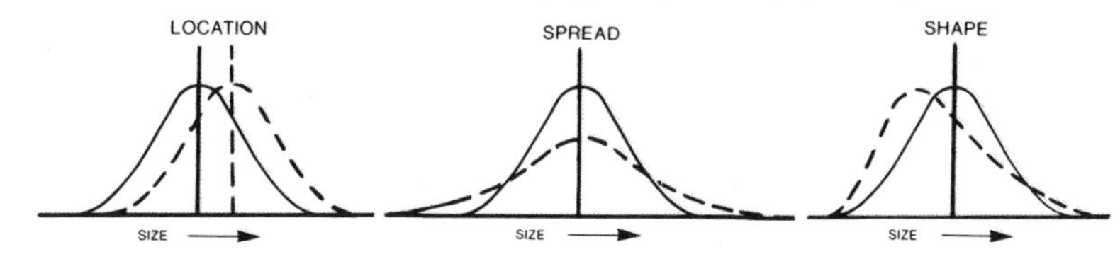

d. If only common causes of variation are present, the output of a process forms a distribution that is stable over time and is predictable.

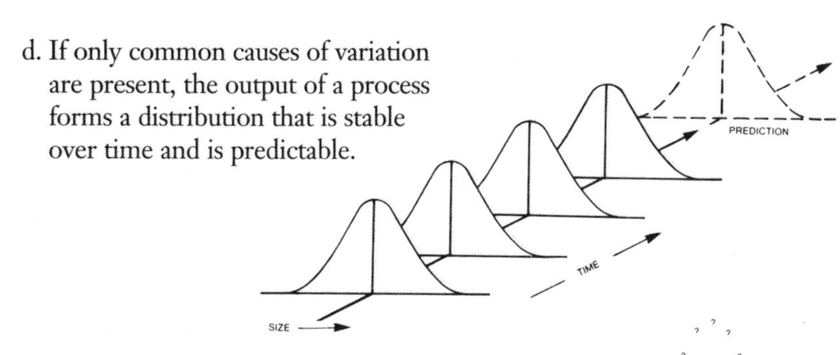

e. If special causes of variation are present, the process output is not stable over time and is not predictable.

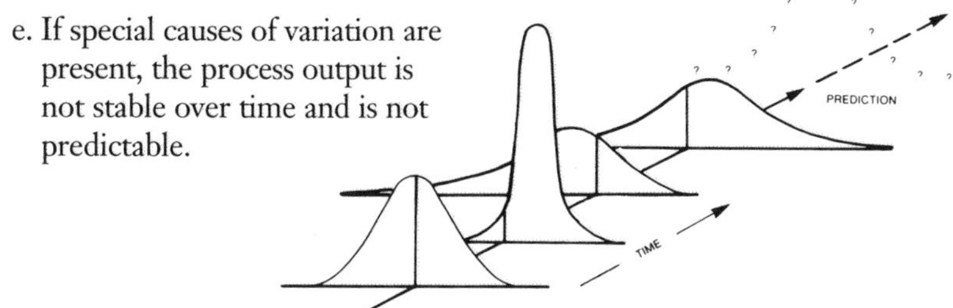

Reprinted with permission of Ford Motor Company.

Figure 19.2 Variation—Common and Special Causes

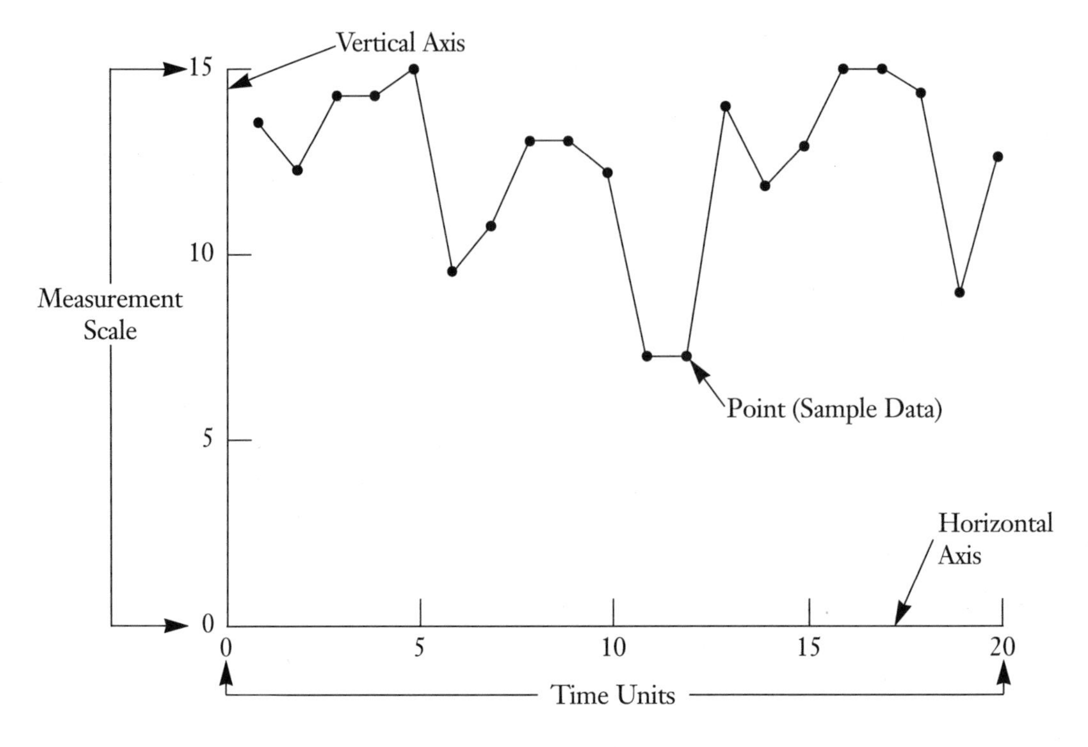

Figure 19.3 Run Chart Example

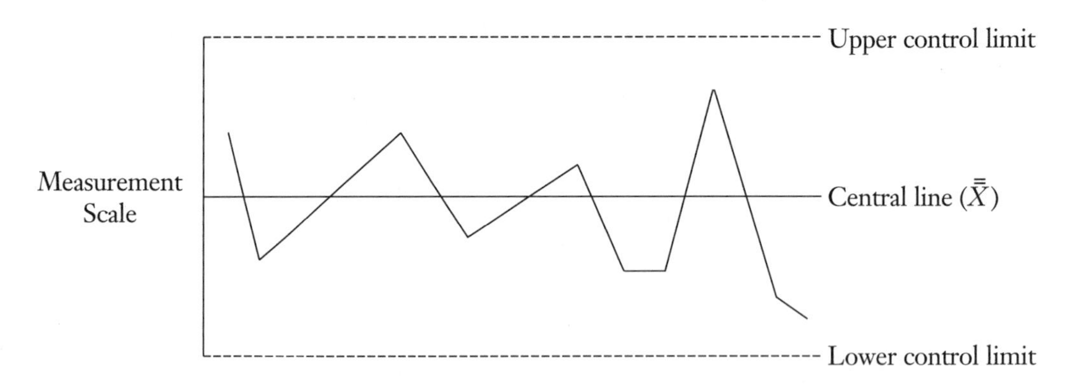

Measured scale—information on some identified process output or characteristic

Control lines

- Upper control limit (UCL) is the highest value a process should produce
- Central line ($\bar{\bar{X}}$) is the average value of consecutive samples
- Lower control limit (LCL) is the lowest value a process should produce
- There is no relation between control limits and specification limits

Figure 19.4 Elements of a Control Chart

4. Recalculate the control limits, after removing the special (assignable) causes of variation, based on new samples.

The control chart is complete. The plotted points show the process variation. The control limits indicate what its performance variation limits should be.

Interpretation. In addition to the ideas presented in Chapter 7, the charts are interpreted as follows:

1. The process, when in control, will continue 99.73 percent of the time to produce within control limits.
2. The process capability is the spread between control limits (the $\pm 3\sigma$ limits as calculated by (Figure 19.6):

$$\hat{\sigma} = \frac{\text{Average Range } (\bar{R})}{d^2}$$

3. The cause should be investigated and corrected, if any sample average falls outside a control limit. Points will fall outside limits by chance alone only 3 times in 1,000.
4. The process capability must be determined be comparing its 3σ spread to the required tolerance spread, which is discussed later in this chapter. Improve the process if it is inadequate. This may require the use of higher order statistical tools, like DOE to remove or reduce common causes.
5. Continuous process variation reduction must be planned by identifying common causes and reducing them. This is the heart of TQM—to drive the process output toward the tolerance nominal. Improve its capability.

COMMON TYPES OF CONTROL CHARTS

Table 19.1 lists the types of control charts most commonly used. The nature of the process and measurement determines which is used.

The chart discussed beginning page 196 is known as an X bar chart ($\bar{X}$) because it is a chart of sample averages ($\bar{X}$).

A chart commonly used with the $\bar{X}$ is the range chart (R) as in Figure 19.6. The range (highest minus lowest) chart is a plot of the range for each sample with calculated control limits. The range chart is sensitive to shifts in process width. The problem doesn't appear as quickly on the $\bar{X}$ chart because of the effect of averaging averages.

The $\bar{X}$ and R charts form the basics of SPC. However, they can be used only when a characteristic, such as inches, pounds, volts, and so forth can be measured. Other charts, based on the $\bar{X}-R$, have been developed for other applications where a process is measured in terms of events or counts, such as defects per unit, errors per

Tables of constants for variables control charts

$\bar{X}$ and R Control Charts					$\bar{X}$ and S Control Charts				
n	A_2	D_3	D_4	d_2	n	A_3	B_3	B_4	C_4
2	1.880	0	3.265	1.128	10	0.975	0.284	1.716	.9727
3	1.023	0	2.574	1.693	11	0.927	0.321	1.679	.9754
4	0.729	0	2.282	2.059	12	0.886	0.354	1.646	.9776
5	0.577	0	2.114	2.326	13	0.850	0.382	1.618	.9794
6	0.483	0	2.004	2.534	14	0.817	0.406	1.594	.9810
7	0.419	0.076	1.924	2.704	15	0.789	0.428	1.572	.9823
8	0.373	0.136	1.864	2.847	16	0.763	0.448	1.552	.9835
9	0.337	0.184	1.816	2.970	17	0.739	0.466	1.534	.9845
10	0.308	0.223	1.777	3.078	18	0.718	0.482	1.518	.9854
11	0.285	0.256	1.744	3.173	19	0.698	0.497	1.503	.9662
12	0.266	0.283	1.717	3.258	20	0.680	0.510	1.490	.9869
					21	0.663	0.523	1.477	.9876
					22	0.647	0.534	1.466	.9882
					23	0.633	0.545	1.455	.9887
					24	0.619	0.555	1.445	.9892
					25	0.606	0.565	1.435	.9896

Tests for Special Causes

1. These tests are applicable to $\bar{X}$ charts and to individuals (X) charts. A normal distribution is assumed. Tests 1, 2, 5, and 6 are to be applied to the upper and lower halves of the chart separately. Tests 3 and 4 are to be applied to the whole chart.
2. The upper control limit and the lower control limit are set at 3σ above the center line and 3σ below the center line. For the purpose of applying the tests, the control chart is equally divided into six zones, each zone being 1σ wide. The upper half of the chart is referred to as A (outer third), B (middle third), and C (inner third). The lower half is taken as the mirror image.
3. The presence of a cross indicates that the process is not in statistical control. It means that the point is the last one of a sequence of points (a single point in Test 1) that is very unlikely to occur if the process is in statistical control.
4. Although this can be taken as a basic set of tests, analysts should be alert to any patterns of points that might indicate the influence of special causes in their process.

Figure 19.5 Formulae for Calculating Upper and Lower Control Limits for All Common Control Charts and Test Patterns for Analyzing Control Charts for Existence of Special Causes.

(continued on following page)

Formulae for upper and lower control limits

Type of data	Control chart	Sample size n	What is to be controlled	Control lines: Central line	Control lines: Control limits	Process standard deviation
Variables	$\bar{X} - R$ control chart	Small normally < 10 usually 3 or 5	$\bar{X}$ – Variation of sample means	$\bar{\bar{X}}$	$UCL_X = \bar{\bar{X}} + A_2\bar{R}$ $LCL_X = \bar{\bar{X}} - A_2\bar{R}$	$\hat{\sigma} = \bar{R}/d_2$
			R – Variation of sample ranges	$\bar{R}$	$UCL_R = D_4\bar{R}$ $LCL_R = D_3\bar{R}$	
	$\bar{X} - S$ control chart	Large usually > 10	$\bar{X}$ – Variation of sample means	$\bar{\bar{X}}$	$UCL_X = \bar{\bar{X}} + A_3\bar{S}$ $LCL_X = \bar{\bar{X}} - A_3\bar{S}$	$\hat{\sigma} = \bar{S}/c_4$
			S – Variation of sample standard deviation	$\bar{S}$	$UCL_S = B_4\bar{S}$ $LCL_S = B_3\bar{S}$	
	X control chart (individuals with moving range)	1 When rational subgroups are impossible	X – Variation of individuals	$\bar{X}$	$UCL_X = \bar{X} + 3\,\bar{R}/d_2$ $LCL_X = \bar{X} - 3\,\bar{R}/d_2$	$\hat{\sigma} = \bar{R}/d_2$
			R – Variation between individuals	$\bar{R}$	$UCL_R = D_4\bar{R}$ $LCL_R = D_3\bar{R}$	
Attribute	p control chart	Large changeable	p: Fraction defective	$\bar{p}$	$UCL_p = \bar{p} + 3\sqrt{\bar{p}(1-\bar{p})/n}$ $LCL_p = \bar{p} - 3\sqrt{\bar{p}(1-\bar{p})/n}$	$\sqrt{\frac{\bar{p}(1-\bar{p})}{n}}$
	np control chart	Large constant	np: Number of defects	$n\bar{p}$	$UCL_{np} = n\bar{p} + 3\sqrt{n\bar{p}(1-\bar{p})}$ $LCL_{np} = n\bar{p} - 3\sqrt{n\bar{p}(1-\bar{p})}$	$\sqrt{n\bar{p}(1-\bar{p})}$
	c control chart	Constant unit	c: Number of defects per unit	$\bar{c}$	$UCL_c = \bar{c} + 3\sqrt{\bar{c}}$ $LCL_c = \bar{c} - 3\sqrt{\bar{c}}$	$\sqrt{\bar{c}}$
	u control chart	Changeable unit	$u = \frac{c}{n}$: Average defects per unit	$\bar{u}$	$UCL_u = \bar{u} + 3\sqrt{\bar{u}/n}$ $LCL_u = \bar{u} - 3\sqrt{\bar{u}/n}$	$\sqrt{\bar{u}/n}$

Test 1
One point beyond Zone A

Test 2
Eight points in a row in Zone C or beyond

Test 3
Six points in a row steadily increasing or decreasing

Test 4
Fourteen points in a row alternating up and down

Test 5
Two out of 3 points in a row in Zone A or beyond

Test 6
Four out of 5 points in a row in Zone B or beyond

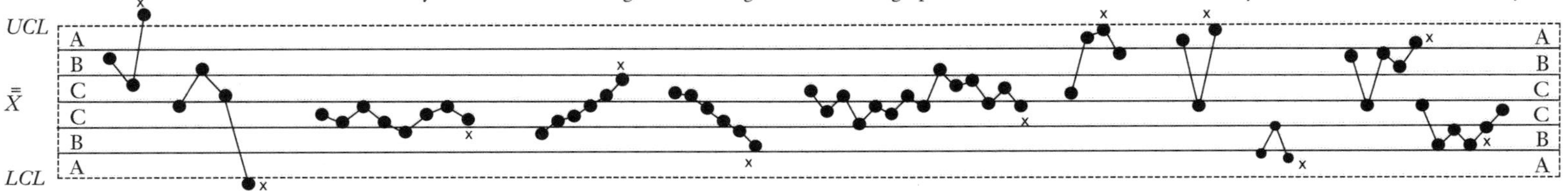

UCL   A B C C B A $\bar{\bar{X}}$ LCL

Table 19.1 Types of Control Charts

$\bar{X}$ (X bar)	Shows average outputs of a process
R	Shows the uniformity of a process
pn	Shows the number of defective products for sample subgroups of equal sizes
p	Shows the fraction of defective products for samples of unequal sizes
c	Shows the average number of defects within each product for sample subgroups of equal sizes
u	Shows the average number of defects within each product for sample subgroups of unequal sizes

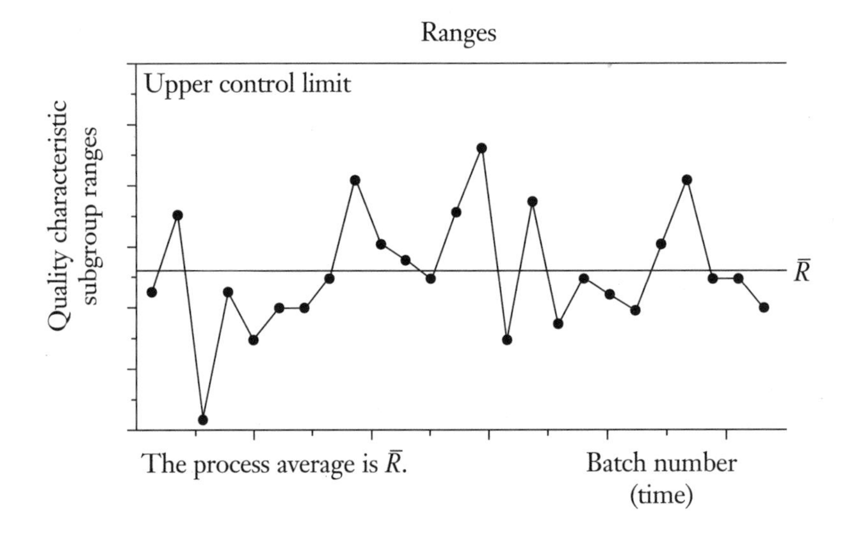

Figure 19.6 Control Chart for a Sample Measurement Range

purchase order, sales per advertising dollar, and so on. They are all evaluated for statistical control the same as the $\bar{X}$ chart using the tests shown in Figure 19.5.

An $\bar{X}$ standard deviation (s) chart combination is sometimes used for large volume processes and large sample sizes.

c *Chart.* This chart (Figure 19.7) shows defects/errors per lot. Each defect (not item) is counted per group, lot, area, and so on. The c chart is used when evaluating items from a process that may have come from different sources. Examples include forms completed by different organizations or a manufactured item after several processes.

u *Chart.* A variation of the *c* chart is the *u* chart. It depicts the number of errors or defects per item from samples that can vary in size (but should be kept to within 25 percent of the average sample size). The process average is $\bar{u}$. The process capability is $\bar{u}$ when in control. Limits are calculated as shown in Figure 19.8.

p *Chart.* This chart (Figure 19.9) depicts the *proportion* (p) of nonconforming items in a sample of items.

pn *Chart.* This chart (Figure 19.10) is similar to the *p* chart except that it measures the *number* of defective items in the sample.

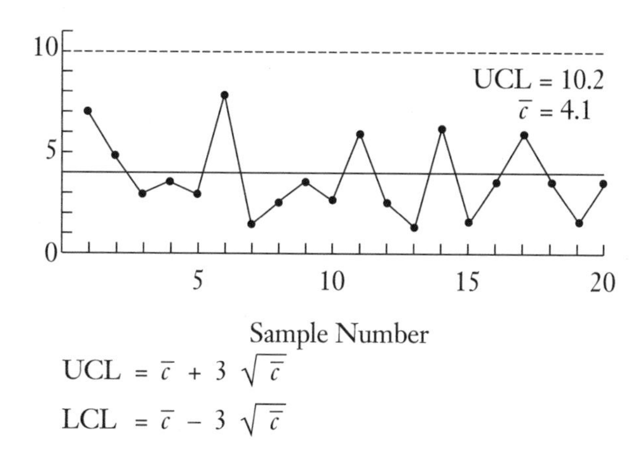

$$UCL = \bar{c} + 3\sqrt{\bar{c}}$$

$$LCL = \bar{c} - 3\sqrt{\bar{c}}$$

Figure 19.7 **c *Control Chart***

- As the subgroup size varies, upper control limits (UCL) and lower control limits (LCL) vary:

$$UCL = \bar{u} + \frac{3\sqrt{\bar{u}}}{\sqrt{n}}$$

$$LCL = \bar{u} - \frac{3\sqrt{\bar{u}}}{\sqrt{n}}$$

- $\bar{u}$ is the central line and equal to:

$$\frac{\text{Total defects}}{\text{Total units}}$$

Figure 19.8 **u *Control Charts***

p Control chart reflow solder machine

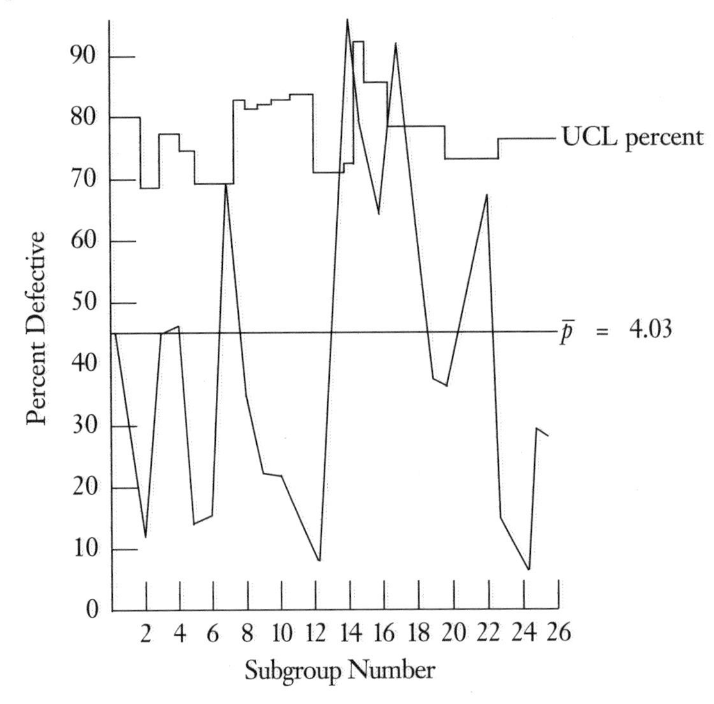

Figure 19.9 p Control Charts

Computations

Control limits are based on the binomial distribution (k = number of subgroups)

Central line:

$$\bar{p}n = \frac{\Sigma pn}{k}$$

$$UCL = \bar{p}n + 3\sqrt{\bar{p}n(1-\bar{p})}$$

$$\text{where } \bar{p} = \frac{\Sigma pn}{\Sigma n}$$

$$LCL = \bar{p}n - 3\sqrt{\bar{p}n(1-\bar{p})}$$

Figure 19.10 pn Control Charts

Figure 19.11 is a diagram to aid in the selection of the correct control chart based on the nature of the data and samples.

CHARTS FOR LOW-VOLUME SHORT RUNS

Many processes operate at a low output volume. In addition, the use of JIT production systems results in smaller lot sizes and more frequent runs. This means more setups, different parts, and different specifications moving through the same operation.

The lot size requirements for using the control charts previously described (requiring 4 or 5 items in 25 or more continuous samples before control limits can be calculated) preclude their application to low-volume, short-run manufacturing. However, there are simple techniques to provide control charts by either operation (with different part numbers) or a small lot of the same part through different operations. They provide a picture of the process variation. Figure 19.12 illustrates an $\bar{X}$ and R chart for the two different parts being cut on the same machine.[12] Control limits are calculated as shown in Table 19.2.

The coded $\bar{X}$ value is derived by using the deviation from the specification nominal value of the part being processed. The nominal (target) value becomes the zero point on the $\bar{X}$ chart. The sample size between parts is kept constant. The control limits are the 3σ limits. The charts are interpreted the same as any control chart.

Another form of short run $\bar{X}$ and R control charts, developed by D. R. Bothe, allows plotting multiple part numbers and different part characteristics on the same chart.[13] Figure 19.13 shows how material is followed through different operations with this chart. Examples of the $\bar{X}$ and R charts of this type are shown in Figures 19.14 and 19.15. The short run control limits of both $\bar{X}$ and R charts are independent of both $\bar{X}$ and R. If a constant subgroup size is maintained, only one chart is needed to monitor all part numbers run through an operation.

Multivariate Charts. Another type of chart used to gain insight into the nature of process variations is called the multivariate chart, developed by Dorian Shainan. It identifies the types of variation. Figure 19.16 illustrates how much is positioned in the manufacturing cycle and with respect to consecutive time periods. Vertical lines show variations within a piece or sample. Averages are connected to show the variation of those averages. The example shows little variation between averages (means) but a large variation within pieces. The time variation shows little variation within pieces and between means, but a large variation from batch to batch or period to period, or both. This information is useful in eliminating variables that could be candidates for further analysis or in planning designed experiments. In using this tool, it is important to collect data sequentially, collect it all, and use only current data.

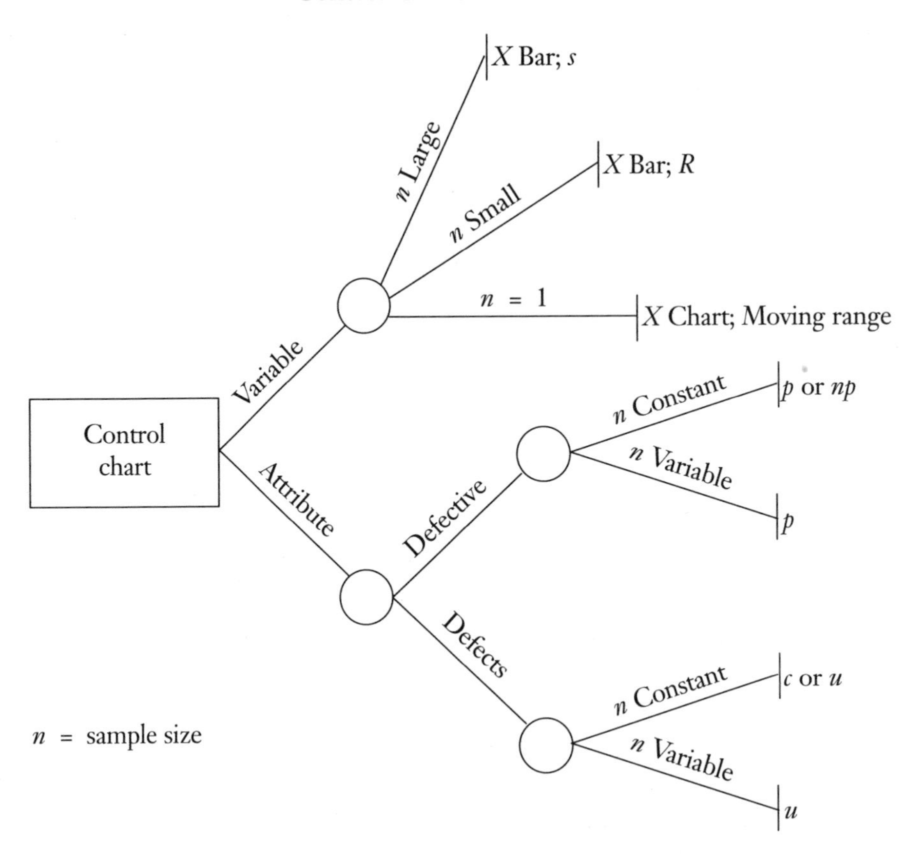

Figure 19.11 Factors in the Decision Process to Select the Appropriate Control Chart

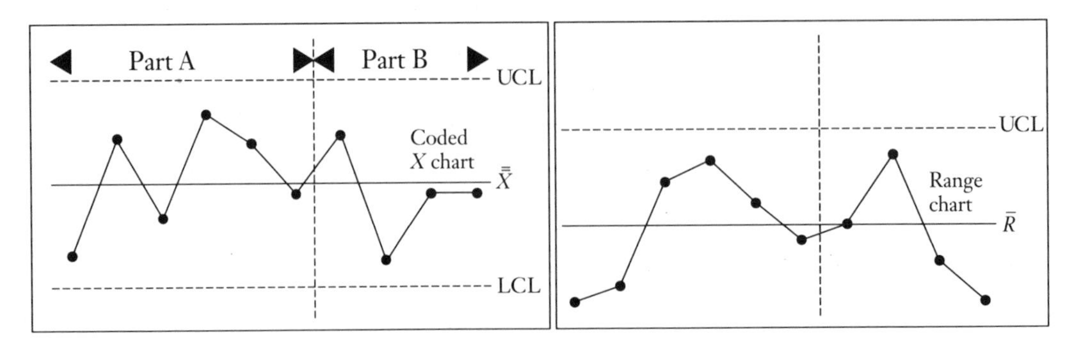

Figure 19.12 The Target **X** *Bar and* **R** *Chart with Control Limits*

Table 19.2 Formula to Calculate Control Limits for Low-Volume Short-Run Processes

$D_3 = 0$ for $n = 1$ to 5

n	D_4	A_2	d_2
1	3.27	2.66	1.13
2	3.27	1.86	1.13
3	2.57	1.02	1.69
4	2.28	0.73	2.05
5	2.11	0.58	2.33

Chart	Control Limits	Center Lines	Plot Point	Sample Size
$\bar{X}$	$UCL = \bar{\bar{X}} + A_2\bar{R}$ $LCL = \bar{\bar{X}} - A_2\bar{R}$	$\bar{\bar{X}} = \frac{\Sigma \text{ coded } \bar{X}}{k}$	Coded $\bar{X}$ = $\bar{X}$ – target value	3 to 5 and constant
R	$UCL = D_4\bar{R}$ $LCL = D_3\bar{R}$	$\bar{R} = \frac{\Sigma R}{k}$	R	

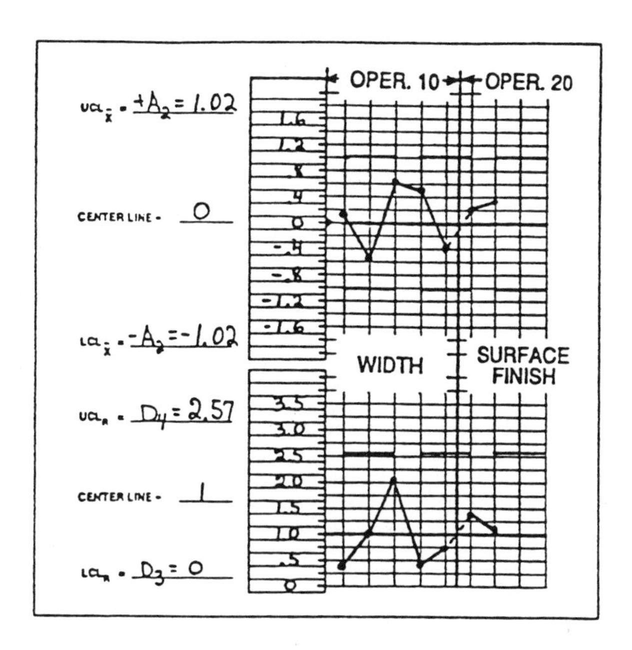

Since the plot points of a short run chart are dimensionless numbers, one chart can follow an order for a part number through a job shop with all the data from different operations plotted on the same chart.

Figure 19.13 Example of Short-Run Control Charts Plotting Multiple Part Numbers and Different Part Characteristics on the Same Chart

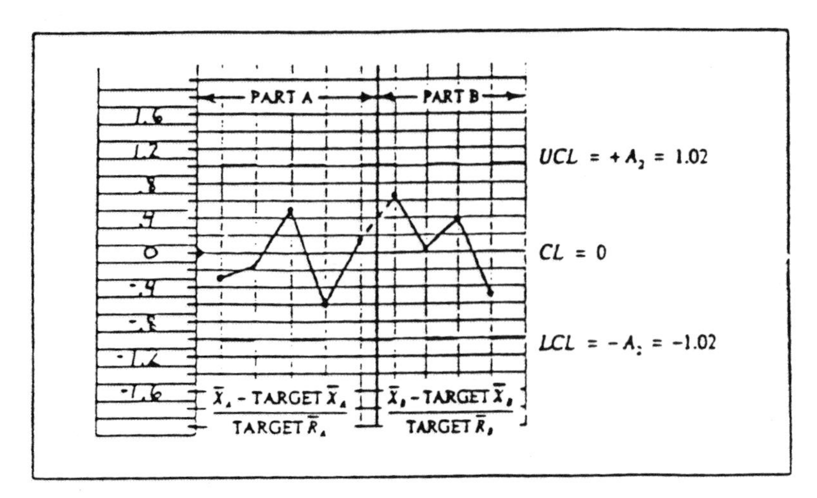

Figure 19.14 The Short-Run $\bar{X}$ *Chart for* n = 3

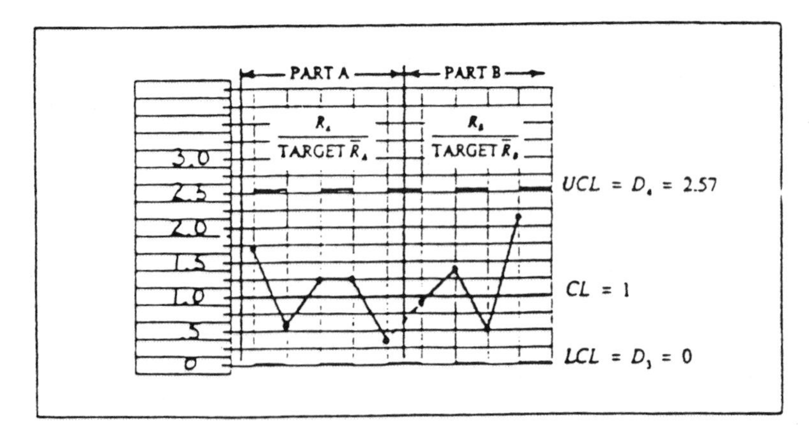

Figure 19.15 The Short-Run Range Chart Where the Ratio R/*Target* $\bar{R}$ *is Plotted*

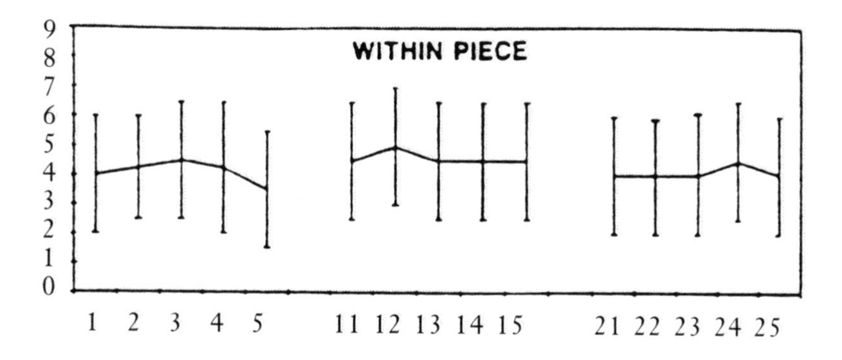

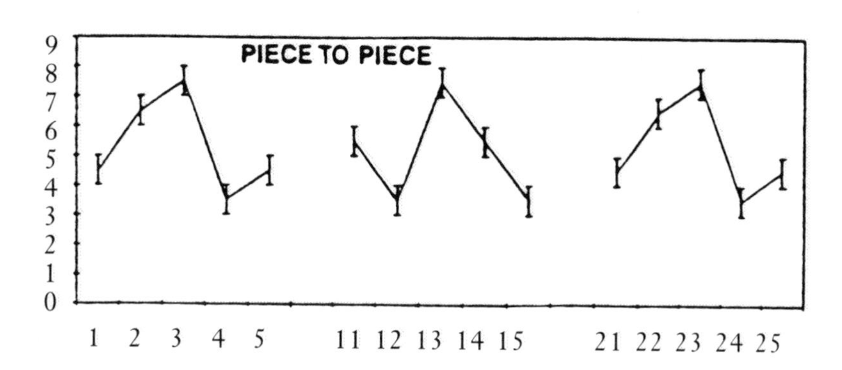

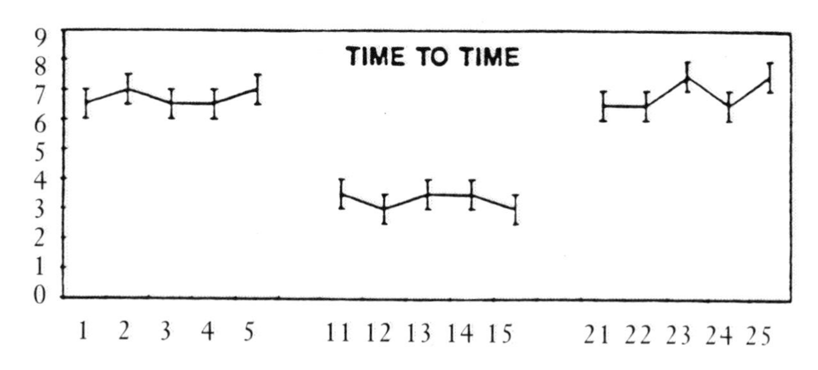

Figure 19.16 Types of Variation

Ratio Control Charts. A control chart for the ratio of two variables is particularly useful in nonmanufacturing (service and support) processes. Figure 19.17 shows its application in the U.S. Department of Labor Unemployment Insurance (UI) Quality Control (QC) program.[14] The objective is to estimate the rate and to identify the causes of errors in the payment of UI benefits. The figure shows the ratios of dollars of UI benefits overpaid to the total UI benefits paid. The chart shows the existence of special causes when the overpayment ratios exceed upper and lower limits. The author of the referenced article suggests other applications for the ratio estimates to include:

- The ratio of charges underbilled, or overbilled, to total billings in accounts receivable.
- The ratio of employee's time spent correcting errors or reworking defects to productive work time.
- The financial ratio, such as savings to disposable income, price to earnings, or debt to equity.

Many of these and other ratios are used by business analysts and managers but they are not treated as data from a process in which expected variation could be calculated and deviations used for rational decision making.

In Figure 19.18, the central line is the ratio (R) computed from all samples selected in consecutive weeks.

$$R = \frac{\text{Total Dollar Errors } (y)}{\text{Total Dollars Paid } (x)}$$

$$\text{UCL} = R + 3\sqrt{v}$$

$$\text{LCL} = R - 3\sqrt{v}$$

$$\text{where: } v = \frac{1}{x^2}\left[\frac{N^2}{N}(n-1)\right]\left[(y - xR)^2\right]$$

Where:

n = number of payment weeks

N = total number of payments in period

FACTORS IN SUCCESSFUL SPC

SPC can't be installed; it's a part of process management. It must be designed to fit the process, people, and organization. Management must understand the concepts, value, and limitations of SPC. A successful SPC program has the following elements:

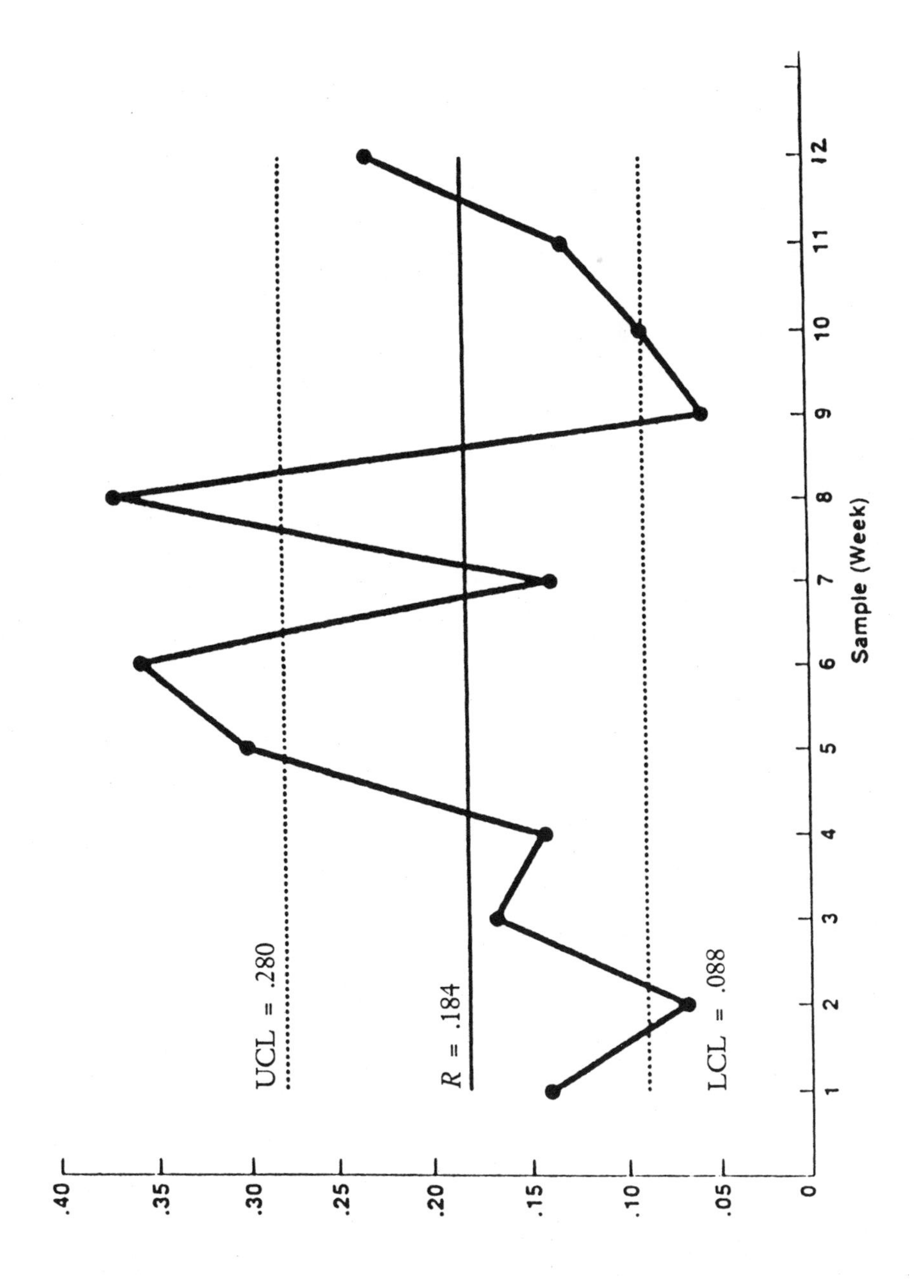

Figure 19.17 Ratio Control Chart for UI Quality Control Data

- Management support of corrective actions.
- Participants with proper training both in the classroom and, more important, on the job.

However, SPC will not solve all production problems. The following factors must be considered:

- SPC has valuable application in administrative (office) processes. This application definitely requires training. This work force is not accustomed to process concepts or measurement; it may be the most difficult activity in which to create a culture change.
- Process operators must be involved in the application, development, implementation, and interpretation of results, as well as corrective action.
- Success involves some "unlearning." People must learn to leave a process alone, not to tamper, and to respond to data.
- Don't have the quality organization install and operate the SPC program. Process operators will not take ownership or responsibility for performance.
- Don't try to chart all product characteristics. Select only those that are critical. Review results periodically to eliminate useless data collection.
- Organizations need to promulgate clear instructions as to what to do when an out-of-control process is recognized.
- Process improvement teams are typically multifunctional. It may be difficult to schedule meetings. Management must show that improvement team meetings have a high priority.
- Senior management must regularly review the SPC program and its results. This is of critical value to the entire company.

PROCESS CAPABILITY

A major focus in TQM is on continuous process improvement, that is, reducing variation. As previously discussed, variation can be depicted using histograms or control charts, a concept already referred to and commonly encountered in process capability. Thus, the variation exhibited by a process with only common causes present—in other words, in statistical control, is the best distribution that can be achieved under a given set of conditions. It is only under these conditions that measuring capability has any meaning.

Determining process capability is the action of studying the causes of variation, separating them into common and special causes and eliminating the latter. Capability cannot be improved until this is done.

After the capability is known the process variables (causes) must be identified and reduced, that is, methods changes, new equipment, different control levels, and so on, if inherent variation is to be improved. The seven QC tools and DOE are the TQM tools to achieve reduced process variation.

There is a difference between having a capable process and being in statistical control and capable. This is illustrated in Figure 19.18 and Figure 19.19. Mathematically, capability is defined as the six standard deviation (6σ) spread calculated from a set of sample measurements. A process capability must be calculated for each characteristic of interest that the process is affecting.

Process capability in administrative applications (processes) is essentially the same concept: eliminating defects and errors. Process variation can be measured and control established (control charts), and that is its capability. It will improve only if the factors causing errors (complexity, poor training, and so on) are removed. The seven QC tools are particularly effective in this application.

PROCESS CAPABILITY RATIO

Capability can be expressed in terms of a number that is a ratio of the width of the engineering tolerance to the capability:

$$C_p = \frac{\text{Engineering Tolerance}}{\text{Process Variation } (6\sigma)}$$

$$C_p = \frac{\text{Upper Limit} - \text{Lower Limit}}{6\sigma}$$

Process variation held to within the engineering tolerance provides a capable process. The terminology used is that, if the ratio is 1.0, it has a 3σ capability. If the ratio is 2.0, it has a 6σ capability. Many companies are adopting a 6σ capability as their long-range improvement goal. The leading industries in Japan have an average 4σ capability and are still improving.

PROCESS CAPABILITY INDEX

The process capability (C_p) is calculated assuming the process is centered between the upper and lower tolerance limits. It measures the *potential* capability. Another ratio, called the capability index (C_{pk}), takes into account the lack of centering of the process. This is a more useful measurement since processes rarely remain fixed at the center:

$$C_{pk} = C_p \, \underline{(1 - k)}$$

$$\text{where } k = \frac{\text{Tolerance Center} - \text{Process Average}}{\dfrac{\text{Tolerance Width}}{2}}$$

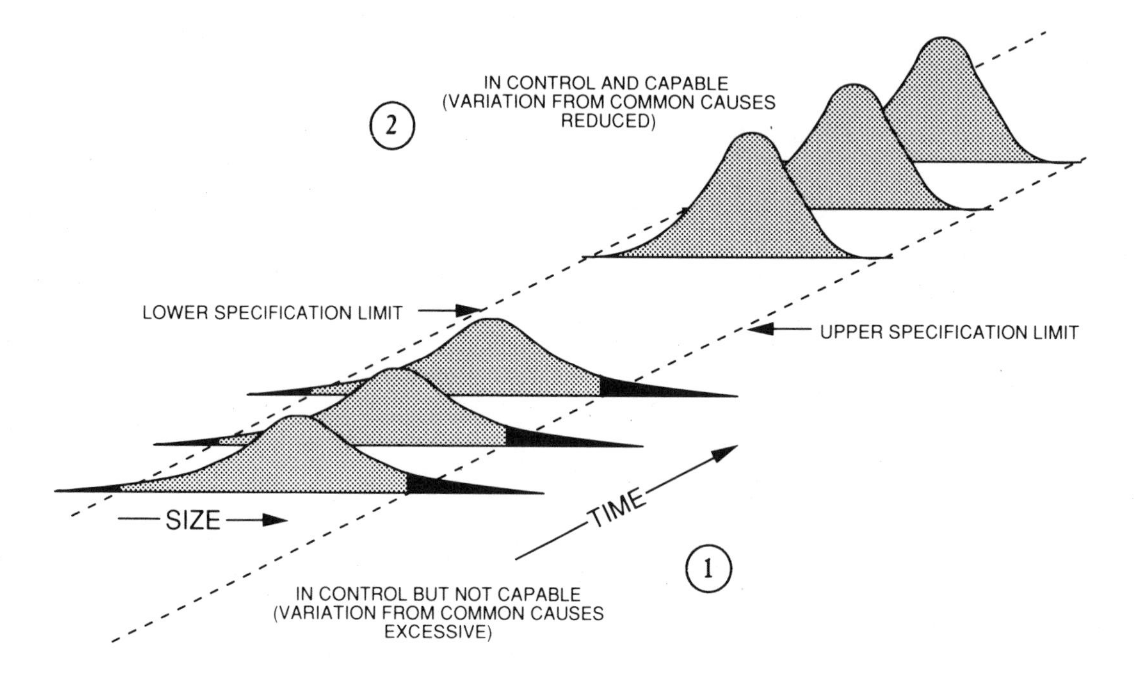

Both processes are in control. Process 1 is not capable of producing a product that is within limits. Some product (solid black) is defective. Process 2 is both in control and capable.

Figure 19.18 Difference Between Process Control and Process Capability

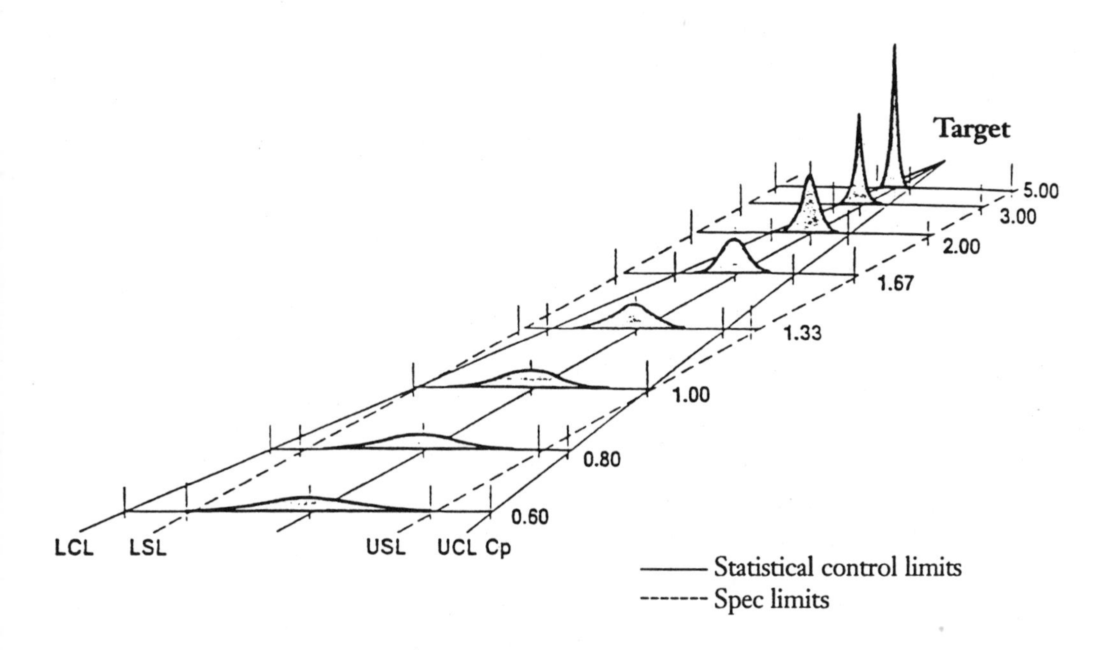

Continuous measurable improvement means reducing the variation of the process with respect to requirements (specification limits). The calculated indicator of improvement is the capability ratio (C_p).

Figure 19.19 Continuous Measurable Improvement

Estimates. The measurement data used for capability determination is typically based on a small sample. This can provide a useful indicator, but it is still an estimate. When making short-term capability studies to get a rough idea where the process is, it is recommended that instead of using the 6σ process range a more conservative estimate of 8σ (±4) should be used.[15]

CONTINUOUS IMPROVEMENT

Perhaps the most profound difference in TQM and other management philosophies is the concept of continuous improvement; improve process quality forever. Considering that "a process" refers to every activity in every organization (business and nonbusiness) it means mass change.

The value of continuous improvement can be illustrated using an industry process. Figure 19.20 represents any business process. It begins with a process that, when measured, is not capable of producing all parts to specification. The process is not in statistical control; there are special, correctable causes of variation at work (Figure 19.20a). Taking corrective action removes special causes and some of the variation (Figure 19.20b). Now, the inherent capability of the process is known. Next, in Figure 19.20c, action is taken to center the process on the specification center. There is no change in variation. It produces more good product with respect to the tolerance requirements. Then, the common causes (the inherent capability of the process) is improved. The result is shown in Figure 19.20d. Variation is reduced. However, any shift in the process would result in producing some defective product. So, further reductions of common causes are made (Figure 19.20e).

The products from this final process have higher quality and lower cost to the producer and customer.

In summary, the steps for continuous improvement are:

1. Measure the process. Develop a histogram.
2. Get the process in statistical control. Remove assignable (special) causes of variation.
3. Center the process operation, if necessary.
4. Use higher order statistical techniques to improve the process if the process is not capable (too much variation).
5. Continue to reduce variation, as long as economically feasible.

The continuous improvement concept is also shown in Figure 19.19. It can also be illustrated in terms of raising the capability index (Figure 19.21).

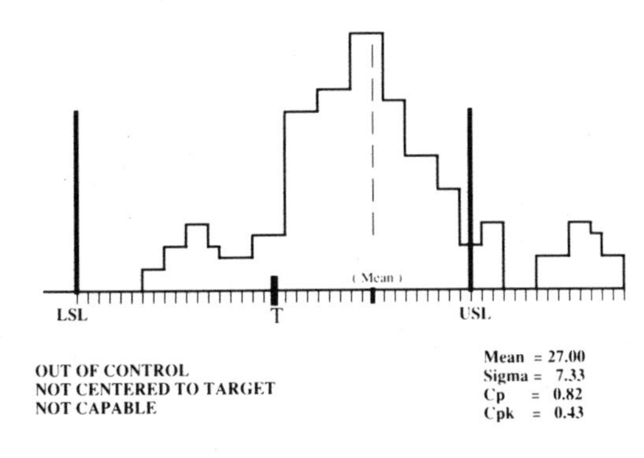

a. Initial distribution

T = Specification target
LSL = Lower specification limit
USL = Upper specification limit

The vertical scale is the frequency of occurrence of a sample measurement.

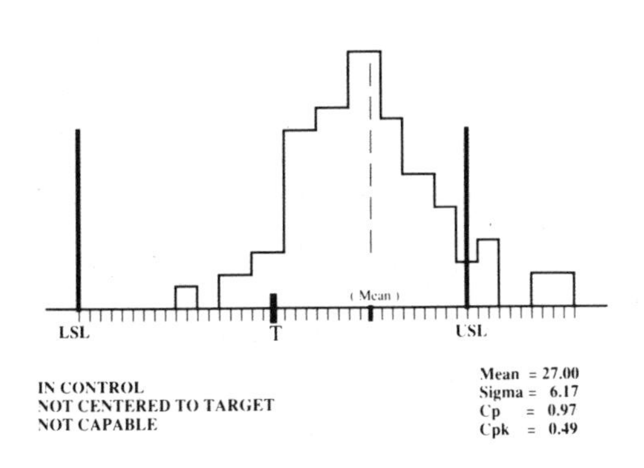

b. After removal of special cause

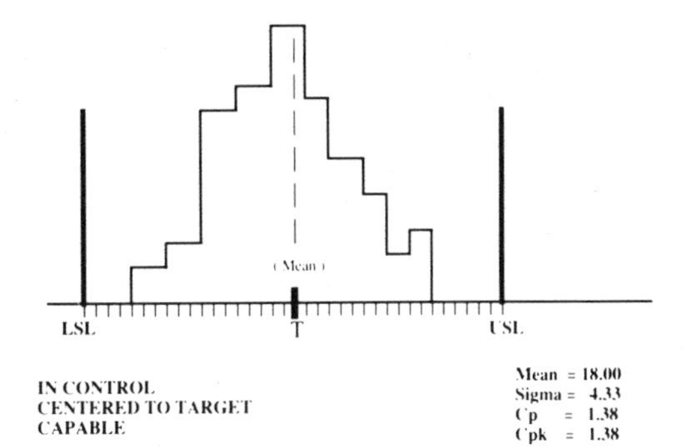

d. After reducing common cause

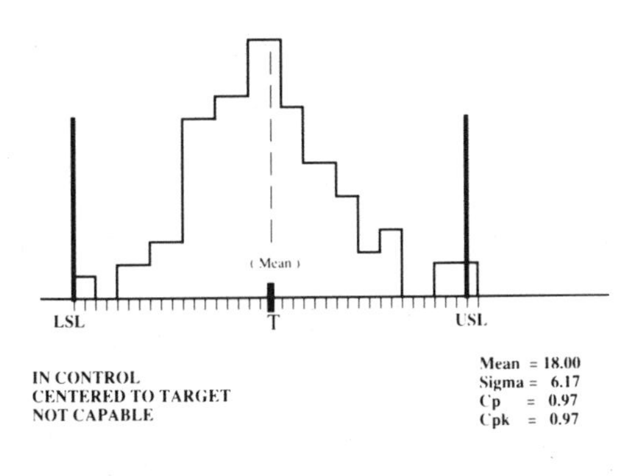

c. After centering to target

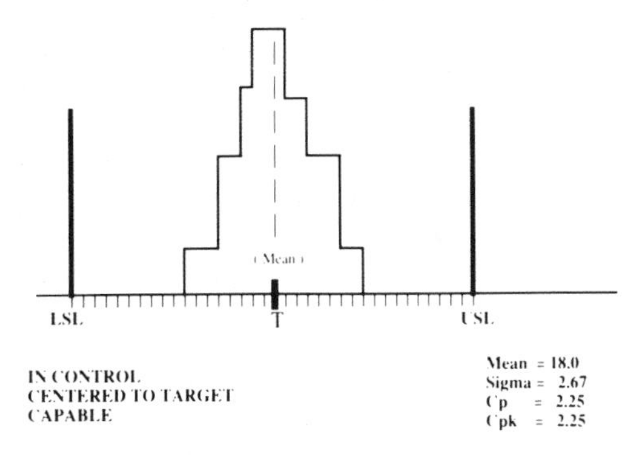

e. After further reduction of common cause

Figure 19.20 Reduction of Variations Around the Target Value

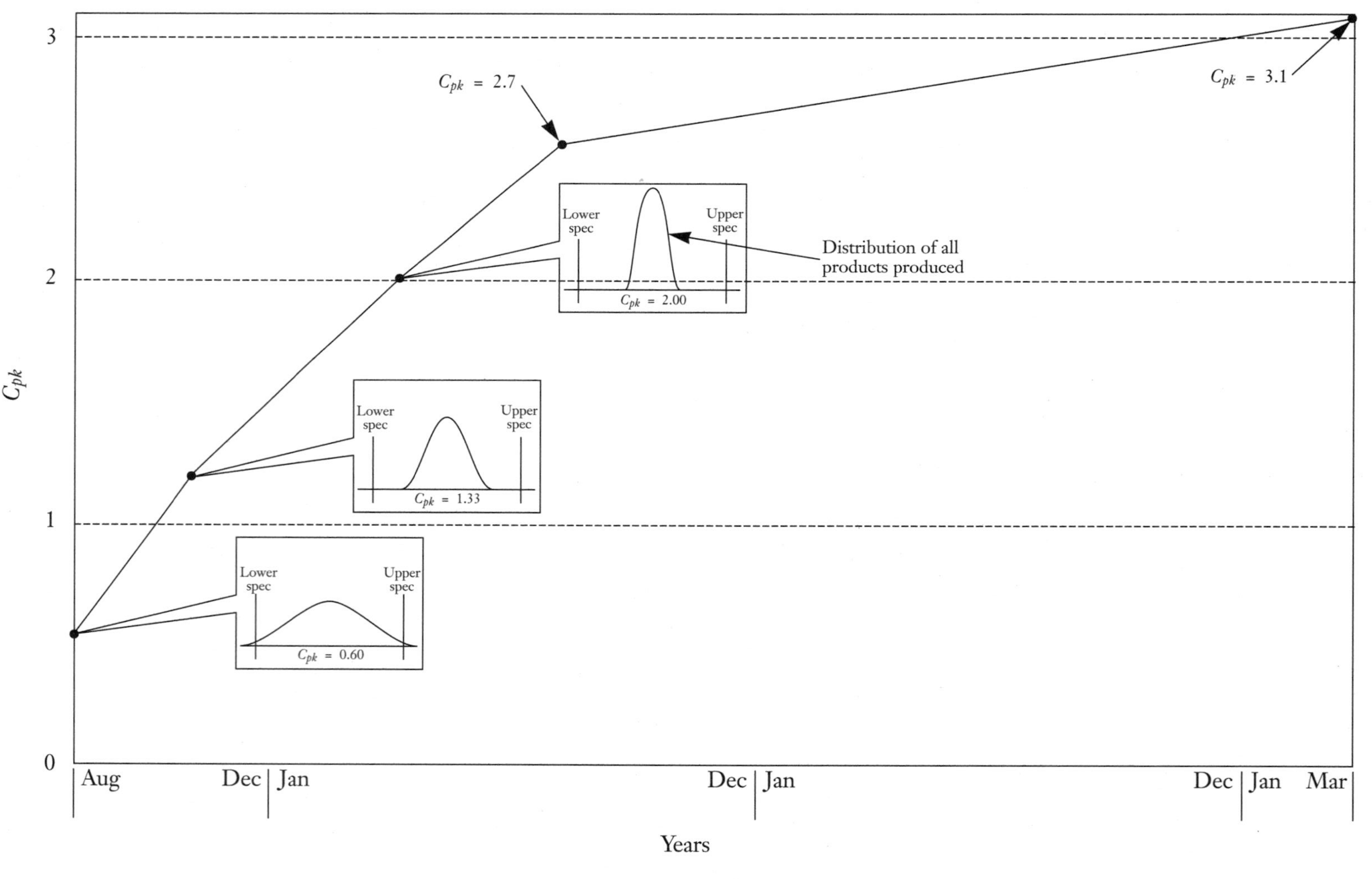

Figure 19.21 Typical* C_{pk} *Evolution

DESIGN AND IMPLEMENTATION

The preceding paragraphs describe the concepts and methodologies used in the adoption of SPC for process control and improvement. Figure 19.22 on page 220 describes a simple nine-step process to follow in SPC implementation. The last step is called advanced SPC. This is the challenging task of improving process capability beyond a C_p of 1.0. This is done primarily by using the techniques identified in Figure 19.1, or sometimes by process mechanization, automation, or technological breakthroughs.

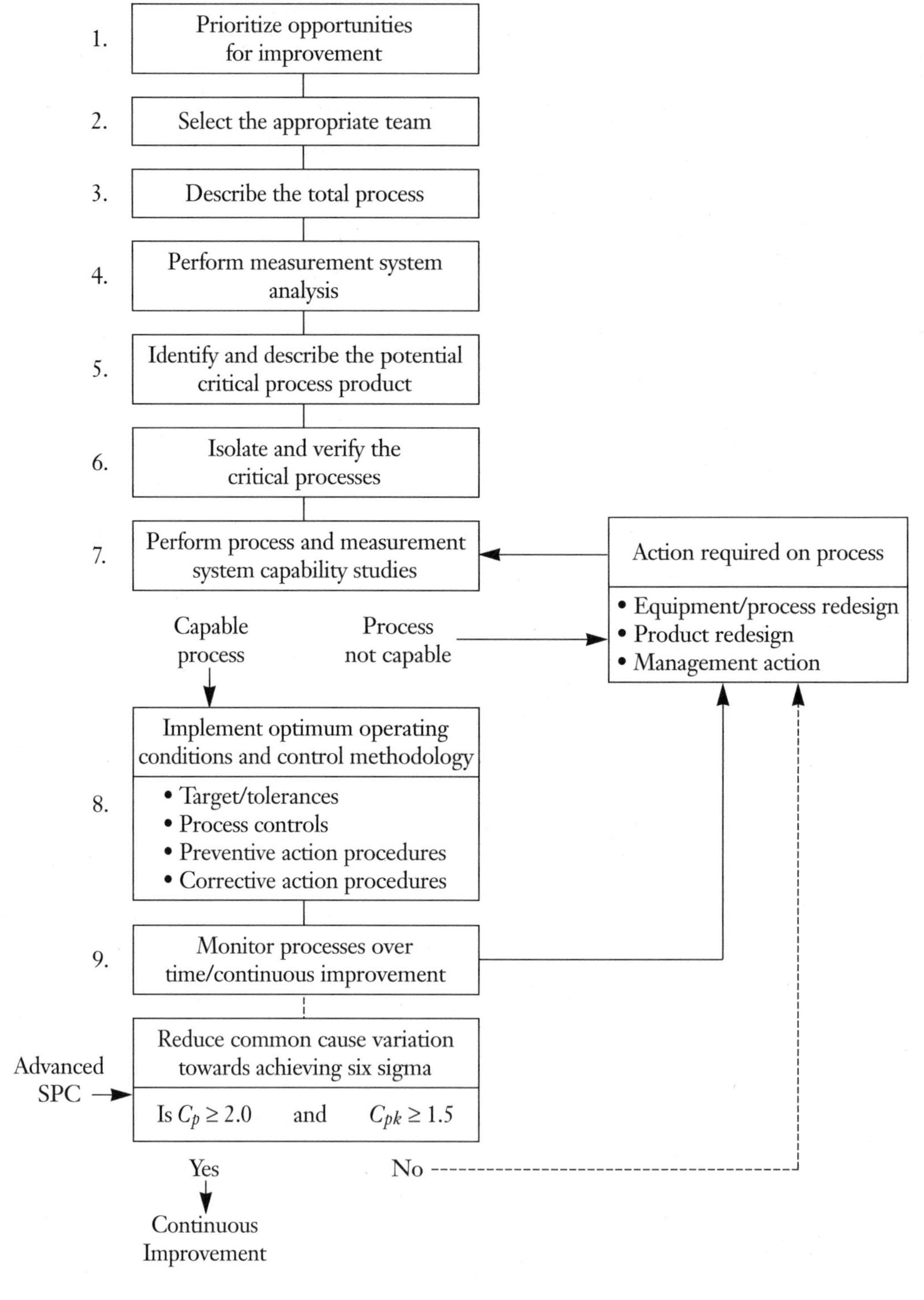

Figure 19.22 Product/Process Improvement Flow Diagram

Chapter 20

Design of Experiments

In the design of products and processes the common approach is to consider one characteristic, or factor, at a time and establish its value and tolerance. The basis for these decisions usually is the designer's knowledge and experience. Sometimes standard practices are involved. Engineers have been taught to use standard practices.

The results were acceptable until recently, when higher quality at lower cost became a competitive requirement. This required a new approach to establish target performance values and process operating levels more scientifically

A statistical technique that Fisher developed in England in the mid-1920s has been available but seldom used by industry. It's known as DOE. As the name implies, it is a structure to perform tests (experiments) that are specifically designed to provide information of product performance in realistic production and customer-use environments. One definition of DOE is: "The planned, structured, and organized observation of two or more process input (independent) variables (factors) and their effect on the output (dependent) variable(s) under study."

DOE provides such things as the product nominal characteristics and process variables settings that produce the best product performance, with minimum variation, while operating in and produced in those environments. The importance of these data cannot be overstated. Product characteristics (parameters) established from these test results provide the best product performance. The resulting process parameter settings provide the least product variation and the highest process yield. There is no other way to find these data. Figure 20.1 shows process variables. It identifies those variables that are typically controllable and those that are expensive

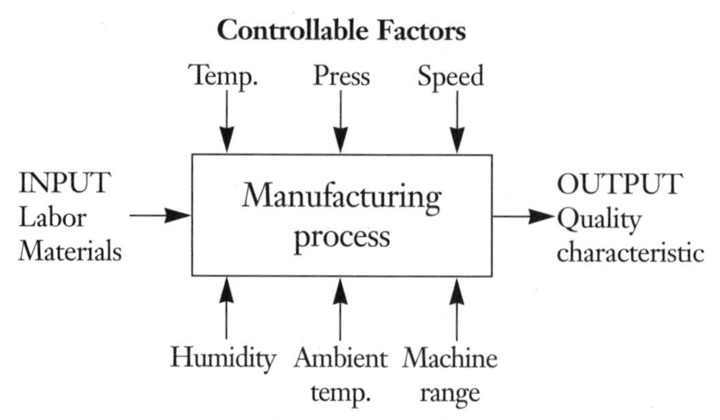

Expensive or Uncontrollable Factors

1. Which inputs affect the output parameters?
2. What is the relationship between the important inputs and the output parameters?
3. How can the output be controlled?

Figure 20.1 Identification of Controllable and Uncontrollable (Actually or Financially) Variables

to control. DOE provides the best settings for the controllables for the product to withstand the uncontrollables.

Compare this to the commonly used "one-variable-at-a-time" approach in which all variables are held constant, except one, and the effects are noted. This may provide useful data, but it is obviously unrealistic. A product is produced and used in a dynamic environment. The variables are constantly changing and these changes are often in unpredictable directions. The "one-variable-at-a-time" approach doesn't simulate this and misses what DOE discloses, that is, the effect of the interaction of different, changing variables.

Fisher sought to determine single effects and interactions when he developed DOE. The application was agricultural. The problem was what effect variations in sun, water, temperature, fertilizer, location, and so on had on growth. The tests were run in the field. A "one-variable-at-a-time" procedure could be followed in laboratory experiments, but it would not disclose what is intuitively known—that those variables don't stay constant. They interact, and that interaction can have a major effect on the outcome. The more complex the process, the greater value of DOE.

The Japanese brought this powerful technique to bear on product and process development through the work of Taguchi. Its application is rapidly growing in the West. Thousands of experiments have been conducted in many industries. The statistical theory and a detailed explanation of the design and conduct of experiments is beyond the intent or scope of this book. It is, however, in the bibliography.

However, the following is a slightly deeper understanding of what DOE is, how it is used, and how it fits with the other TQM tools and practices.

DOE OVERVIEW

The objective of DOE is to select critical product characteristics (factors) and the factor levels (values to be selected from) at which to assess performance response, organize factors and level combinations into test matrices (arrays), and perform the tests. For example, factors could be three casting alloy ingredients, and the levels could be two different mixtures. The different combinations of factors and levels would be set up in a matrix according to a plan. Castings would be poured and the results would indicate which combination of ingredients and mixture produced the best castings.

The Taguchi Method

The name Taguchi has become synonymous with DOE and its use in Japan. Taguchi's contribution made the technique more practicable and affordable compared to the classical, purely statistical approach. In brief, he developed some fixed arrays (experiment matrices) that significantly reduced the number of experiments required for various combinations of factors and levels. The tradeoff was an increased risk of not detecting some important interactions. He developed some other supportive analysis techniques, however, referred to as the signal-to-noise ratio to reduce this risk. The risk is also reduced by using knowledgeable process specialists to assist in designing the experiment by selecting the controllable factors that most likely affect variation. CE and the role of Taguchi's off-line and on-line quality control in that approach was discussed in Chapter 12. Taguchi's summary is shown in Table 20.1.

Some statisticians have found some difficulty with this shortcut approach to DOE. Taguchi's position is that it is better to do this level of experimentation than none at all. This practical approach was acceptable to engineers who had often taken greater risks in estimating factors using previously acceptable design methods. However, significant progress has been achieved in developing experimental methods for design that maximize the amount of reliable information and minimize the number of tests required. This requires a thorough understanding of the design method before it is attempted, beginning with simple experiments to learn the methodology.

The Experimental Process[16]

Each process and experiment is unique. There are some basic steps that need to be performed when designing and conducting experiments, and they are included to

Table 20.1 Means of Functional Countermeasures

Department Countermeasure			Type of noise		
			External	Internal	Unit-to-unit
Off-line quality control	R&D	(1) System design	●	●	●
		(2) Parameter design	●	●	●
		(3) Tolerance design	○	●	●
	Production engineering	(1) System design	×	×	●
		(2) Parameter design	×	×	●
		(3) Tolerance design	×	×	●
On-line quality control	Production	(1) Process diagnosis and adjustment	×	×	●
		(2) Prediction and correction	×	×	●
		(3) Measurement and action	×	×	●
	Customer relations	After-sales service	×	×	×

Source: G. Taguchi, Introduction to Quality Engineering, 1986.

give some insight to the method. They are shown in Figure 20.2 and summarized briefly as follows:

- Preparation. The main objective of this step is to identify key sources of variation, identify the problem and objectives, and select a team that represents all the skills required to understand the problem and process thoroughly. As a minimum, team members should be trained in problem-solving techniques and the seven QC tools. The team identifies process inputs, measurable process characteristics, and outputs. It must identify the impact of each input factor on the output. If any factors appear difficult to change, hold them constant during the experiment.
- Selection of design. Engineers trained in the fundamentals of DOE do not usually have difficulty selecting an adequate design (number runs, order, levels, and so forth), but the team should have access to someone with a comprehensive theoretical knowledge of DOE. Major contributors to process variation can usually be isolated using one or several common designs with a surprisingly small number of runs.

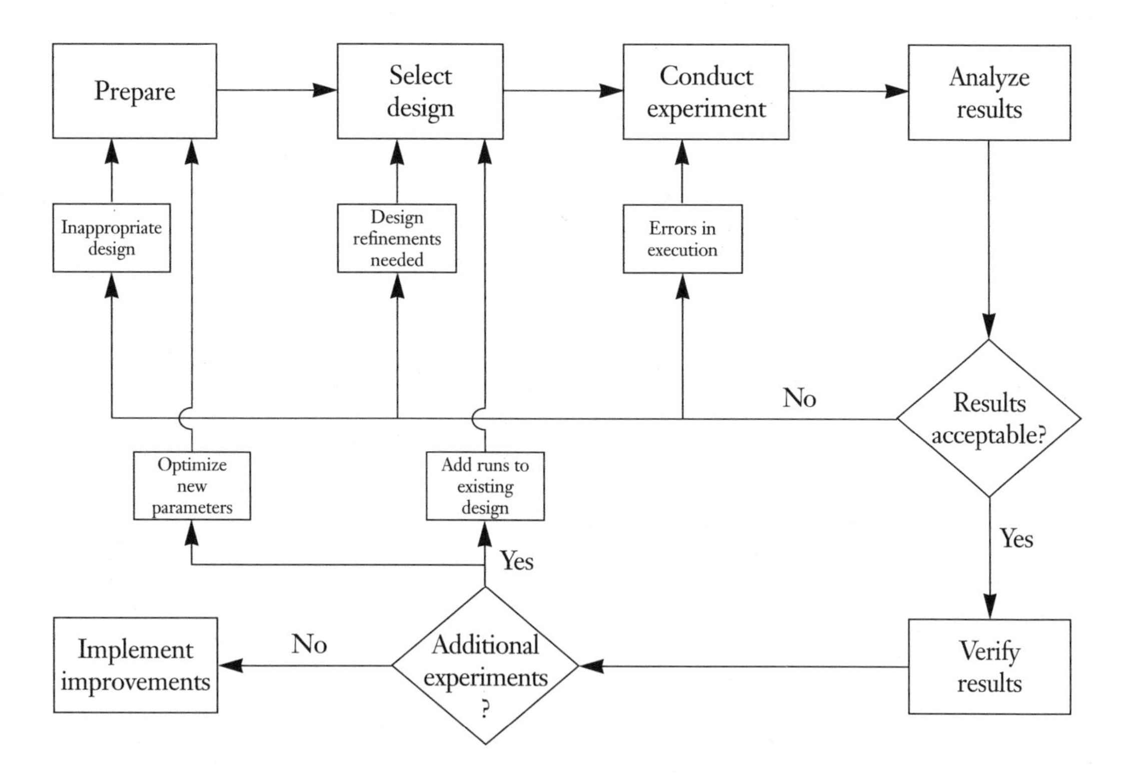

Figure 20.2 Steps in the Experimental Process

- Conduction of the experiment. This step occurs when the objectives of the experiment are recognized. Data interpretation should identify the input variables that most affect the output. A mathematical model can then be prepared that predicts outputs as a function of inputs. If results indicate some interaction between variables, a few more runs would be made to separate them.
- Verification of the tests. In this step, a few runs are made using the values of the variables determined in the experiment to verify that the results can be replicated. This is to gain assurance that the indicated relationship truly exists.

This is a highly simplified description of how experiments are conducted. Someone knowledgeable in DOE fundamentals should be involved in every step.

Chapter 21

Concurrent Engineering

CE was discussed in Chapter 12 with relation to TQM and the factors in product design. This chapter discusses more of the factors involved in performing CE.

CE is a methodology for the design, development, and manufacture of products that meet the market/customer demand for high quality, low cost, and fast delivery. From the internal customer standpoint, higher quality includes satisfactory functional performance, reliability, and maintainability. The internal customer of a design is the manufacturing process, whether internal to the company or those of suppliers. Their requirements are completeness, producibility, and, in the case of many products, what is called testability. This is a product that can be thoroughly and economically evaluated for performance in the production cycle.

Lower cost results from design simplicity and the avoidance of design changes once the production begins. It is also dependent on understanding and planning for the important product control parameters and levels.

Faster deliveries—the time from concept to shipment—is a result of satisfying the requirements just discussed. It has become of critical importance as a competitive factor. The highest profits for new products are realized in the initial periods after introduction, that is, until competition arrives and drives prices down. A rapid development-production cycle will ensure high profits and product leadership, as the Japanese automobile industry has demonstrated.

CE is the application of TQM philosophy, tools, and techniques to the design-manufacturing process in combination with the tools and techniques of computer-aided design and manufacturing. It provides a methodology for managing and conducting the activity.

The most important CE management method is the use of multifunctional teams from product concept to manufacturing stability. It supersedes the traditional serial method of design and manufacturing whereby marketing gave engineering the specifications for a product, engineering gave manufacturing its answer to the requirements, and manufacturing then figured out how to make it and what it would cost. Suppliers, who typically provide a large percentage of the final product content, were in the same boat. Frequently, engineering had also already determined which suppliers would be used. Organizational functional barriers were at their strongest. The marketplace got whatever came out of this sequence. It wasn't always what was wanted.

What was missing was a systematic integrated approach to utilize fully all the untapped knowledge and skills of the people in an organization in a timely and effective manner. Timely does not refer to schedule but to getting the proper type of inputs to the design-manufacturing process at the time they can be most effective in decision making. It involves asking the important questions about function, complexity, materials, tolerances, processes, and so on in the early design phases by specialists who can contribute to the answer and by using techniques like DOE to obtain the correct answers. Clearly, what this all involves is also effective communication and useful information systems.

GETTING STARTED

Initiating a CE methodology isn't easy. A significant portion of this book describes the difficulties in converting to a TQM philosophy. It involves changing the beliefs of what people have been taught and practiced. Achieving this with a highly intelligent and educated technical group that was accustomed to being in control and that was educated to solve difficult problems and make independent decisions may be the most difficult of all. But it must, can, and is being done.

1. The first step is to expose top key managers and technical decision makers to the CE concept, elements, process, and benefits. Companies already using TQM will find this relatively easy to do since it will be obvious that CE is a special and comprehensive application of the TQM philosophy. If a company is not using TQM principles and practices, the job is more extensive. TQM and CE principles will have to be introduced together.
2. The top-level group should identify an important new product to be developed using CE. Boeing Commercial Aircraft Company, for example, is using it to develop its new 777 aircraft. It's critical that Boeing achieve the benefits CE can provide.
3. A team of key decision makers and specialists should be formed to plan the CE application. The team should represent marketing, engineering, manufacturing, procurement/subcontracting, finance, and quality engineering.

4. The team must be given fundamental training in all the TQM elements covered in this book. These are the foundation for CE application.

   A CE team is not just a group of specialists who are assigned to bring their technical skills and traditional way of operating to design a new product. They *must* understand TQM. The subjects of the training include:

   - TQM principles
   - Team training
   - Seven QC tools
   - QFD
   - Design for manufacture and assembly
   - DOE

   The training assumes that team members are knowledgeable of the available and appropriate computer tools.

   If the company has a CAD-CAM-CIM capability, the CE process may highlight the need for modification, particularly with respect to intersystem access and information exchange.

5. The team should identify the other special knowledge that may be required and identify the individual who will be on call to supply it.

6. Develop a design plan and target schedules.

   The cost of the effort will be difficult to determine with accuracy because the organizations have no previous experience to use as reference. However, using CE requires extra effort and takes longer than the serial approach. This will create some management anxiety, but management must accept the proven fact that the manufacturing cycle will be shorter and cheaper since there will be few engineering changes and few surprises. The final product will also exhibit few problems in the hands of the customer.

   For example, Hewlett-Packard found that, on a small project that might require from two to five full-time design engineers, it needed only half the time of a production engineer, one-third of a quality engineer's, one-tenth of a buyer's, 20 to 40 percent of a materials engineer's, 10 percent of an accountant's, and 10 percent of an electromagnetic compatibility engineer's.[17] There were others who used even less time. Their contributions are more valuable in design and cost less than to fix mistakes later.

7. Organize the other working teams required to work on the different facets of the development. Train them to apply TQM tools.

8. Follow the general concept represented by Figure 12.2 in Chapter 12.

9. Identify key suppliers and make them members of the appropriate teams when the time is right.

FACTORS FOR SUCCESS

1. Train all team members in the objectives, methodologies, and tools being used.
2. Communicate with all affected functional organizations as to what the team is doing and how it will operate. If the company or element is not accustomed to this independent method, managers will not likely welcome unplanned interference in the operation of their organizations.
3. Colocation of at least the key team members is almost a requirement for successful communication and cooperation. Organizations and even company-wide electronic communications would support communication.
4. Develop adequate database networking and implement the latest design automation.
5. Include and use supplier knowledge and expertise.
6. Encourage the disclosure of serious problems or limitations.
7. Don't delay developing a CE capability because of limited capital for modern tools. Great benefits can be realized by training and organizing the teams to work together. It's a natural part of the continuous process improvement activities.

NOTES

1. Bemowski, K. "The Benchmarking Bandwagon." *Quality Progress* (January 1991): 19.
2. Camp, R. C. *Benchmarking: The Search for Industry Best Practices that Lead to Superior Performance.* Milwaukee: ASQC Quality Press, 1989.
3. Cohen, L. "QFD: An Application Perspective from Digital Equipment Corporation." *National Productivity Review* (Summer 1988): 197.
4. King, B. *Better Designs in Half the Time.* Meuthen: GOAL/QPC, 1989.
5. Ishikawa, K. *Guide to Quality Control.* Tokyo: Asian Productivity Org., 1971.
6. Kamikubo, H. "New Way of Management Tools for CWQC." In *Annual Quality Congress Transactions.* Milwaukee: ASQC, 1989.
7. The affinity diagram originated from the KJ © method developed by J. Karvakita and H. Kamikubo. 1989.
8. Kamikubo, H. "New Way of Management Tools for CWQC." In *Annual Quality Congress Transactions.* Milwaukee: ASQC, 1989.
9. Excerpted from a series of articles in *Quality Progress,* June-November 1990.

10. "The Tools of Quality: Check Sheets." *Quality Progress* adapted from the Quality Improvement Tools workbook by Juran Institute, Inc. (October 1990): 51.
11. Bajaria, H. J. and R. P. Copp. "Statistical Process Control." *Quality* (December 1988): 24.
12. The Quality Breakthrough; for Boeing Suppliers, 4th quarter. 1989.
13. Bothe, D. R. "A Powerful New Chart for Job Shops." In *Annual Quality Congress Transactions.* Milwaukee: ASQC, 1989.
14. Spisak, A. W. "A Control Chart for Ratios." *Journal of Quality Technology* (January 1990): 34.
15. Siegel, J. C. "Managing with Statistical Methods." Society of Automotive Engineers Technical Paper Series Number 820520, 1982.
16. Bingham, T. Boeing Quality Breakthrough Magazine. Number 9, 1st Quarter, 1990.
17. Rosenblatt, A., and G. Watson. "Concurrent Engineering." *IEEE Spectrum* (July 1991): 22.

BIBLIOGRAPHY

Quality—Markets Management

Cartin, T. J. *Quality—The Old and New Testament.* Washington, D.C.: AIAA/ADPA/NSIA, First National TQM Symposium, 1989.

Deming, W. E. *Out of the Crisis.* Cambridge, MA: MIT Press, 1986.

Feigenbaum, A. *Total Quality Control,* 3d ed. New York: McGraw-Hill, 1991.

Naisbitt, W. *Megatrends.* New York: Warner Books, 1982.

Ouchi, W. *Theory Z.* Reading, MA: Addison-Wesley, 1981.

Critical Role of Management

Conner, D. R., and R. W. Patterson. *Building Commitment to Organization Change.* Atlanta: O. D. Resources Co., 1983.

Deming, W. E. "Improvement of Quality and Productivity Through Action by Management." *National Productivity Review.*

Garvin, D. *Managing Quality.* New York: Free Press, 1988.

Mizuno, S. *Company Wide Total Quality Control.* Tokyo: JUSE, 1988.

Mohrman S., and T. Cummings. "Implementing Quality of Work Life Programs." Graduate School of Business Administration, Los Angeles: University of Southern California, 1982.

Roberts, H. V. "Quality and Productivity Implication for Management." Selected Paper No. 65. Chicago: University of Chicago, 1987.

Systems Approach to Management

"Managing Quality and Productivity in Aerospace and Defense." Defense Systems Management College. Washington, D.C.: U.S. Government Printing Office, 1988.

Melan, E. "Focusing on the Process: Key to Quality Improvement." In *Annual Quality Congress Transactions*. Milwaukee: ASQC, 1988.

Total Employee Involvement

Blake, R. R., and J. S. Mouton. *Productivity the Human Side.* New York: AMACOM, 1981.

Scholtes, P. P. *The Team Handbook.* Madison, WI: Joiner Associates, 1988.

Quality of Design

Taguchi, G. *Introduction to Quality Engineering.* Tokyo: Asian Productivity Org., 1986.

TQM Tools

Ishikawa, K. *Guide to Quality Control.* Hong Kong: Nordica International, Ltd., 1968.

Kamikubo, H. "New Way of Management Tools for CWQC." In *Annual Quality Congress Transactions.* Milwaukee: ASQC, 1989.

Sink, D. S. "Total Quality Management Is." *VPC Magazine* 8, No. 2 (1990): 14.

Design of Experiments

Barker, T. B. *Quality by Experimental Design.* Milwaukee: ASQC Quality Press, 1985.

Barker, T. B., G. E. P. Box, G. Taguchi, and R. Kacker. "Controversial Aspects of Taguchi Methods: A Panel Discussion." In *Annual Quality Congress Transactions*, Milwaukee: ASQC, 1989.

Ross, P. J. *Taguchi Techniques for Quality Engineering.* New York: McGraw-Hill, 1988.

SPC

Berger, R. W., and T. H. Hart. *Statistical Process Control.* Milwaukee: ASQC Quality Press, 1986.

Ott, E. R. *Process Quality Control.* New York: McGraw-Hill, 1975.

Manufacturing TQM

Shores, R. A. *A TQM Approach to Achieving Manufacturing Excellence.* Milwaukee: ASQC Quality Press, 1990.

JIT

California Department of Commerce Supplier Improvement Program. *JIT Instructor's Guide and the Student Work Book.* Sacramento: California Department of Commerce, 1990.

QFD

Akao, Y. *Quality Deployment.* Series. Methuen, MA: GOAL/QPC, 1987.

King, R. *Better Designs in Half the Time.* Methuen, MA: GOAL/QPC, 1987.

Sullivan L. P. "Quality Function Deployment." *Quality Progress* (June 1986): 39.

Zultner, R. E. "Software Quality Function Deployment; Applying QFD to Software." In *Rocky Mountain Quality Conference Proceedings.* Milwaukee: ASQC, 1989.

Managing Variation

Flynn, M. F. "All Answers Are Approximate . . . and Temporary. Statistical Thinking and Total Quality Management." In *Annual Quality Congress Transactions.* Milwaukee: ASQC, 1990.

Joiner, B. L., and M. A. Gaudard. "Variation, Management and W. E. Deming." *Quality Progress* (December 1990): 29.

Nolan, T. W. and L. P. Provost. "Understanding Variation." *Quality Progress* (May 1990): 70.

Supplier Quality

Burt, D. N. "Managing Suppliers Up to Speed." *Harvard Business Review* (July-August 1989): 17.

______. "Partnering with Suppliers, It Works." *Purchasing* (July 28, 1988).

Benchmarking

Camp, R. C. *Benchmarking; The Search for Industry Best Practices that Lead to Superior Performance.* Milwaukee: ASQC Quality Press, 1989.

Quality Cost

Cooper, R., and R. S. Kaplan. "Measuring Costs Right: Make the Right Decisions." *Harvard Business Review* (September-October 1988): 96.

O'Guin. M. C. "Activity-Based Costing: Unlock our Competitive Edge." *Manufacturing Systems* (December 1990): 35.

CE

Rosenblatt, A., and G. Watson. "Concurrent Engineering." *IEEE Spectrum* (July 1991): 22.

Turing, J. *Concurrent Engineering.* Campbell, CA: Logical Solutions Technology, 1991.

Index